# THE PEOPLE'S ROAD REVISITED

# THE PEOPLE'S ROAD REVISITED

## ON THE TRAIL OF THE NEWFOUNDLAND RAILWAY

### WADE KEARLEY

**CREATIVE PUBLISHERS**

St. John's, Newfoundland and Labrador
2007

© 2007, Wade Kearley

**Canada Council for the Arts**  **Conseil des Arts du Canada**  **Newfoundland Labrador**

We gratefully acknowledge the financial support of The Canada Council for the Arts, The Government of Canada through the Book Publishing Industry Development Program (BPIDP), and the Government of Newfoundland and Labrador through the Department of Tourism, Culture and Recreation for our publishing program.

All rights reserved. No part of this work covered by the copyrights hereon may be reproduced or used in any form or by any means—graphic, electronic or mechanical—without the prior written permission of the publisher. Any requests for photocopying, recording, taping or information storage and retrieval systems of any part of this book shall be directed in writing to the Canadian Reprography Collective, One Yonge Street, Suite 1900, Toronto, Ontario M5E 1E5.

Design and layout by Joanne Snook-Hann
Printed on acid-free paper

Published by
CREATIVE PUBLISHERS
an imprint of CREATIVE BOOK PUBLISHING
a division of Transcontinental Media
P.O. Box 1815, Stn. C, St. John's, Newfoundland and Labrador A1C 5P9

First Edition
Printed in Canada by:
TRANSCONTINENTAL PRINT

**Photo Credits:** All photographs, except where otherwise noted, are by the author. The author's complete collection of images from the cross-Island walk is housed in the Wade Kearley Collection at the Centre for Newfoundland Studies Archive, Queen Elizabeth II Library, Memorial University of Newfoundland.

Library and Archives Canada Cataloguing in Publication

Kearley, Wade, 1956-
  The people's road revisited : on the trail of the Newfoundland Railway / Wade Kearley. -- Rev. ed.

Includes bibliographic references.
ISBN 978-1-897174-14-2

1. Kearley, Wade, 1956- --Travel--Newfoundland and Labrador.
2. Newfoundland and Labrador--Description and travel.
3. Railroads--Newfoundland and Labrador--History.
4. Newfoundland Railway Company--History. I. Title.

HE2809.N4K43 2007        917.1804'4        C2007-903799-2

*To my father, Albert Walter Kearley,
who taught me the value of holding
on to the things you love.*

# TABLE OF CONTENTS

**FOREWORD** .................................................. ix
**ACKNOWLEDGEMENTS** to the original version ................... xi
**INTRODUCTION** to the original version ..................... xiii

**WRECKHOUSE TRAIL**
    Wreckhouse Trail Map ...................................... 2
    Wreckhouse Trail Introduction ............................. 3
    Ch. 1    The First Spike ..................................... 5
    Ch. 2    Wind Man ............................................ 8
    Ch. 3    Soul of the Boot ................................... 12
    History Siding One: The Work of the Country .............. 15

**LONG RANGE TRAIL**
    Long Range Trail Map ..................................... 18
    Long Range Trail Introduction ............................ 19
    Ch. 4    The First Scars .................................... 20
    Ch. 5    Salmon Backs ....................................... 23
    Ch. 6    Zing ............................................... 27
    History Siding Two: A New Vision for a National Railway .. 32

**LOGGER'S TRAIL**
    Logger's Trail Map ....................................... 34
    Logger's Trail Introduction .............................. 35
    Ch. 7    Waiting for the Rain at Black Duck Siding .......... 36
    Ch. 8    Fish Stew .......................................... 39
    Ch. 9    Helltrot Pipes ..................................... 43
    Ch. 10   "Trains are Gone" .................................. 45
    Ch. 11   Petries Undercrossing .............................. 50
    History Siding Three: From Nowhere to Nowhere ............ 52

**HUMBER VALLEY TRAIL**
    Humber Valley Trail Map .................................. 54
    Humber Valley Trail Introduction ......................... 55
    Ch. 12   Unlikely Ambassador ................................ 57
    Ch. 13   Lost in No Man's Land .............................. 60
    Ch. 14   At Humbermouth .................................... 64
    Ch. 15   When Stories Come Tumbling ......................... 69
    History Siding Four: The Reid Deal ....................... 74

**TOPSAILS TRAIL**
   Topsails Trail Map . . . . . . . . . . . . . . . . . . . . . . . . . . . . . . . . . . . . . . .76
   Topsails Trail Introduction . . . . . . . . . . . . . . . . . . . . . . . . . . . . . . . . .77
   Ch. 16  Trapper's Lounge . . . . . . . . . . . . . . . . . . . . . . . . . . . . . . . . . 79
   Ch. 17  On Patrol in the Gaff . . . . . . . . . . . . . . . . . . . . . . . . . . . . . . 82
   Ch. 18  Taking up the Rails . . . . . . . . . . . . . . . . . . . . . . . . . . . . . . . 84
   Ch. 19  Pyjamas with Rockets . . . . . . . . . . . . . . . . . . . . . . . . . . . . . 87
   Ch. 20  Stone on Water . . . . . . . . . . . . . . . . . . . . . . . . . . . . . . . . . . 92
   Ch. 21  The Land Speaks . . . . . . . . . . . . . . . . . . . . . . . . . . . . . . . . . 99
   Ch. 22  Lesson of the Map . . . . . . . . . . . . . . . . . . . . . . . . . . . . . . . 103
   History Siding Five: Of the People, by the People,
   for the Reids . . . . . . . . . . . . . . . . . . . . . . . . . . . . . . . . . . . . . . . . . .106
**RED OCHRE TRAIL**
   Red Ochre Trail Map . . . . . . . . . . . . . . . . . . . . . . . . . . . . . . . . . . . .108
   Red Ochre Trail Introduction . . . . . . . . . . . . . . . . . . . . . . . . . . . . . .109
   Ch. 23  Skull Hill . . . . . . . . . . . . . . . . . . . . . . . . . . . . . . . . . . . . . . . 111
   Ch. 24  What's in a Name . . . . . . . . . . . . . . . . . . . . . . . . . . . . . . . . 116
   Ch. 25  Halfway to Nowhere . . . . . . . . . . . . . . . . . . . . . . . . . . . . . 121
   History Siding Six: The Heart of the Matter . . . . . . . . . . . . . . . . . .125
**TWO RIVERS TRAIL**
   Two Rivers Trail Map . . . . . . . . . . . . . . . . . . . . . . . . . . . . . . . . . . .128
   Two Rivers Trail Introduction . . . . . . . . . . . . . . . . . . . . . . . . . . . .129
   Ch. 26  New Pants for Joey . . . . . . . . . . . . . . . . . . . . . . . . . . . . . . 131
   Ch. 27  The Sign on my Forehead . . . . . . . . . . . . . . . . . . . . . . . . . 136
   Ch. 28  Gandhi in Gander . . . . . . . . . . . . . . . . . . . . . . . . . . . . . . . 139
   Ch. 29  Of Horses and Floods . . . . . . . . . . . . . . . . . . . . . . . . . . . 142
   History Siding Seven: Stretched to the Limit . . . . . . . . . . . . . . . . .145
**CROSSROADS TRAIL**
   Crossroads Trail Map . . . . . . . . . . . . . . . . . . . . . . . . . . . . . . . . . .148
   Crossroads Introduction . . . . . . . . . . . . . . . . . . . . . . . . . . . . . . . .149
   Ch. 30  Walking Backwards . . . . . . . . . . . . . . . . . . . . . . . . . . . . 151
   Ch. 31  Fibre-Optics Darkly . . . . . . . . . . . . . . . . . . . . . . . . . . . . 154
   Ch. 32  Coyote Warning . . . . . . . . . . . . . . . . . . . . . . . . . . . . . . . 158
   Ch. 33  Just the Wind . . . . . . . . . . . . . . . . . . . . . . . . . . . . . . . . . 160
   Ch. 34  Welsh's Camp . . . . . . . . . . . . . . . . . . . . . . . . . . . . . . . . 162
   History Siding Eight: Death of a Thousand Cuts . . . . . . . . . . . . . . .167

**EASTERN EDGE TRAIL**
    Eastern Edge Trail Map . . . . . . . . . . . . . . . . . . . . . . . . . . . . . . . . . . . . .170
    Eastern Edge Trail Introduction . . . . . . . . . . . . . . . . . . . . . . . . . . . . .171
    Ch. 35 "Nar Worm" . . . . . . . . . . . . . . . . . . . . . . . . . . . . . . . . . . . . . 173
    Ch. 36 Rabbits' Hotel . . . . . . . . . . . . . . . . . . . . . . . . . . . . . . . . . . 178
    Ch. 37 "Do Not Distroy" . . . . . . . . . . . . . . . . . . . . . . . . . . . . . . . . 184
    Ch. 38 At the Stationhouse . . . . . . . . . . . . . . . . . . . . . . . . . . . . . 190
    Ch. 39 Pirates . . . . . . . . . . . . . . . . . . . . . . . . . . . . . . . . . . . . . . . . 193
    Ch. 40 How to Drown a Horse . . . . . . . . . . . . . . . . . . . . . . . . . . . 195
    Ch. 41 A Private Place . . . . . . . . . . . . . . . . . . . . . . . . . . . . . . . . . 199
    History Siding Nine: Recommendation 29 . . . . . . . . . . . . . . . . . . . . .202
**ISTHMUS TRAIL**
    Isthmus Trail Map . . . . . . . . . . . . . . . . . . . . . . . . . . . . . . . . . . . . . . .204
    Isthmus Trail Introduction . . . . . . . . . . . . . . . . . . . . . . . . . . . . . . . .205
    Ch. 42 Our Valley . . . . . . . . . . . . . . . . . . . . . . . . . . . . . . . . . . . . . 207
    Ch. 43 Father and Sun . . . . . . . . . . . . . . . . . . . . . . . . . . . . . . . . . 214
    Ch. 44 Fiddler's Green . . . . . . . . . . . . . . . . . . . . . . . . . . . . . . . . . 219
    Ch. 45 "Sure, what's on a bog?" . . . . . . . . . . . . . . . . . . . . . . . . . . . 222
    History Siding Ten: End of the Line . . . . . . . . . . . . . . . . . . . . . . . . .226
**TRAIL OF AVALON**
    Trail of Avalon Map . . . . . . . . . . . . . . . . . . . . . . . . . . . . . . . . . . . . . 228
    Trail of Avalon Introduction . . . . . . . . . . . . . . . . . . . . . . . . . . . . . .229
    Ch. 46 Autographs from Mahers . . . . . . . . . . . . . . . . . . . . . . . . . . 232
    Ch. 47 Out of the Past . . . . . . . . . . . . . . . . . . . . . . . . . . . . . . . . . 239
    Ch. 48 A Ride on the Ghost Train . . . . . . . . . . . . . . . . . . . . . . . . . 244
    Ch. 49 The Last Spike . . . . . . . . . . . . . . . . . . . . . . . . . . . . . . . . . 248
    History Siding Eleven: Surviving Former Railway
    Stations in Newfoundland . . . . . . . . . . . . . . . . . . . . . . . . . . . . . . . . .250

**EPILOGUE** to the original version . . . . . . . . . . . . . . . . . . . . . . . . . . . . .251
**ENVOY** to the original version . . . . . . . . . . . . . . . . . . . . . . . . . . . . . .259

# FOREWORD
## to *The People's Road Revisited*

No matter how well planned, every journey reveals the unexpected, exposes things we could not have known about ourselves, about others and about the world. Because these experiences shape our perceptions, a journey once begun, never really ends. What I'd planned as a simple hike across the island of Newfoundland in the summer of 1993 is now an integral part of who I am.

It began on a cool July morning near the Port aux Basques ferry terminal when I set out to make the 547-mile trek to St. John's. The highlights of that journey, the people I met, and the lessons I learned the hard way, were captured in the book *The People's Road* published in 1995. The book became a provincial bestseller but the publisher, Harry Cuff Publications, for reasons that were never explained to me, elected not to do another print run. They have since closed their doors and *The People's Road* is now a collector's item.

In this new book, I've regrouped an edited and revised version of that story into eleven geographic sections. Each section includes a new introduction and a map, an update on trail conditions, and current interviews with some of the people I first featured in 1995. (Special thanks here to Terry Morrison, executive director of the T'Railway Council, who contributed greatly to these introductions). At the end of each of the first ten sections, I've added a short "History Siding" on various stages of the Newfoundland Railway's rise and fall. And lastly, on page 250, you'll find an updated catalogue of Newfoundland's remaining railway stations as compiled by Randy P. Noseworthy.

One thing this journey has proven to me is that, no matter how important the heritage of Newfoundland may be, unless it has some relevance to our daily lives, then its meaning and its memory will be lost. Perhaps with that danger in mind, the government declared the railbed an island-wide provincial park in 1997. But giving it relevance is not enough. If we wish to be true to our heritage, then we must integrate it into the modern context in a coherent and informed way. The alternative is decay, corruption, and forgetting, the erosive forces of which now threaten the route of the former Newfoundland Railway twenty years after it was derailed.

One way to integrate the legacy of that route into our lives today is to protect and re-build the long thin community which, as you will discover in these pages, connects St. John's to Port aux Basques through some of the most scenic, and some of the most devastated landscape in the province.

I call that community the Newfoundland T'Railway. And one group whose aim is to protect it is the Newfoundland T'Railway Council. Since 1995 the Council has struggled with some success to hold this route together. I have done what I could to help. In addition to the trek and the first book, I served ten years as a volunteer on the Council, including two terms as president. And I speak out on the importance of protecting this historic corridor whenever I have the opportunity. This book is another step along that path.

I invite you now to join me on the journey, to see what has been gained, what has been lost, and what is at stake for those whose lives have been touched by the people's road.

# ACKNOWLEDGEMENTS
## to the original version

In the research and writing of this book I came to depend on the generosity of hundreds of people, many of whom you will encounter in the following pages. And while I am reluctant to dispense gratitude as if it were a commodity, nevertheless there are certain groups and individuals whose support was crucial in pushing me to the completion of what has been a joyful but arduous three years.

My heartfelt thanks first and foremost to my wife and friend Katharine. Without your hard work, critical editing, and strong shoulders, this book would never have seen the light of a reading lamp.

A special note of thanks to the volunteers and staff of the Newfoundland and Labrador Development Council and the rural development associations, especially to Otto Goulding and Terry Morrison.

For funding assistance, thanks to the Newfoundland and Labrador Arts Council, the Canada Council Explorations Program, the Johnson Family Foundation, Ed Redmond and Val Hodder, Daisy Burry, and George and Bernice Legrow. And thanks to Anne Hart and Patrick O'Flaherty for supporting my funding applications.

Thanks to each of you who invited me into your homes, cottages, and businesses along the route. To each of you who shared a part of the walk with me, a special thank you. Your companionship helped renew my resolve. Thanks to my brother Geoff whose gifted hands carved my walking stick, Clara. Thanks also to Fred Earl of the Department of Natural Resources who donated the railway maps. Thanks to Janice Udell for sharing her hiking expertise and her friendship, and to my extraordinary cousin Chris Hammond. Thanks also to Neil Dawe, Heddy Peddle, and Randy P. Noseworthy.

To the staff of Enterprise Newfoundland and Labrador, my co-workers, thank you. It is a pleasure to work with people who cared enough to ease my journey.

Thanks to Clifford Grinling and Gordon Rodgers for your critical reading of the final manuscript and for your helpful and constructive suggestions.

Thanks to my editor Bob Cuff. Your patience and insight made the process of fashioning this book a pleasant one.

And there are others to whom I owe a debt of gratitude, so if I haven't thanked you yet, please let me thank you now.

Finally, to all those people who live, work, and play on the long thin community known as the Newfoundland Railway, thank you sincerely for sharing your stories with me. I have tried in good faith to recreate them here.

# INTRODUCTION
## to the original version

In 1957, Ralph Balsom presented a brief to the provincial Cabinet on behalf of the Union of Locomoters, Firemen, and Engineers, recommending ways to cost-effectively improve railway services. After the meeting, then-Premier Joseph R. Smallwood called Ralph aside. "He complimented me on the brief, said it was very detailed and complete. Then he told me, 'Ralph, it won't work you know. The island is not big enough for a railway and a highway. And the people want a highway. In ten years you'll see grass growing on the rail line.'"

Joey may have been right about the closure—though the line lasted twenty-one years longer than he predicted. But he was very wrong about the grass. As the rails were lifted, between 1988 and 1990, the railbed became a back road across the province—a 750 mile corridor, including the 547-mile main line and various branch lines.

Following the closure there were pressures on government from lobby groups, including municipalities, businesses and other interested parties, to break up the railbed for recreational, commercial and industrial uses. All the proposals had one thing in common, a narrow local focus. The provincial and federal governments and Canadian National Railway (CN), by the lack of any co-ordinated action, appeared uncertain of how best to proceed. One group came forward with a broader vision to preserve the right-of-way for the entire trans-island corridor. The Rails to Trails Coalition, formed in 1990, lobbied for a study of alternative uses for the entire rail line. The Coalition argued that the tourism and recreational potential of an intact trans-island trail could have positive economic and social benefits for the entire province, long-term benefits that would outweigh any short-term gains from a piecemeal approach to development.

Among the more influential supporters of the Coalition was the Newfoundland and Labrador Rural Development Council (NLRDC), an umbrella organization for the fifty-nine rural development associations across the province. These grassroots associations are committed to the belief that the way of life in rural Newfoundland and Labrador is of value and ought to be preserved and fostered. For 107 years the railway was an important feature of that rural life.

With the enthusiastic support of NLRDC's executive director, Terry Morrison and its board, the Coalition gained government funding for a feasibility and inventory study of the railbed. The detailed two-volume report "The Newfoundland T'Railway: Opportunities and Feasibility," was released in 1992. It supported the contention of the Coalition that the rail line offered a unique opportunity to develop a multi-purpose system of trails on the island.

With the T'Railway report in hand, Otto Goulding, a community volunteer and Western Zone director for the NLRDC, kept the Council in the forefront of those groups pushing for implementation of the T'Railway. Initially he met with a great deal of stonewalling from CN and from both levels of government. No one seemed able to answer his questions. Who had jurisdiction over the rail line? Who policed the route? Who was liable for accidents due to damaged or missing infrastructure? Who was granting commercial licences to logging, excavating, and quarrying companies actively using the rail line for commercial purposes? Under whose authority were the Province and municipalities expropriating railway lands for roads?

After the initial flurry of attention following the release of the T'Railway Report, it seemed as if the issue was being derailed by the difficulties of determining exactly who was accountable for the railbed. That is where things stood in December of 1992.

Intrigued by the controversy and looking for a way to get involved, I revived a dream of mine to make the cross-island trek on the railbed and began planning to make it happen. In the winter of 1993 I met Otto Goulding. When he heard my plan was not just to walk the line, but to listen to the people I met along the way and to write a book about that experience, he pledged support. For Otto this was an opportunity to help pull the T'Railway issue off the bureaucratic siding and gather momentum for action through media attention, perhaps even force government and CN to take a public stance. Otto agreed to arrange contacts for me in each of the twenty-two development association areas along the route. In return, he asked that I speak out on what I saw. We shook hands. Five months later, on July 6, 1993, I set out on the trail of the Newfoundland Railway.

# WRECKHOUSE TRAIL
## PORT AUX BASQUES TO CODROY VALLEY

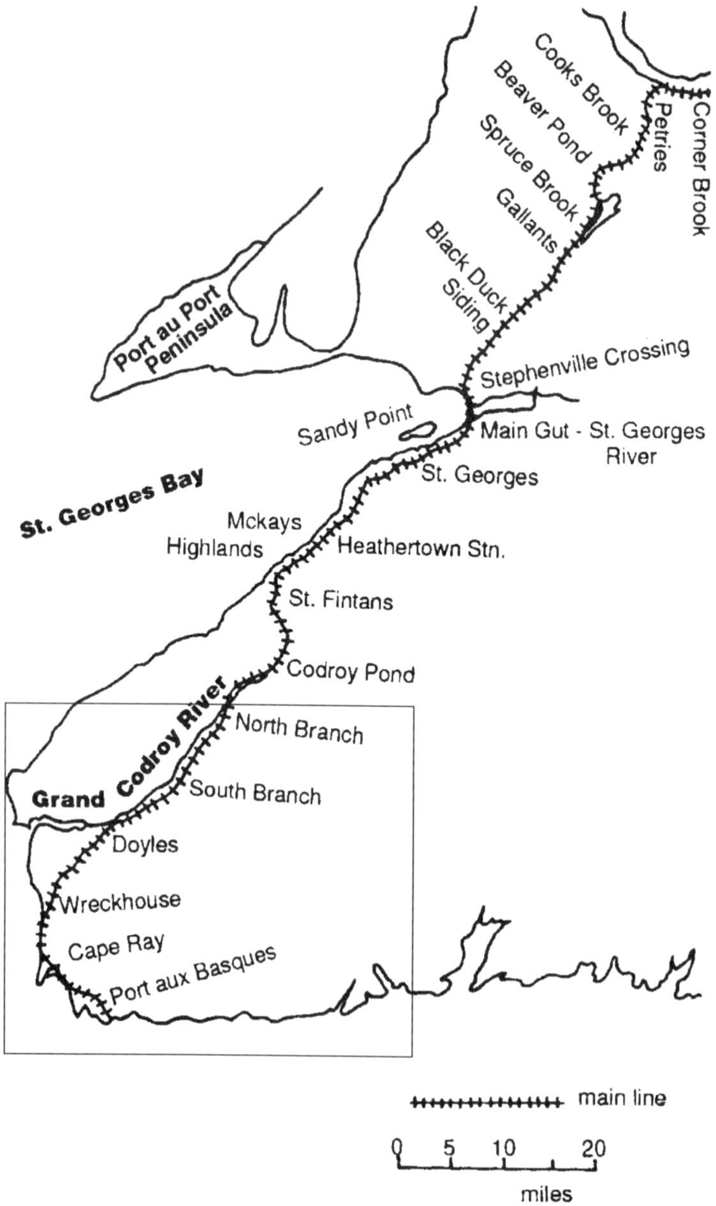
Cooks Brook
Beaver Pond
Spruce Brook
Gallants
Black Duck Siding
Petries
Corner Brook
Port au Port Peninsula
Stephenville Crossing
Sandy Point
Main Gut - St. Georges River
St. Georges
St. Georges Bay
Mckays
Highlands
Heathertown Stn.
St. Fintans
Codroy Pond
Grand Codroy River
North Branch
South Branch
Doyles
Wreckhouse
Cape Ray
Port aux Basques
main line
0 5 10 20
miles

# WRECKHOUSE TRAIL INTRODUCTION

Stepping out on that cool June morning fourteen years ago, I had no idea what an incredible experience the trail ahead held for me. The stark beauty of the coastline and the distant grandeur of the mountains made the first day on the trail unforgettable. And since then, this section of the T'Railway has been refurbished from Port aux Basques to South Branch. I only wish the improvements made here were typical of what's happening along the rest of the cross-island route, but I'm getting ahead of the story.

The improvements in the Wreckhouse Trail are courtesy of the T'Railway Council. Taking advantage of a federal program that offered money to hire unemployed fishermen, the Council developed an ambitious project. They created hundreds of short term jobs upgrading the trail, resurfacing the trestles and trying out new technology. At Overfalls Brook, for example, they decked and railed the trestle using recycled-plastic lumber. According to Terry Morrison, executive director for the Council, it is holding up well. "Even though it's a bit more costly, we're hoping there'll be less need for maintenance," he says.

Among the most significant trail projects is the Red Rocks bridge. For years, a large washout there prevented trail users from following the route. But, as part of the upgrade, a new bailey bridge now spans that troublesome breach.

The South Branch trestle was badly damaged by fire shortly after the upgrade. Four young people admitted to lighting a fire on the beach close to the bridge but claimed they had no intention of catching the bridge on fire. Morrison says that when the T'Railway Council came up with the additional funds and materials to fix the damage, "the local community got behind the effort with volunteer labour and cooked meals."

North Branch is still an issue. When the highway was expanded it took in a portion of the railbed. Since then, according to local reports, ATVs leave the trail, follow along the shoulder of the Trans-Canada and cross the highway bridge "when no one is looking," before turning back onto the railbed.

The popularity of the T'Railway has encouraged others to enhance resources along the route. For example, a local development group is working on a boardwalk trail extending from the T'Railway across the windswept fen to the base of the mountain at Wreckhouse. The long-term plan is to reconstruct the house of the legendary wind man, Lauchie MacDougal and develop an interpretive site.

When I first met Dave Kitchen at the start of my journey in 1993, he was an enthusiastic supporter of anything to do with trail development, active with the Codroy Valley Development Association and pushing to develop for the Cormack Trail as a part of the T'Railway on the west cost of the island. When I reached him by telephone, in April of 2007, he told me he has no contact with the T'Railway. Since rural development was radically altered by government in the mid-1990s, he gradually withdrew. "As far as I'm aware," he said, "there are no gaps and the people who want to use it, on ATVs and skidoos and the likes, are using it."

Caboose in Port aux Basques park.

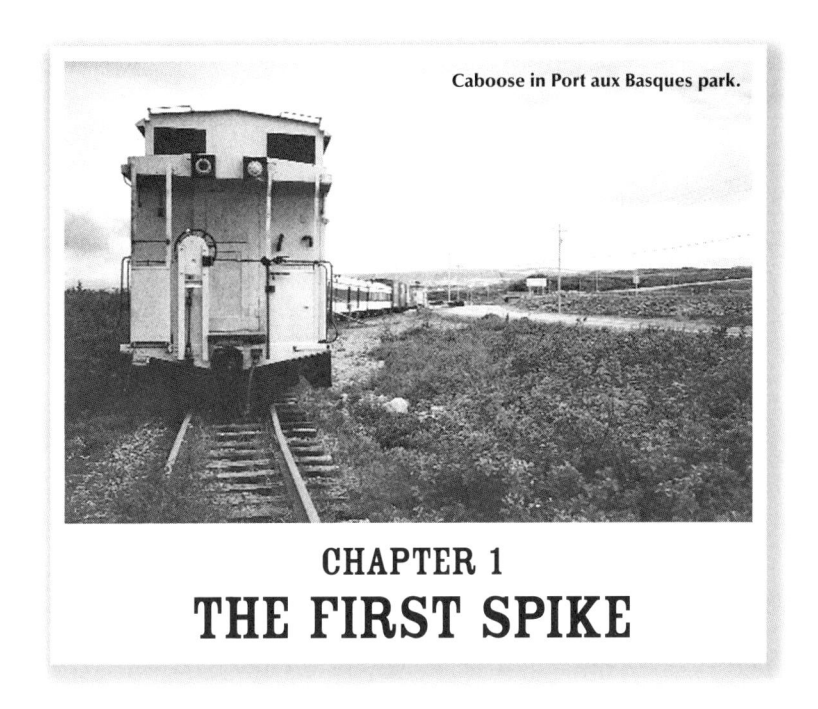

# CHAPTER 1
# THE FIRST SPIKE

### 6 JULY, 8:10 A.M., 1993

There is snow along the ridge of Table Mountain. A cool wind pushes at my back as the "crowd" of three people, turned out so early on this chilly July morning, bids me good luck on my journey. Ahead is a 547-mile hike along the abandoned railbed to St. John's, where the Newfoundland Railway began construction in August of 1881. The Port aux Basques ferry terminal falls behind as I trudge around the first bend. My skin tingles. Unanswered questions rise unbidden like goose bumps. "Will my knee hold up? Who will I meet? Can I make it?"

Where the roadbed passes along the foot of an eroded embankment, below a row of bungalows, rail ties lie embedded in the road gravel. Hop-stepping to match the ties' uneven spacing, I recall hot July afternoons of twenty-five years ago on the other side of the Island. The diesel engines still ran then and the railway was our shortcut to the swimming hole. Heat waves distorted the air ahead, raising the sweet stench of creosote. The crushed granite was our ammunition for picking off the dozens of glass insulators mounted on every pole, rows of wire strung between them. If a stone struck any of the thin, uncovered wires, a ping reverberated in either direction. No poles here now. No rails, not since 1990 when the last of the track was torn up and shipped to South America.

I hated the uneven steps it took to match the irregularly spaced ties. Sometimes, risking a skinned ankle, I'd teeter along on the steel rail, reaching across the narrow gauge to hold a buddy's hand as he balanced on the opposite rail. During the endless summers, my brothers, and a few of the other boys from Neil's Line would plan a day hike on the track. Torn between the promise of adventure and the drudgery of hopping along the rail ties for a day, I always stayed home, opting to risk being stuck with garden chores.

*A loon floats like waterlogged driftwood. Two ducks fly around a low hill and, angling their wings, plop into the water.*

Rain has gouged washouts in the line just outside Port aux Basques. Over one of these washouts, guard rails are laid at the right width for ATV tires. At a nearby "railway park" several neglected rail cars on a rusty siding. Onto the first bridge, Grand Bay Trestle (Mile 546.2), patched with plywood. These trestles will be my mileposts across the Island. The name and mileage for each one is printed on my maps. From the left a speedboat races in through the salt pond, tracing an arc of foam beneath the trestle. A strong smell of seawater drifts up in its wake.

Outside town, on the way through an industrial park—which is more park than industry—the sight of the first long, straight stretch sends a chill through my body, colder than the early morning wind. The point of a railway spike protrudes from the crushed stone. I pry it loose and shove it into my day pack.

To ignore the doubt that mingles with my excitement, I repeat into my tape recorder the things I see and hear: purple swamp orchids, pitcher plants, mean alders, buttercups, bog. Rooster crowing, crunch of crushed stone, whispering bird song. Swift little brooks. Ferns, low spruce. White bellflowers, the early promise of blueberries. Granite outcrops. A loon floats like waterlogged driftwood. Two ducks fly around a low hill and, angling their wings, plop into the water. A sandpiper scuttles just ahead of me, feigning a broken wing, then hops into the air. Muddy sand. Seesawing grasses. Seapeas. Two young boys wearing long rubber boots carrying their fishing poles tromp in the opposite direction. A nod and on they go.

In Cape Ray a group of children play softball. It is so windy the pitcher has to throw the ball overhand to reach the batter. A small thin boy leaves the field and crosses the railbed.

"What's the name of this road we're on?" I ask him.

"That's the track," he says, walking backwards away from me. "We took up the rails."

Deb's Variety in Cape Ray is a dark, cheerless convenience store. With a diapered child clinging to her shirttail, a tired looking young woman rings in the price of my fishing line and rat-tail comb. She chats with me in a high, pleasant voice.

"You'll notice a big change in the weather as soon as you get up into the Valley," she says, meaning the Codroy Valley. I admit I would not mind a little less wind.

By mid-morning Sugar Loaf Mountain towers on my right and the track turns slowly westward towards the coast, away from the shelter of the alders. Even from this distance I can see the ocean churning. My left knee feels a little hot so I stop long enough to pull on an elastic knee support and set off again, leaning a little more heavily on my stick.

All my life I have loved to walk. Where I grew up, on the south side of Conception Bay, there was plenty of room for that, along woods paths, the one paved highway, and the many dirt roads. Later, as an army cadet at camp near Banff, Alberta, I learned I could survive in the bush. When we were not in Banff, agog at the young women from the art school, we were hiking in the mountains for days at a time. Or canoeing on the Bow River. That was one of the happiest summers of my adolescence. For the first time I learned I could take care of myself.

Near Wreckhouse.

## CHAPTER 2
# WIND MAN

After two hours in the relentless wind I shelter in the gully of a small stream in the area known as Wreckhouse. Trout roll on the surface of the dark pool. Ten miles done, eight miles to go before camp at Mummichog Provincial Park. What a landscape from Port aux Basques! Across wind-blown barrens, sand dunes, along sandy beaches, over inlets, and along the coastal cliffs from Black Head Rock, granite rising straight up out of the white-capped waves. I had budgeted for eight photographs today. I took thirty-six. Along the cliffs the wind-shaped bushes—tuckamore—are so dense the branches look like textbook diagrams of blood vessels.

A small blister pinches my right heel when I finally hobble into Mummichog Park. Once the tent is up I don't know quite what to do next. Is this to be my routine for the next month? I can handle it well enough but there is one difference from other camping trips: I would like to stroll around but I can't take another step. I feel like a member of one of those religious sects with an allotted number of footsteps each day. Eighteen miles is my limit, and that is with just the day pack and canteen. What about when I strap on the full sixty-pound pack? There are days when my itinerary demands twenty-six miles. The thought scares me a little and I have to dig deep for a reason to go on.

This journey has been a dream of mine, ever since CN began to take up the rails in the fall of 1988. The only train rides I'd had were the few times I had managed to cling to the outside of boxcars when the diesels pulled their slow length past our swimming hole. I first confessed my dream to walk the length of the Newfoundland railway two years ago at a New Year's Eve party. But then it was just a vague hope, with the teaser of gathering enough material for some kind of book. Just this past winter, talk in the media began to heat up that the trestles were deteriorating. The overland route might be lost. It was now or never.

And so began the long weeks and months of planning. But it was not until May, when the plans were in place, that I actually took my first extended walk—fourteen miles—on the railbed from St. John's to Manuels. Perhaps, if I had gone on those hikes with my brothers years before, I would never have planned this trip. It took five hours instead of the three hours I had predicted and it was exhausting. Walking on the crushed stone was like tripping over a rocky beach. And the next day my left knee felt hot. I waited two days then walked the route again. The knee was hurting before I reached Manuels. I waited a week and then walked again. Next day the knee was stiffish—no pain, but taut. But this was mid-June and less than a month before my scheduled departure. So I bought a knee support and got on with preparations.

A new thought begins to seep into my plans. "There may be ways to make this easier. I could hitch rides on all-terrain vehicles." Three of them passed me today, riding the undulating roadbed like dories on the waves. One triker, in a red plaid shirt and black helmet, drove past, went on for a quarter mile, then turned and came back.

"You that fella walking across?" he said, squinting at me and smiling. I introduced myself. John Osmond held out his hand. It was big, leathery, smooth. John himself was about sixty, grey grizzle of a beard, paunch. We chatted about the weather and he drove away. I thought, "That's an opportunity lost. I should have asked him for memories about the railway." I know that the Osmonds worked the line along a section called (what else?) Osmond, now a cluster of shacks squeezed between the pond and the ocean, just south of Cheeseman Park. I vowed not to let such chances slip by again.

Only two of the thirty-eight campsites at Mummichog are occupied tonight. Despite strong protest from my muscles, I walk up as far as the warden's shack. Mary, the duty warden, says camping has been way down for several years. Many former campers have cabins along the rail line.

After a supper of rice and beans I'm starting to feel a little more optimistic about my chances of at least making one more day. Dave Kitchen stops by the campsite in his big Pontiac V-8. He is a tall, sturdy man in his sixties, with Buddy Holly glasses on an oval face and a rolling smoker's laugh. I first met him yesterday when he picked me up at the airport to drive me to Port aux Basques. Dave grew up in Millertown, in Central Newfoundland, but he has lived on the West Coast for years.

Dave is a volunteer with the local rural development association and is involved in a project to develop the Cormack Trail. Newfoundlander William Cormack and his Micmac guide, Sylvester Joe, set out from eastern Newfoundland in September of 1822 and, after an arduous journey across the unmapped interior, reached St. Georges Bay in November. Desperate for a berth to St. John's, Cormack sailed in fishing skiffs down the west coast and east along the south coast until, at Fortune, he finally found an ocean-going vessel that could take him back to the capital.

As Dave drove me south towards Port aux Basques, he talked about the natural history of the area. He told me about the wind. How studies on the knee-high tuckamore along the coast revealed that some of the dwarf trees are over 300 years old. How the wind, accelerating up the sides of the mountains, has shaped the forest into a natural phenomenon called wind waves. Dave told me about Wreckhouse and Lauchie McDougall, the legendary wind man, who lived with his large family in the path of a ferocious wind.

This nameless wind has its genesis in the Gulf of Mexico. From there it blows up through the central United States, twists over Maine and along the Atlantic Coast, hits Cape Breton Island, accelerates eastward across the open water of the Cabot Strait, builds a swell, and sends waves crashing into the southwest corner of Newfoundland. The wind howls through the streets of Port aux Basques. People must bend into the gales and fight the stinging rain to make headway. The wind swirls over the rocky landscape and up the slopes of the Table Mountains. Churns along the mountaintops, the rushing air swoops down a pass on the western face. Thus confined it gathers speed, whistling among the boulders like a runaway steam engine. It strikes the plain at the base and hurtles westward towards the sea five miles distant. This wind-blasted plain, between the base of the mountain and the ocean cliffs, is Wreckhouse. It is here, in the 1930s, that Lauchie McDougall built his home, a low house dug into the earth.

To reach Port aux Basques the railroad crossed this plateau within a stone's throw of McDougall's home. There he witnessed the unseen wind, like a distracted boy tired of his dinkies, lift train cars into the air and knock them on their sides. Each derailment meant days of work for the railway workers and lost revenue for the railway. During the 1940s and

1950s the railway agents to the north and south of Wreckhouse relied on MacDougall's report before they dispatched the trains to or from Port aux Basques. Legend has it that MacDougall would gauge the strength of the wind by pushing open his front door. Depending on how hard the wind pushed back, he knew whether or not Wreckhouse was safe for the trains. MacDougall is dead now, his family scattered, and all that remains of their small house is the wind-blasted foundation.

The Trans-Canada Highway runs through Wreckhouse close to the former rail line. When the wind sweeps down from the mountains, experienced transport truck drivers, unless they have a heavy load, wait for the wind to subside—however many hours or even days that may take. Dave said that a few years ago a new driver heard the warnings but decided, since he had a full trailer, that he would risk it. The wind picked up his truckload of potato chips and flung it across the road.

Dave's tail lights bump out of sight up the dirt road and I am alone with the dust and the mosquitoes. Quietly massaging my feet at the edge of the campsite, I'm startled when a rabbit pops out of the woods within arms reach, brown and thin, then scampers across the grass. The feeling of desolation slowly fades to a dull ache, like the ache in my blistered heel. I try not to think about the whole journey, focus instead on tomorrow's goal, South Branch, sixteen miles to the north.

St. Andrew's

# CHAPTER 3
# SOUL OF THE BOOT

*Our worth is determined by the deeds we do
rather than by the fine emotions we feel.*
– Elias Magoon

### 7 JULY, 5:00 P.M., MILE 498.4

The North end of Codroy Pond is ideal for my second night. It takes fifty paces on the sandy bottom to get to waist depth. The air is warm, but each splash of water raises goose bumps. Fish ripple the surface. From the shore large spruce and birch hide the steep hillside to the east. About 300 yards back I can just see the dirt-cut of a logging road. Above that only birch and an occasional patch of spruce stand above the brush of the logged slope. A quarter mile away to the west is the rail line where several overgrown cabins are all that remain of Codroy Pond Siding.

Not wanting to think, I do laundry and listen to crows bawling to each other. On the way back up the path I see a crow stabbing at the plastic bag with the last of my bread in it. I chase the bird off and salvage half a loaf.

I am one day ahead of schedule. But it is not due to any miraculous walking. About two hours ago I made it as far as South Branch, fourteen miles southwest of here. My full pack was waiting for me at the local post office, where the waitress from the Chignic Lodge had dropped it off. Staggering under the weight of the pack, I panicked. There were camper trailers on all the likely camping spots. I felt lost and slumped on the doorstep, grappling through fatigue for the right decision. I needed a break.

All day I had slogged over loose crushed stone. Gruesome walking. And to make matters worse, the taps were beginning to separate from the rest of my $170 hiking boots. I had the name of a contact in South Branch, a Mr. Muise, so I called him. He showed up in his pickup truck within ten minutes of my call. I told him I needed a ride "back" to Codroy Pond.

The day started well enough. Warm, with a gentle breeze and crows bawling "up, up." I left Mummichog by 8:00. To the right, shadows in the mountains made giant staring faces. I was an insect scrambling among the aspen and buttercups. For the first mile the track was worn smooth by the vehicles of cabin owners. Then the loose granite again. My knee began to tighten and the blister on my heel soon doubled in size.

Just as Deb had told me yesterday, the change in vegetation was remarkable. By noon the wild strawberries were red on top, while the previous day I had seen only strawberry flowers. The farmland of St. Andrews and Tompkins, with mountains on either side, was so lush it reminded me of the Fraser Valley in British Columbia. Yellowhammers, small birds with black-trimmed wings, darted through the trees and over the weed tops like swallows. Could the wind-blasted bleakness of Wreckhouse be less than a day's walk behind?

There's nothing like ninety-degree heat on a railbed and blistered feet to strip away romantic notions about this trip as a stroll across the Island. As the shadows retreated into the mountain crevices, my feet began a protest which lasted to South Branch. Every time I stopped, a host of mosquitoes greeted me. I was soon punch-drunk from slapping at the stouts (or deerflies, also known on the West Coast as blowflies) that dive-bombed me constantly. Later, thick alders made a roofless tunnel, blocking any view of the countryside, slowing the wind and concentrating the heat.

Twice the track ran close to the Trans-Canada and I danced on the pavement, such a relief after the stone on the railroad. Streams of traffic whipped past at sixty miles an hour. They had driven their damned cars off the ferry twenty minutes before and had already reached the point that took me several blisters and bouts of depression to reach.

The TCH has taken a couple of quarter-mile chomps out of the track west of Doyles. Who approves this kind of destruction to the rail line when its fate is still uncertain? A road sign: Corner Brook 182 kilometres. Grand

Falls 422 kilometres, and that's only half way. Try not to think about it—South Branch, here I come. Tableland Mountain melted into the distance behind as the rail line turned inland up the Codroy Valley.

By noon I reached the Grand Codroy River, running shallow and broad to the left. At every pool, salmon fishermen flicked their spider strands across the surface, reeled in their flies. The heat was almost blinding and I was ready to collapse when I reached the Chignic, where an off-duty warden had dropped off my full pack for me. The waitress for the restaurant at the lodge lives near South Branch and volunteered to cart the pack on to that community, if I would lift it into her truck. By 3:30 I stumbled into South Branch, where I planned to spend the night. My feet, and my trip, were in serious trouble. So I called Muise and hitched the ride with him to Codroy Pond.

As Muise drove away from my camp, I had to wrestle the urge to quit, to drag my monster of a pack to the highway and hitch home. The distant rush of the transport trucks echoed across Codroy Pond. I could be in St. John's tomorrow morning. Demoralized, not yet hardened to the trail, and discouraged by the flaw in my boot soles, I'm that close to cashing in the trip. Instead, I eat, hang up the laundry, take another very brief, breathless swim.

My pack might be too heavy to carry, but at least it has everything I need, including the right goop for repairing the soles of boots. I squeeze some of the glue into the opening and lodge a large rock on top of the boot to press the sole to the upper.

At twilight an ATV races up the track. They are the gods of this terrain, these people astride their ATVs, like the Spaniards on horseback who subdued Central America, like centaurs. Because of the mobility it lends them, the iron steeds give the drivers the kind of power over the trail that is a prelude to possession.

Despite the panic attack, the black flies, mosquitoes and stouts—and the blisters—I am happy. Twelve miles to St. Fintans tomorrow and my first scheduled rest day. Taking the ride has really given me a boost. A loon calls again from Codroy Pond. And from the logged hillside the wild chainsaw calls into the twilight…voom voom whooon.

## HISTORY SIDING ONE
# THE WORK OF THE COUNTRY

Stretching in a narrow, interrupted line for 547 miles across the island of Newfoundland is a ribbon of crushed stone and precarious trestles—the impressive fragments of a tiny nation's leap of faith into the age of steam and iron.

It began in the closing decades of the nineteenth century. Newfoundland's 200,000 people eked out an existence in coastal fishing villages. Roads were scarce. Transportation, freight and communication were limited to coastal boats. But there was a prospect of new industry and a diversified economy, if a means could be devised to reach the unexploited timber, mineral and agricultural resources in the interior.

In 1880, Newfoundland's Prime Minister William Whiteway confidently told the House of Assembly that the construction of a national railway from St. John's to Halls Bay, on the Northeast Coast, was to be, "the work of the country. And in its bearing on the promotion of the well-being of the people, in which the returns are alone sought and will be found, [a railway] eminently commends itself to our judgment."

The following year Whiteway's government received two bids. They rejected a proposed standard-gauge line, though most suited to the extremes of the Newfoundland winter; in favour of a bid, from New York lawyer Albert Blackman, for a cheaper but less suitable narrow-gauge line. Within three years the Blackman Syndicate was bankrupt and Whiteway had less than 100 miles of track, from St John's to Harbour Grace, to show for his vision.

Work on the main line ceased and Whiteway was defeated in 1885 by the merchant-dominated Reform Party under Robert Thorburn. He was opposed to the railway. However, upon Whiteway's re-election in 1889, the national ambition was re-invigorated, thanks largely to the cunning and ability of a Scottish stonemason turned railway builder and financier.

# LONG RANGE TRAIL
## CODROY VALLEY TO STEPHENVILLE CROSSING

Map of the Newfoundland Railway main line from Corner Brook to Port aux Basques, showing stations: Corner Brook, Petries, Cooks Brook, Beaver Pond, Spruce Brook, Gallants, Black Duck Siding, Stephenville Crossing, Main Gut - St. Georges River, Sandy Point, St. Georges, Heathertown Stn., Mckays Highlands, St. Fintans, Codroy Pond, North Branch, South Branch, Doyles, Wreckhouse, Cape Ray, Port aux Basques. Also labeled: Port au Port Peninsula, St. Georges Bay, Grand Codroy River.

++++++++++++ main line

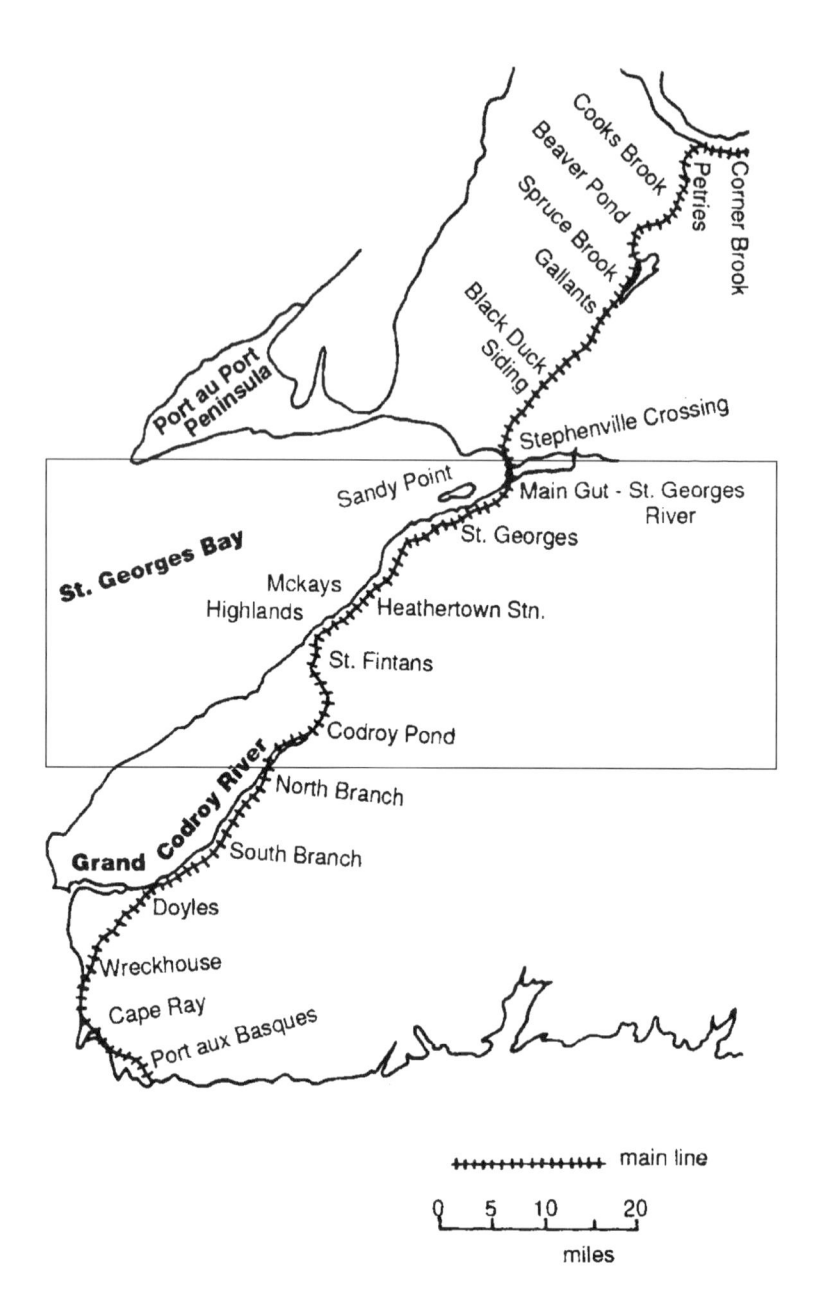

0  5  10    20
     miles

# LONG RANGE TRAIL INTRODUCTION

In 2004, Johnny Macpherson and his wife Cathy bought St. Fintans Grocery, the small store where he first rescued me from my backpack. When the trains were running, this small structure was the railway station house. In recognition of that tradition, the Macphersons renamed the store Station Grocery.

Sitting right next to the railbed like that gives Macpherson a front row seat for traffic on the T'Railway. "We're seeing more and more ATVs every year on the trail," he says. Local traffic is too frequent to calculate but even out-of-province ATV traffic is up. "At least 300 to 400 a year are stopping at our store," he says. These come through in small groups as part of ATV tours sold by adventure tour operators in the Maritimes. Because the trail is not groomed in winter the snowmobile traffic is slower than it might otherwise be. But when it comes to hikers Macpherson says, "I could count on the fingers of one hand, the number of hikers that are after going by there since we bought the store."

In contrast to the Wreckhouse Trail, the Long Range Trail is badly in need of upgrading. This area is blessed, or cursed, with the greatest concentration of large trestles of the entire T'Railway. These don't respond well to neglect. The Main Gut Trestle near Stephenville Crossing is closed to all traffic. The nearby highway bridge is fine for hikers or bicyclers, but it is illegal for ATVers and snowmobilers to use it. But they do anyway. And with an estimated cost of over one million dollars to either remove or replace the trestle, there is no solution in sight. The North Branch River Trestle is also impassable.

But it is not all bad news. A few years ago Robinsons River Trestle shifted downstream. In response, the Three Rivers Snowmobile Association raised enough money to pay for the work necessary to stabilize the trestle. They are now using it again. Other large trestles in the area, though badly in need of a great deal of work, were decked over in 2007 thanks to the fundraising success of the T'Railway Council. In addition, the Bay St. George South development association has a project, through Service Canada, to cut back the heavy alder growth in the Codroy Pond area.

In communities like Stephenville Crossing, where the trail passes close to residential areas, dust is a real problem for residents. The T'Railway did solve a similar problem in Norris Arm using recycled asphalt, the cost, though relatively inexpensive, is prohibitive for now.

# CHAPTER 4
# THE FIRST SCARS

A cloud of dust streams up into the late afternoon sky and roars along the gravel road. Galloping towards me the cloud suddenly spews a black pickup truck. One-handing the steering wheel is a thick-armed young man with longish hair. He brakes slightly to nod, then roars past into the inwardly whirling dust. He is the first person I have seen since I staggered into the straps of the knapsack at Codroy Pond early this morning. According to the map this is supposed to be the railway.

The road into St. Fintans runs parallel with the railbed to the intersection with Route 405, where a small convenience store offers an end to the misery of my own stupidity. When I drop my pack outside I feel like I have run a marathon, though my top speed for the day was only about two miles an hour. After guzzling a soft drink, I phone Johnny MacPherson, the coordinator with the local development association and my contact here.

Within fifteen minutes, Johnny pulls into the parking lot. He's thick-boned, of medium height, in his forties, with a full head of black hair and clean-shaven face. A gold crucifix swings out as Johnny bends and lifts my knapsack into the back of his little blue pickup with an ease that I find disappointing. I want him to struggle, at least a little. I climb stiffly into the cluttered cab and we scoot down the highway on a twenty-minute drive to a hot shower and a soft bed.

Luckily for me Johnny proved to be a patient listener. I talked about the hell of walking on crushed stone, talked about washed-out culverts, felled trees and tangled branches, the deep tracks of skidders too close to the track, talked about singing long rambling songs loudly, talked about how ecstatic I was just to have the bloody knapsack off my back. He probably thought I was nuts. I could not stop talking, even apologized a couple of times. But Johnny waved it off. Words just kept pouring out of my mouth.

*In the warm embrace of the shower I shut my eyes and it is a baptism of images and sounds.*

When I finally talked myself out, I learned that Johnny was from nearby Highlands, and had lived "up-along" for several years. One year he came home on a visit and never went back. He has volunteered with the development association for twenty years, and has worked full time as coordinator for the last four. Johnny proudly pointed out local landmarks: Robinsons Head, the old-age home built and operated by the development association, the new bridge between McKays and St. Davids.

Ruby Gillam's home, where Johnny has arranged my room and board for a few days, is a tidy, two-storey house in Crown Lands, inland from McKays. She hosts guests for the development association. Ruby has lived here since she and her husband danced their wedding night away, forty years ago. He died in 1984. But she has kept up the property with help from a son who lives down on the main road. There's a pile of unchopped wood near the back shed. Ruby's blue eyes study me through black-rimmed glasses under tightly controlled grey hair. After setting the table for me and serving baked beans and buns, she leaves to help cater a wedding at the Lions Club.

Dragged down with fatigue, I'm overcome with a bad case of "poor me" as a dirty man stares back at me from the dresser mirror. He has black stubble thick enough to make shaving tough, brown eyes a little too focused, streaks of dirt on the neck. A flattened mosquito is stuck with blood to my thigh. The left knee is slightly swollen and when I peel off a sock there are two newborn blisters.

In the warm embrace of the shower I shut my eyes and it is a baptism of images and sounds: the leaves of birch and aspen trace the wind, stones crunch like marbles underfoot, the rhythmic click of the walking stick, the marooooom of bees so close they sound like transport trucks, the tiny buzz of mosquitoes, blood in my ears. Behind it all is a tapestry of bird songs, as colourful and intricate as a hooked rug.

Under River Brook Trestle, Mile 491.5, in the smooth thin smell of fish, I watched a red ant struggle across the footing with a cocoon three times its size. The ant tries to climb up the concrete wall and falls down, picks itself up and starts again. I wonder how his knees are holding up.

In the sweltering heat, under the killing weight of a knapsack only slightly less than three times my size, something changed for me today. Despite the blisters and drudgery, I realized, for the first time, I could complete the trip.

I imagine what it must have been like to rumble in a passenger car down to St. Fintans. Along Rainy Brook and River Brook, where spruce ease their huge branches out over the water, the train wheels screech and rattle as the engineer brakes with every turn in the line. Suddenly a shale cliff rises sheer...bushes, shrubs and spruce growing in the cracks. At the foot, the track is littered with small rocks the roots have thrown down. Veering westward towards the coast, the mountains drift backwards to the right. The tall spruce and fir grow stunted. Old stumps, earth chewed to black ruts by logging trucks and skidders.

I shut off the shower and the images swirl down the drain.

Fischells Brook

## CHAPTER 5
# SALMON BACKS

Just before dusk, in November of 1822, a weary party of three men "led" by William Epps Cormack scrambled down the ice-crusted shore of Crabbes River to the community of Jeffreys on St. George's Bay. They were in the final hours of the two-month expedition which made Cormack the first white man to cross the unmapped interior of Newfoundland. His companions were Sylvester Joe and a second Micmac, who served as guide during the last few weeks. From the Crabbes River Trestle—486 miles from St. John's—high over the wide shallow river, 171 years later, I can scan their crooked path down to the sandy estuary.

There is a large bridge there now, built in 1987 to connect Jeffreys on the north bank to St. Davids and Crabbes Hill. At breakfast this morning Ruby Gilliam told several local stories including one about that bridge. Before it was built the only way to travel between the two communities was either by boat across the river or by road to the nearest bridge, a fifteen mile round trip. The people from Jeffreys could hear the St. Davids Anglican church bell almost as loudly as they could hear the bell of their own Anglican church. With an amused smile Ruby recounted how devout Anglicans on either side of Crabbes River fought the proposed bridge.

They were afraid one of the churches would have to go. Today there are still people who, when they want to get to the "Other Side" will drive the old route rather than use the bridge.

Resistance to change is not new here. In the kitchen with us is Johnny Macpherson. He recounts how his great-grandfather, John Macpherson, sailed into St. George's Bay from Cape Breton in the late nineteenth century and set up a farm on the wind-blasted earth in Highlands, south of here. He and his neighbours fought successfully to keep the new railway out of their coastal community to protect their free-range sheep and cattle. So the line was diverted up the river valley through St. Fintans. Ironically, a few years after their victory over the railway, the people of Highlands saw their sheep herds decimated by a disease that was spread by blowflies.

Ruby has vivid childhood memories of a singer called Leonard Hulan. He is a legend on this part of the Island. The Hulans, of Jersey descent, were one of the first resident families on the West Coast. Leonard lived in Jeffreys and was renowned for his ability to strike up songs, a cappella, about local people, places and events. Like many, he farmed and fished. Unlike many, he kept oxen. Ruby Gillam remembers him as a good-humoured man, in his middle years when she was a child. He made frequent household visits on both sides of Crabbes and was always ready to sing. He would stay on late into the evening, regardless of the chores waiting for him at home. Ruby remembers one evening Leonard looked thoughtful for a moment, then remarked:

"Here I am, up here singing, and my oxen are home starving." Johnny says if Leonard was alive today he would be a folk hero, just like fiddlers Emile Benoit and Rufus Guinchard, recently deceased musicians from a slightly younger generation.

This morning I've been following the rail line as it runs between the Long Range Mountains and the coast as it crosses three major rivers and several smaller ones in one ten-mile section. That makes the rail line an ideal back road for salmon fishers. "If it's too wide to jump across, there's probably salmon in it," one ATV rider told me. When Cormack reached this section of the west coast he found small but thriving communities where the inhabitants made a good living in the salmon fishery.

Stepping off Middle Barachois Trestle, Mile 482, I'm startled when the alders call to me in a thick male voice.

"Good morning." A black-haired man in long green rubbers and a green forestry jacket steps out onto the track. He's studying me up and down with his one good eye and asks, in an almost conversational tone, where I'm coming from and where I'm headed. It is my turn to catch him off guard.

"Port aux Basques and St. John's."

"You're walking right through on the track?"

"Yeah."

A second voice laughs from the bushes, and another fisheries officer steps onto the track. He's in his mid-fifties, with grey hair and a green baseball cap tipped back to reveal a bald forehead.

"You got more guts than I do," he says, and we shake hands. He's John Downey. His partner—mid-thirties and badly in need of a shave—is Ron Barry. They are staking out the river to nab salmon poachers. And there's no shortage "as long as salmon is fetching a good price and the rivers are so low."

"Last night we made a good catch. We got a fella with a whole sack full of salmon," chuckles John. There seems to be more salmon since the commercial fishery ended—but that is a coincidence, John tells me between drags on his cigarette. Ron agrees. They've clearly had time to discuss the ways of the Atlantic salmon, as they lie in wait.

"I think it's a cycle. Five years. It was a bad year 1988, and this is five years gone by. But last year there was a lot of salmon," says Ron as I drop my knapsack to the ground. They both glance over it casually but intently.

John spits out loose bits of tobacco. "There's a lot of salmon no doubt. But we're losing them in the fall eh, from the spawning grounds, because [all the fisheries officers] will be laid off just as the fish gets on the spawning ground. The government is saving a thousand dollars in salaries and losing a hundred thousand in fish stock."

Ron throws his arms wide, "There's salmon on the spawning ground that big."

"That's five feet!"

"I've seen 'em go to sixty to sixty-four pounds, in the spawning pools from Twelve Mile Pool and on up the river," says John. Then he looks angry. "You can catch more in twenty minutes than you can take in a pick-up. That's how much salmon is there."

"And there's a bridge goes right over the pool," adds Ron, taking off his hat and turning it round and round. He knows people who have gone to places like Twelve Mile Pool, and taken enough fish to block their freezers. "They eat the fish all winter and then what's left in the spring they just throw on the dump and go out and do it all over again."

"There's lots of salmon there, but there's not going to be in five or six years because they're taking the spawning stocks," John says, throwing down his smoke and scuffing it out.

"And the fines are so expensive! You get a guy half drunk and he's just liable to try and hit you over the head with a stick or a rock or something. You fall in that river, you drown," Ron says.

"That's a two-way street." John clenches his jaw. "That's why we're together." They both lapse into silence for a moment. "You missed that wildlife right there, it was either a meadow vole or a lemming, one or the other," says John, pointing north along the track.

Crossing Robinsons River at Mile 481—in the shadow of the trestle several fishermen are casting across a wide pool. I caution them that wardens are in the area, then grow angry at myself for the betrayal. The river is shallow in the heat of summer, but residents say each winter and spring it boils with unstoppable rage. The trestle is forty feet above the surface of the river right now, but with the spring thaw it occasionally catches the ice. It was here in 1986 that a flood took out a pier and shut down the railway for a month and a half. The piers in these large rivers need yearly inspection. In the rail days, grouting-gang divers would stuff bags of anchorite—a kind of cement—under the footings to halt the erosion. Nothing has been done here since 1988.

Shortly after noon Heatherton Station appears ahead, surrounded by forest. This area thrived as a farming center in the nineteenth century, supplying the soil-less Southwest Coast. Heatherton was a busy farmers' market and shipping point for farm produce up and down this section of the coast. Now the station is boarded up and graying. There's a small blue pickup beside it and I can just make out Johnny's profile through the heat waves. Dripping sweat, I finally reach the station and Johnny snaps a few photos before we take the shore road to Ruby's. The last three miles from Robinsons Road to the Heatherton Station was hell to walk on, all very loose crushed stone. From the tire tracks I guessed a front-end loader had scooped off much of the stone. Johnny already knows about it.

"As you saw, a local contractor has been quite busy," he says. "The CN police were called in. But CN don't give a goddamn." He slaps the steering wheel with his thick hand.

Jutting out from this shore, Robinsons Head stretches huge and sphinxlike into the bay. Once forested, the hill is mostly meadowland today. Across St. George's Bay, the Port au Port Peninsula is a low line on the horizon. Johnny says that from the top of Robinsons Head, on a clear day, "you can see twenty-four miles up the bay to Stephenville, and the mountains behind."

Hush! Puppies in the zing.

# CHAPTER 6
# ZING

Three men and a woman pose as a tight group in the viewfinder. The mid-morning sun is masked behind clouds so there are no shadows. We've walked four miles since 8:00. There's another mile to the Station House in Stephenville Crossing, where we will go our separate ways. My jaws ache from laughing. What I had feared would be a stressful hike turned out to be a very enjoyable stroll.

The compact man on the right of the frame is Bud Hulan, a great-great-grandson of the Hulans from Jeffreys whom Cormack mentions in his memoirs. Bud is balding and has a trim grey beard around his affable, but professional, smile. He is the provincial member for the area. Bifocals hang from a strap around his neck. His khaki shorts and white socks at mid-calf emphasize his stature.

Immediately to Bud's right is Maudie MacDonald. She is a political assistant to Bud and a second or third cousin. Forty-something, she's the only one of the four smiling enough to show teeth. From under her crop of dark-blond hair, she regards the camera with an amused gaze. Baggy shorts cover her knees, blue socks rumple around her ankles.

With his left arm around Maudie is Howard Skinner, St. George's mayor. Under dark glasses and a sunburned nose, his bushy mustache rides a wide smile. Howard's blue jogging jacket is unzipped, revealing a robin-red tee shirt.

On the far left, hands deep in his jogging pants pockets, is Hayward Young, blond and white as a Norse adventurer. He's mayor of Stephenville Crossing—the "Cross Zing" or simply "the Zing" to locals. Hayward is telling yet another story, even as I prepare to take the photo. "A friend of mine is a biologist in Nova Scotia and I was visiting him one time when he had just finished comparing skulls of bears. He said 'You know Hayward, the skulls of Newfoundland black bears are different from Nova Scotian bears.' The two skulls didn't even lie the same way. 'Look at the Newfoundland skull, the brain cavity is bigger,' he said. And I said, 'You didn't have to tell me that, it's the same with the humans.'"

We all laugh and I click the shutter, freezing their grins in the middle of a wide dirt road. Immediately behind, the trusses of Main Gut Trestle—453 miles from St. John's. A pole line cuts across the frame in the middle distance, and beyond that dabs of white are the houses on the outskirts of Stephenville Crossing. Behind it all, green ridges rip their way across a grey sky.

The five of us met earlier at Barachois Brook Trestle—Mile 457. The local politicians were already there when Danny Conway and I arrived. Danny is the president of the Barachois Development Association. He worked with Otto Goulding to set up this morning's group walk and made contacts for me in Gallants, the community I hoped to reach before dark. (Otto was one of my main supporters in organizing this walk. You'll meet him later when we get closer to Pasadena where he lives). Danny was pale and sweating—chest pains every time he breathed. But he wanted to drive me to the trestle and introduce me to my walking companions.

After a brief interview by a local journalist, the five of us—Bud, Maudie, Howard, Hayward and I—set out. The crushed stone was thick, so walking was tough. At first there were a lot of questions about my trip. I took particular delight in describing how I gutted my knapsack after the ordeal between Codroy Pond and St. Fintans, removing at least twenty pounds of food and useless supplies, such as the spatula and extra fuel.

At the mouth of St. George's River, Sandy Point Island hunches a few hundred metres offshore. Though deserted now, it was the largest town on the West Coast in the era prior to the railway. But the steam engine changed all that. Howard says the settlers moved across the inlet from the Point to the rail line and St. George's became the unofficial West Coast capital and a major watering station for the steam trains. "Right down here," continues Howard "that's Tank Hill. A lot of people don't know why it has that name. It's because of a big water tower down at the bottom of it where the steam engines took on water."

Nearby is a site called Seal Rocks. It was a Micmac settlement for a century beginning in the early 1800s. "The Micmacs used to live in Conne River, Baie d'Espoir, in the winter and then come over to St. George's Bay for the summer," explains Howard.

"The railroad drove all the Micmacs inland," says Bud pointing east to where the morning sun is a dim disk above the Long Range Mountains. And the talk turns again to hiking and the journey of Cormack and Sylvester Joe across the interior of Newfoundland.

Bud believes the important point is that Cormack made the first recorded journey across Newfoundland, describing geology, flora and fauna. "I don't know if you have ever seen the original book, I have a copy of it. It is very interesting to me because three pages in the center are devoted to my great-great-grandfather and grandmother," says Bud. Cormack stayed with them and he describes how they lived, making yogurt, making cheese. "That's all gone now," says Bud. He lives in the old house and is carrying out extensive renovations this summer.

We slog along for another while, Bud in the lead, me flitting from person to person. Hayward mentions his admiration for Mayor George Saunders of Bishop's Falls, a railway town in Central Newfoundland. The town was paid $7 million in compensation when the railway shut down. The Zing got zip.

"The railway wasn't a major industry in the Crossing when it finally closed. Not like Bishop's Falls. All we had was a railroad running parallel to the town's main road. That's all," says Hayward. CN handed over the land they used in the town. "Our main concern is that we don't lose control of the right-of-way through town. We don't mind sharing it with snow mobiles and ATVs but we want to send a clear message that the old rail line 'is not a highway for ATVs' going right through town,'" says Hayward, as I hand him my canteen of water.

He says there is another larger concern for the council. Their municipal area includes the Main Gut Trestle and two smaller ones. Hayward admits that they are concerned about the liability as far as injury and maintenance goes for people using the trestle. "The bridge has been there that long that, sooner or later, it will deteriorate to the point that it has to be removed. And we don't want to be responsible to move that. You are talking a million dollars."

Bud has stopped ahead and points down at the track. "You see that flower there?" At his feet is a pale plant with a yellow flower that resembles a buttercup, except the petals are larger and several flowers grow from one central stalk. I had noticed them growing through the crushed stone all the way from Port aux Basques.

"That's the evening primrose. The seeds contain a unique amino acid, found nowhere else in nature." Bud stoops and plucks a blossom. He explains that the amino acid is used for medical purposes such as treating severe acne and migraine headaches. It is also involved in protecting the heart from vascular disease, and in counteracting inflammatory disease, such as arthritis. This knowledge comes from his experience ten years before when he was part of a research team in Kentville, Nova Scotia. "It started off as a little industry. Last year their business plan showed $140 million. We encouraged Nova Scotian producers of evening primrose, but it didn't work out. It's now grown in England, where they extract the oil and then ship it to Kentville."

*Two miles outside the Crossing the roadbed crosses a large wetland. The mid-morning clouds are thinning.*

The grade is slightly downhill from St. George's, through the town of Barachois Brook, on past Black Bank Provincial Park and north along the shore. The Bay stretches westward on our left towards the distant Port au Port Peninsula. Two miles outside the Crossing the roadbed crosses a large wetland. The mid-morning clouds are thinning. As we round the end of the Bay, heading towards Main Gut Trestle, several ATVs roar past us. Walking is easier because traffic has pushed the crushed stone aside. Hayward points to a pond to our left on the beach side of the track.

"I'm going to give you a lesson in wildlife here now," he says. The jibe is not missed by Bud. "See a bunch of ducks... right out in the middle? Those out there are greater scaup." For the last five years the greater scaup males have been spotted in the pond. "The females are off having their broods or whatever. So the boys hang out here. Like a bar, I suppose," he says looking around for a laugh.

According to Hayward there are another ten varieties of ducks that nest there including American widgeon. "Last week I passed here and there were two guys from the biology department. They said they don't know what it is about this Little River Pond, but it attracts several species of rare birds."

"Are they protected from hunting?" Maudie, although a local, is intrigued.

"No. But they are this time of the year, from everyone other than the poachers," Howard tells her. "They haven't been bothered lately.

Anyway, from what the biologists told me, they're trying to get some type of bird reserve here." The conversation stirs one of his concerns with conservation in the area. "Birds from Sandy Point come here," he says and this is an issue because the Point is a protected area, but "protection over there means very little, if they're not protected in Little River Pond." There's a guy named George Kitchen from Robinsons (Dave's brother) heading up the effort to extend the protected area.

Spreading inland on our right is Little River. It is well-known locally for big trout at certain times of the year. The overhead supports for the long Main Gut Trestle are clearly visible just ahead and the closer we get the more nervous Maudie becomes. She does not want to cross the trestle. We pause on the south bank for a few photographs. They bunch together in the viewfinder, Bud, Maudie, Howard with his arm around her, and Hayward. Then we step onto the trestle, Maudie too. Howard holds her arm, Bud holds her hand.

The determined current of St. George's Bay rushes black and deep just a few feet beneath the trestle. Boots clump heavily on the ties and Maudie titters nervously. To ease Maudie's discomfort, Howard tells how a young man from the area committed suicide last year when he leaped from the trestle.

That puts Bud in mind of another story. "It was before your time Howard, but I remember Plum Bennett. Did you ever hear of him? From Stephenville Crossing?" None of us had heard of Plum, but Bud continues. "He was a tough fella and the RCMP were after him, pinned him between them on this trestle. It was very cold, early in the spring, but he jumped in and swam right out to the other side," says Bud, waving across Little River Pond to the wave-heaped rocks of St. George's Bay. "Climbed out on the beach and got away."

We made it across without further incident, or stories, and reached the Station House Inn where we posed for another local journalist, shook hands and then slipped back into our private lives.

## HISTORY SIDING TWO
## A NEW VISION FOR
## A NATIONAL RAILWAY

In 1889, Robert Gillespie Reid stepped ashore on a finger pier in the bustling seaport of St. John's. The forty-seven-year-old Reid, who began as a stonemason in Scotland, had used his natural ability for engineering and business to earn his fortune as he constructed rail lines in the United States and in Canada.

Undaunted by Newfoundland's extremes of weather and difficult terrain, the railway contractor saw opportunity in the Island government's difficulties. That same year he signed a contract with Whiteway to construct 261 miles of rail line to Halls Bay within five years for $4.07 million in government bonds.

From Whitbourne, Reid directed 3,000 men in three gangs: one to slash the right of way through thick spruce and scrub brush; one to work with pick, shovel, wheelbarrow and dynamite, to grade the way through rocky soil and treacherous bogs; and behind them, one to build trestles, sling ballast, lay ties and rails, and hammer spikes.

Working for a dollar a day (and paying two dollars and fifty cents a week for room and board) the men pushed ahead at eighty miles a year until, in 1893, they halted on the banks of the formidable Exploits River, across from what is now the town of Bishop's Falls.

The Whiteway government now had a change of plan for their national railway. The copper mining region of Halls Bay was no longer of primary concern. They drafted a new contract which directed Reid to divert the main line 285 miles south to Port aux Basques, taking a direct, but exposed route across the Topsails, the snowbound roof of Newfoundland. In a second contract the government obliged Reid to operate the railway between Whitbourne and Port aux Basques for ten years in return for the rights to 5,000 acres of land per mile. Reid knew the operation of such a line was a money-losing proposition but the profits of construction and the additional land rights proved a sufficient incentive. Work began on the Exploits Trestle.

# LOGGER'S TRAIL
## STEPHENVILLE CROSSING TO CORNER BROOK

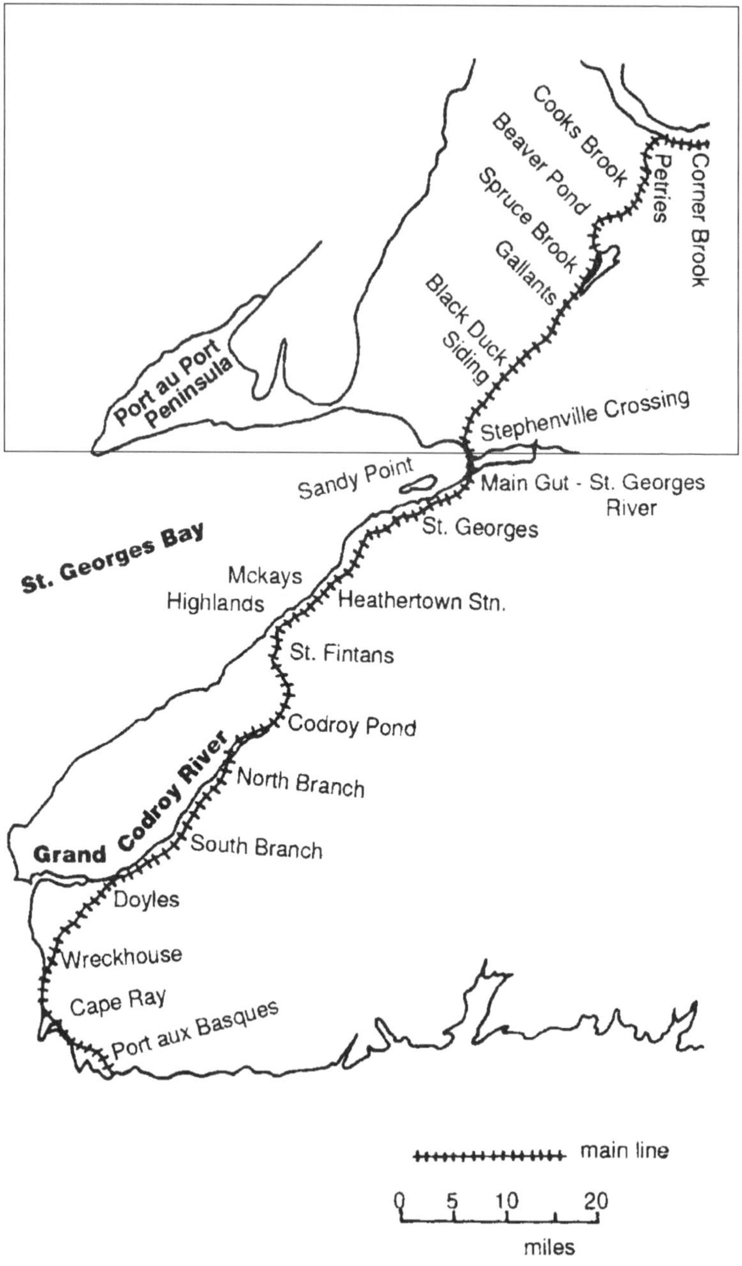

# LOGGER'S TRAIL INTRODUCTION

Jim Collier says it's hard to tell these days whether the trail is busier in the winter or in the summer. It is just a stone's throw from his door and the dust from ATVs can be daunting, even though the T'Railway Council supplies the town with dust-suppressing calcium each year. Collier lives in the same home, near the western end of George's Lake, where he lived when I sat down with him to a meal of fish stew in 1993. His widowed daughter-in-law had just moved away to Stephenville Crossing with his three young grandchildren including a baby granddaughter for whom he was very concerned. The daughter-in-law is now remarried and living in Stephenville where the granddaughter he was so concerned about is "graduating from grade eleven and doing well."

Collier's buddy and former railroader Ted Hickey died of a heart attack in 2005. He owned a cabin just up the road. The working model train and track that Hickey laid in the woods is gone.

At the eastern end of George's Lake, the Spruce Brook railway station that Garfield Connock converted into a home has been abandoned since Garfield caught the last train for the coast. But, says Collier, the development along the shores of George's Lake has continued. "People building homes have got every part of it filled right in," he says.

Collier doesn't use the trail much himself, but one person who does is Kevin Sweetland. He's with the Bay St. George Snowmobile Association (*www.bsgsa.ca*). They are part of a provincial snowmobile group that works together to keep as much of the trail groomed as possible across the island from November to May—snow permitting, says Sweetland. The conditions for traveling are ideal in winter because the west coast is a snow zone. The T'Railway is the main east-west corridor for snowmobilers, not only from the island but "the ones visiting from Nova Scotia, New Brunswick, Great Britain and Germany."

The trail is much rougher in the summer with a lot of the dips and low mounds known locally as "yes'ems." There are also several culverts missing. According to Sweetland, Newfoundland Power will be putting in new poles along the section from Gallants to the Crossing, and "we've asked them to replace the few missing culverts and to fix up the washout near Beaver Pond while they are taking their heavy equipment through the area." But, Sweetland says, "by rights, in order to fix up the trail for ATVs, the whole length of the trail needs to be ploughed."

Ted Hickey's model train.

# CHAPTER 7
# WAITING FOR THE RAIN AT BLACK DUCK SIDING

### 12 JULY, MILE 446

Clouds are rolling in from the west. Everything is still. The railway is a dirt road intersecting another dirt road. Soaked in sweat, I wrestle my way out of the pack. Yesterday the flies feasted on me through my spandex pants, and today I feel like I've fallen into a cactus hedge. I try to resist scratching and survey the four houses nearby for a likely candidate to approach for fresh water.

Two hours ago, at the railroad intersection with Whites Road, I met a member of an endangered species. Eating canned fruit while leaning against his ATV, he wiped his hand on his coverall before we shook hands. "Junior Cumby. I work with the railway," he said. How many other men are there today, along the whole 547 miles, who can make that claim? Junior left Corner Brook that morning in order to record the number and location of discarded railway ties and rails between that city and Port aux Basques.

"If you had a strong enough magnet, you could get enough spikes between here and Port aux Basques to start a scrap yard," I tell him. Junior is more interested in scraping the last of the fruit from inside the can.

Based on his inventory of remnants from the railway scattered along the railbed, Canadian National in St. John's will call for tenders to collect everything left behind by the demolition crews. Junior finishes his lunch, packs the remains away in a box on his ATV, and, after offering me a ride to Gallants (which I reluctantly decline), he drives north along the trail.

One thing his inventory will not show is the damage along this portion of the route. Though many sections of the railbed are passable, the washouts are a real hazard. Beavers are quite active in this area and regard the railbed as a prefab wall for damming operations. And when the beavers' reservoirs overflow, the loose dirt of the 'prefab' is the first to go, creating washouts thirty feet wide, all virtually invisible to drivers until they are at the very edge of the steep drop. At every washout people have tied cloth or survey ribbons to small trees, or piled branches or other debris on either bank as a sign of danger to approaching drivers.

There is a small patch of strawberries in the meadow at Black Duck Siding. Strawberries grow all along the track. Some are overripe, but today is the first day I've eaten them. There's probably no threat of poison anymore but I'm still leery about eating anything that grows along the line. The railway used Agent Orange and other chemicals to control the vegetation. From my childhood I can recall work crews riding their speeders slowly down the track spraying both sides of the line. I remember seeing the berry bushes, small spruce, alders and other wild shrubs wither and brown. Yesterday, after I discovered Bud Hulan was a chemist, I asked him if it was okay to eat the berries. He said the only danger from the Agent Orange was to the workers who sprayed it.

The sky is hidden now behind the clouds and the stillness is shattered. Several vehicles, including a brand new luxury car, rattle down the track from the direction of Gallants, twelve miles to the north and turn to head for Route 460. The leaves on either side of the roadbed are white from dust.

Heavier and heavier clouds blot out the blue. I can almost feel the rain falling, smacking the leaves. But it doesn't. A woman nearby in her neatly tended backyard bends stiffly over a flower bed. Tied to a lead is a spotted crackie that yaps defensively when I enter the yard with my empty canteen.

"You know that dog very seldom barks at anybody that comes here. But he barked at you."

"Is that a good sign or a bad sign?"

"I don't know," she laughs pushing her wire-rimmed glasses back into position. She introduces herself as Eileen Matthews and shows me to the garden hose. She says the dog runs away so she has to keep it tied on. "When she was in heat, she used to run down the road. And there is a dog down on the farm," Eileen says, gesturing westward across the track "what kills little dogs."

"Who owns the farm?"

"There used to be three farms down there.  Mitchell's, Captain Campbell's and Major Duwiess's.  And the man who bought Major Duwiess's, he has big dogs. And one of them is after killing three small dogs. So I keep Frisco tied on." Hearing his name, Frisco wags his body furiously and sniffs my boots while I fill the canteen.

Eileen and her husband, who is away this afternoon, have lived here since the 1940s. She says it hasn't changed much except for the railway. The train used to stop here for passengers until passenger services ended in 1968. Then the freight trains just rumbled on through. "Used to be a big station there," she says pointing to the clearing on the other side of the track where I ate lunch. "That went after they took the passenger trains off the line. They tore it all down. Used to be a big coal shed over there one time too. That was before the diesels.  For the steam."

### Postcard from under a Trestle

> *The thumb-sized beetle pulls its brown body from the brook onto a rounded stone, clings there as it pushes and shoves at the damp husk of its underwater history. New flesh emerges, emerald stones gleam and shimmer, wired by dark lines of silk to four transparent wings. It waits there, wings clasped together above its back, a jet on a carrier. Buffeted by the gentle gusts, the wings are antennae decoding ancient secrets. The insect's bright aqua green slowly fades to blue, dark blue, black. Then the wings unfold, flick, as if in response to the careful instruction of the wind, then flick back, then spread again. Almost lifted from the rock by the wind, it drags itself to the boulder's highest point and, its lesson at an end, the dragon flies.*

## CHAPTER 8
# FISH STEW

A half-ton truck with a wooden box approaches, headed back towards Black Duck Siding. The driver, his weathered face sporting a three-day salt-and-pepper beard, pulls up alongside and leans out the window, asks if I'm "that fella." Behind him his friend, in a stained tee shirt and trousers, tells me they own cabins in the area. They have read about my trip and want to talk about people using the railbed. The driver says people are hauling a lot of lumber out. About twenty miles north around Harry's Brook and Spruce Brook and that area, "they have got it crucified." When I asked him who "they" were, he said "just the public" looking for pulpwood and firewood.

There are cabins every half mile or so along the line from Robaires Brook north to Gallants, which explains the heavy traffic at Black Duck Siding. Every so often there is a slash of domestic cutting. Just north of Robaires Brook Trestle, Mile 444, a teenager in jogging clothes hauls a five-gallon bucket of water up from the brook. He lays down the bucket when he sees me, takes off his cap and wipes his forehead with his arm.

"Some warm."

"Too warm. I'm sweating like a pig now, but it keeps the flies away."

"Yeah, you wants to jump in a brook every now and again," he laughs. A child crying nearby, and a woman's impatient voice demands that someone "Get over here!" He asks what I'm doing and I explain that I am walking to Corner Brook and mention that I expect to get a boat ride up George's Lake.

"Oh, so you're not walking."

"Yeah. No." His matter-of-factness confuses me, revives memories of my near defeat at Codroy Pond. "I'm camping at the head of George's Lake and then I'm walking into Corner Brook tomorrow." A puppy runs out of the woods from the direction of the crying child.

Blackberry bushes tumble in a profusion of white blossoms. Just beyond the bog-drainage ditches are the tall larch and spruce. I imagine squadrons of mosquitoes lurking there. Always over the next ridge a pond. Mistaken pond, or am I mistaken? The line turns slowly inland as Indian Head Range to the west slopes down into hills. To the east rise the Long Range Mountains, the most easterly section of the Appalachians. Gusts of wind fill the silence between the gentle clamour of birds and the crunch of crushed stone under boots.

By mid-afternoon I keep turning to see if there are any signs of Danny Conway's blue pickup. Unless he is sicker than he was this morning when he drove me out to Barachois Brook, he's going to drive out and introduce me to my contact in Gallants. I would like to cover the remaining five miles before he catches up, so I walk hard and forego rest stops. My knee is sorer than it has been but the swelling has gone away.

"No shooting in this area, private property," declares a large plywood sign nailed to two high posts stuck in the bog. Through the trees gleams the truck driver's yellow cabin. He complained about the country being crucified by people cutting wood, yet he has stacked two cords beside the cabin and another half cord by the gate. The road to his cabin is corduroyed with a hundred or more railway ties.

A mile or so shy of Gallants two men, side by side on ATVs, approach up the track. They stop and switch off the motors. Fly rods flag their intentions. Bernard, about fifty, wears hip rubbers pulled up all the way. Ted looks to be thirty, with a thin beard and mustache. He lives in Gallants. Bernard has a cottage there, but is from Stephenville. He has worked for the town council there for longer than he cares to remember.

"This used to be a farm," Bernard tells me, pointing to where decayed railings separate us from a large meadow wild with the reds, oranges, yellows, and whites of native flowers. "All rose trees and apple trees. When the woman who owned it died they went in there and destroyed everything and they burned her house down. Look at the mess they have made there," he says, turning his head away from the long-dead trees beyond the neglected meadow.

The talk turns to injuries of a more personal nature. Bernard astride his ATV says, "I have a bad hip," and puts his hand on the small of his back. "If I walk against the tide of a river—after that, for a full week, my hip is good. I don't know what the hell it does." While he is talking Danny pulls up in his truck and slides out. He looks very pale under his close-cropped blond hair.

Once in the truck I notice Danny can't even hold the steering wheel with his left hand, his side hurts that much. He's driving uncomfortably close to the shoulder of the railbed.

Gallants is a small, tidy community of about two dozen houses and several cottages. The low evening sun gives a brilliance to the white fronts of the bungalows. Everything seems so pastoral until we swing into Jim Collier's yard. Danny brakes hard. A rusty green car, front wheels six feet off the ground, hangs by a chain from the bucket of a front-end loader. Half-hidden in the shadows of the cab, the tractor driver signals for us to keep back, and then rattles off up the road with the car in tow. "That's Jim Collier," says Danny.

Within fifteen minutes Jim returns, minus the old car. He climbs down nimbly from the cab and walks over to shake hands. He is pale, with a sleeveless tee shirt stretched out over his impressive middle-age spread and tucked in his green work pants.

The large driveway is layered with crushed stone which Jim admits came from the railbed. "Sure the section where I took the stone between Gallants and Black Duck Siding is the best part of the track for driving on," he says matter-of-factly. "And make no mistake, people do drive on the line. But that is nothing new here," Jim says. "People used to drive their trucks on the railbed even before the trains stopped running. At the trestles they would drive down into the riverbed or, depending on the level of their liquid courage, they'd listen carefully, then dart across the trestle." Jim believes that if the trestles are lifted then they'll just start driving through the streams.

When he notices me scratching, Jim asks about the flies and we exchange remedies. My best tip so far to keep the flies at bay is "don't wash." Apparently the flies hate the salt on the skin, or maybe it is just the smell they hate. Jim says woods workers coat a plastic bread bag with motor oil and pull the bag onto their hard hats. By the end of the day the bag is black with flies.

He invites me in for a supper of stewed codfish with potatoes. Two big platefuls, half a loaf of fresh bread, two or three frozen molasses buns, and several cups of tea later, I push back my chair. "If only I had known we were having company," Mrs. Collier says, by way of apology for the frozen buns.

Their twenty-nine-year-old son died in January. In late spring his widow left Gallants for Stephenville Crossing with the Colliers' three grandchildren, two boys, aged six and one, and a four-year-old girl who is mentally delayed, and not adjusting well to her new home. Jim and his wife are concerned about her. One of the last things that Jim says to me, when we part at Beaver Pond, is that he thinks the granddaughter may be coming to live with them. And he seems pretty happy about the idea.

On George's Lake.

## CHAPTER 9
# HELLTROT PIPES

Several people had warned me that Jim Collier is probably the grumpiest man alive. I never heard anything further from the truth, although when he starts on the subject of government, he gets a steely look in his light blue eyes and tenses his jaw.

After supper Jim drives me on the railbed along George's Lake on a guided tour, sketching his childhood for me. He talks about his business plans and the potential of the George's Lake area for tourism: for example, a barge on the lake as a floating hotel. The Reids, when they operated the railway, had big plans for tourism in this area as well, and produced several fancy brochures to market the area between 1908 and 1916. When CN announced the closure of the rail line Jim tried to buy a portion of it before the rails were lifted. He and his friend Ted Hickey planned to haul fishermen back and forth to the salmon rivers west of Gallants. All he got out of it was "the bureaucratic runaround."

Ted Hickey used to work for CN. He lives in Corner Brook but his cabin is about five minutes' drive from Jim's place and, though Ted is not around, Jim takes me up to the cabin for a "surprise." Ted has built a working model train large enough to seat two people in the cab and pull several small flatcars up the mile of track that he and Jim have laid into the woods.

George's Lake is at least five miles south to north and a mile wide. From the train track along the western shore Jim and I have an unsurpassed view of the steep and forested hills on the far side. He tells me the Boy Scouts have a camp there. Many of the "cottages" look more like expensive homes. I count at least five under construction.

Spruce Brook—Mile 429—is a former logging community and hunting and fishing resort along the track, that was vacated in the 1960s. It's been resettled since the 1970s and 1980s when people began moving back, "even though the road is only ploughed to Gallants in the winter," Jim says. And today there are several families of livyers, including a million-dollar-lottery winner. There's nothing to distinguish his bungalow from the others except for the five ATVs parked by the back door. The former Spruce Brook railway station, made of logs, is still standing. In fact it is in good shape. The owner, Garfield Connock, a former railway worker from Corner Brook, moved it back from the tracks and converted it to a cottage.

At the farthest end of George's Lake, Jim shows me the remains of a wharf spur where pulpwood was lifted from the lake and onto waiting flatcars. He stops the car in another spot to show me the concrete remains of a small water chute system that once supplied steam engines with water from a spring in the hill. It is grown over, but Jim finds it easily. As a boy, he and his buddies would use the water pipe to shower each other on summer days.

There is a four-foot-tall plant, with huge leaves and flowers like Queen Anne's lace, growing throughout the region. Called helltrot locally, it is common in the wet ditches along the track. The canes are hollow and in the fall young Jim and his friends would collect them to make "helltrot pipes." By cutting the main stem an inch or two above a joint they fashioned an airtight bowl. Smaller hollow canelets served as pipe stems. This autumn ritual was accompanied by the harvesting of "dried leaves, any kind, we weren't fussy." These dried leaves they would crunch up fine like tobacco and hide along with their pipes, to have a smoke during the winter.

Jim and I part ways at the head of George's Lake. He heads the pick-up back to Gallants and I tromp up the trail to a nearby camping spot he told me about.

*Looking for hawks.*

# CHAPTER 10
# "TRAINS ARE GONE"

### 13 JULY, 8:40 A.M.,
### THREE MILES NORTH OF BEAVER POND

The trail traverses a wooded hill, which drops steeply to the left offering a vista of lush lowlands. At the base of the hill is a large rushy pond with a beaver house near its centre. A quarter mile beyond the opposite shore a dirt road ribbons its way along the base of the far hills that slope back into the thinning fog. That's the Logging School Road. The school did not last long. They brought in new people, fresh out of training courses in adult education, to teach veteran loggers how to log. From the map I can see that Logging School Road is a collector for more than fifty miles of logging roads that snake among the hills.

The forest leans over the rail line. Occasionally the crashing of large animals unseen in the brush. The early sky grows bright. Suddenly, around a sharp turn, I startle two men crouched over a small portable stove in the middle of the road. The pickup nearby has a canoe lashed to the roof. And farther back a pup tent glows bright orange in the grassy clearing. The smell of bacon.

The two are biology students from Memorial University. They're researching hawks and owls for the Wildlife Department. They have a cabin at Little Grand Lake for the summer and came into this area three days ago. Yesterday they spotted a family of hawk owls and a kestrel. They invite me to stay for breakfast, but I have miles to go before I eat, so I thank them and set out again on the heavy crushed stone, prepared for a tough slog into Corner Brook. But less than a mile beyond the students' camp I get the first real shock of the journey. There the track intersects with the Logging School Road and ceases to be a rail line. The narrow, overgrown path disappears, as does the crushed stone, to be replaced by a two-lane dirt road, indistinguishable from the Logging School Road. Though the walking is now much easier, almost leisurely, I'm horrified at this transformation and what it portends.

By 10:00 the shadows are pulling back fast, when I spot movement ahead on the broad dirt road. Through the wavering heat a distorted shape, like a turtle, wobbles forward for twenty steps or so on two bowed spindly legs, stops and looks around, wobbles a few more paces, stops, then wobbles on again. As we approach each other, the turtle slowly morphs into the shape of a hunched old man in a stained blue tee shirt, shorts, no socks and new runners. He squints out at the world from beneath the black bill of a baseball cap.

"Out for a stroll are you?" I ask as we approach. He smells even riper than I do.

"Eh?"

"Out for a stroll?"

"That's all, yeah."

"You got a cabin around here?"

"No. I got a cabin yes, about ten minutes' walk down the track."

"Down the track? This sure doesn't look like the track does it?" I say, glancing up and down the hard-packed road.

"No, it's gone, hard to believe it though. Once I put it on, I got a hard job to take it off."

"Put what on?"

"Weight. I'm overweight," he says rubbing his slight paunch with both hands. There's no fat on his arms or legs, though the skin sags a little. "The only way to get it down is to cut down on my food and walk a bit. I got diabetes and it makes matters worse, hey." Unsure of what to say in response, I introduce myself, to which he responds "Good day sir, good day, good day."

"You are?"

"Jack Leitch." We shake hands.

"So, you living out here?"

"No, I live here, about ten minutes from here on that side," he says indicating the west side of the track.

"How long have you lived here?"

"Oh, about ten or fifteen years."

"So you've seen some changes then?"

"Well, trains are gone," he says, as if I might not be aware of this key fact.

"Yeah. How come the road is so wide?"

"They were hauling wood see. They had to ballast the sides hey."

"Who's hauling the wood?"

"They're not hauling it here no more."

"Stopped are they?"

"Oh no, they're not stopped. They're down to Alder Pond down that way," and he gestures to the southwest.

On the east side of the track is a large pond with a few sites cleared for camping, and a few camper trailers. "Is that Cooks…?"

"…that's Big Cooks Pond," he says, and spits. Mile 418.

"So do you get much traffic down here now that they're not logging anymore?"

"Oh we gets traffic, but this is the wrong time of the week hey, Tuesday. Mostly Saturdays and Sundays, hey. When the stores is closed, Sunday, you know."

We chat for a few more minutes, small talk, then start in opposite directions. I've only gone a few paces when he calls to me. I turn. "You stayed to Beaver Pond last night," he tells me.

"Yes. How'd you know that?" I stammer.

"I lived there years ago. Went up to see the cabin a couple of weeks ago and it was flattened right to the ground. Must have been the snow I expect," he says by way of explanation. Then he spins dangerously on his thin legs and waddles off.

By the time I reach Cooks Brook Trestle—Mile 416—I can bear witness to the devastation of clear-cut logging. The scope of it is overwhelming. I can smell the churned mud, a thick smell, almost like cow shit. Tree roots have been torn and the branches strewn so the land is impossible to walk over. The boughs are blasty red and the stumps clutch the soil like hands severed at the wrist. The trench-like skidder trails go back so far they become thin lines across the stripped hills, where the only thing left standing is the scattered birch, white trunks stark as skeletons.

This destruction stretches as far as I can see, to the west and to the north. A crow bawls, and in this landscape the sound takes on a strange almost demented sound that echoes in the narrow band of forest. The crow bawls its warning again. Tiny juncos, sparrows, and warblers flick in and out among the dead branches.

The slow but steady decline towards Petries is Burtons Grade. When this section of the railbed was laid in the mid 1890s it was named after an experienced railway walking-boss from Ontario. Cooks Brook tumbles down beside the track, dropping faster than the roadbed, so the riverbank grows steeper with every step. Eight miles out of Corner Brook I hit the municipal boundary. All along the way the forest is scarred by patches of domestic cutting, piles of treetops and stumps, but the clear-cut has ended. And there are a lot of decaying rail ties around. I take refuge in a dry culvert under the track to escape the stouts.

*By mid-afternoon I spot the scattered houses on Mount Moriah, above Petries. There I collapse in the shade of a huge spruce tree.*

After a brief rest I climb out and scramble back onto the track, which is more like a rail line again. The weight of my knapsack reminds me of that character from the Arabian Nights: the old sorcerer who tricked Sinbad into allowing him onto his back. The old man then locked his legs around Sinbad's neck and refused to climb down. So Sinbad had to carry the little man wherever he went. Then I think of Newfoundland's own little old man, the one from Gambo, the Father of Confederation, the man who claimed to have walked these tracks during the fall of 1925 in a failed effort to unionize the section crews. Joey Smallwood. He would have been only twenty-five at the time, unaware that he was fated to be the first Premier after Newfoundland and Labrador joined Canada in 1949. In 1925 he was working as a journalist and labour organizer when he struck upon the idea of walking across the rail line to organize the section crews of the newly nationalized Newfoundland Railway. And in September of that year he set off from Port aux Basques, suitcase in hand, to do just that.

An idea occurs to me and I laugh out loud. My knapsack is Joey! The little man tricked me into allowing him on my back, and now I must carry the blighter. I stop to shift Joey's weight and lean on my walking stick. Sometimes the stick is the only thing that keeps me upright. The copper tip is already worn off it and the journey less than one third complete. My only support the walking stick? Joey's support? Why Clara Oates of course, the fiancée who awaited him in the newly founded town of Corner Brook in 1925, at the end of the first leg of his journey. My supporter and companion must be Clara too. Joey on my back and Clara beside me, chuckling to myself, I rattle along through the heat and dust towards Petries.

By mid-afternoon I spot the scattered houses on Mount Moriah, above Petries. There I collapse in the shade of a huge spruce tree. Lulled by the buzz of insects and the distant rush of Cooks Brook, I slip into a semi-conscious dream. All the towns, the faces, the names and the miles and miles of railroad blend into one. I feel as though it is the roadbed that is moving. I just stand, lifting my feet, lifting my stick as the road grinds past, like the tide sweeping around the piles of a wharf. I should get up, but I'm too relaxed. I think of my wife Kathy and our two daughters. I think of Petries Undercrossing. A shower and a full body massage. If I have learned anything on the journey thus far, it is how useless good intentions are and how important right action is. Slowly I pull Joey onto my back and watch as once again the railbed flows beneath me.

Approaching Corner Brook.

## CHAPTER 11
# PETRIES UNDERCROSSING

Every time I felt like quitting today I chanted, "Petries Undercrossing," as if it were a mantra. But when I finally reach what the map says is the undercrossing—Mile 408.8—the rail line is replaced by a gradual gravel slope to a busy highway intersection. What I am to discover is that, for the next three miles into Corner Brook, the railway is gone, except for a few brief patches, replaced by Marine Drive.

There is no ride waiting for me at Petries and I'm filled with grumbling self-pity. But instead of calling for a taxi, I set out to walk the additional three miles into Corner Brook. I do try to hitchhike, but people are more inclined to speed up at the sight of me. Or maybe it is the little man on my back that is scaring them off. I soon abandon that effort and settle down for the walk when a thin man with long blond hair runs up the side of the road shouting my name. He introduces himself as Steve. "You know her, Janice," he says and points to a woman fifty paces behind him. Getting only a blank stare, he adds, "Janice Udell."

Last winter while looking for a hiking companion, I learned that Janice had her own plan to walk across the Island. But our timetables did not match. All the same, we became friends and she had helpful hiking tips. In 1989, after the railway closed, Janice and a friend, Eric West, hiked the Avalon section of the rail line. The rails were still in place so the hiking was much more difficult than it is now. One day, in the middle of the trip, they were trudging along, both plugged into a walkman on full volume. Eric asked Janice if she could feel the track shaking. No she couldn't. So they continued on until the shaking was so insistent they pulled off the ear plugs. Bearing down behind them, its whistle blowing furiously was a diesel engine. Janice and Eric leapt to the side and narrowly missed becoming the last people struck by a train in Newfoundland.

The sulfurous smell from the paper mill intensifies as it comes into sight. The Reid brothers (who took over the railway when their father retired) were key figures in the original effort to start up this mill in the early 1920s. They were able to use their position and their considerable land holdings to shape a deal to force the government of Richard Squires to bolster the sagging Reid Newfoundland Company. There was a fear in the government that the "Humber deal" would fall through and create a political disaster. But the deal did go through, the government took the railway off the Reids' hands, and the mill has been in production since 1925.

Today huge stockpiles of pulpwood rise up like great walls. Giant cranes nip bites from the top and transfer them to trucks. On the wind, mixed with the mill's stench, is the sticky-sweet fragrance of spruce logs. I feel the same rage welling up that I felt when I witnessed the clear-cut at Cooks Pond. A wind-blown scrap of the lichen known as "old man's beard" with twigs stitched into it, tumbles across the pavement and catches in my boot.

## HISTORY SIDING THREE
## FROM NOWHERE TO NOWHERE

The first train left St. John's for Port aux Basques, June 29, 1898 and chugged its way across the 547 miles at the average blistering speed of 19.5 miles per hour. The overland route was complete.

Operating the railway proved to be more of a challenge than building it. The many twists and turns severely limited the number of passenger and freight cars that the steam engines could haul along the steep grades of the narrow-gauge line. Heavy snows played havoc with the schedule, especially in the Topsails where excessive drifting regularly closed the line for days, sometimes weeks, at a time. In the spring great torrents swept away sections of the line, even trestles.

Financial efforts to maintain the fledgling line helped push Newfoundland's public debt from $4.1 million to $17.3 million. Meanwhile, Reid's influence gained momentum as the millions he spent on supplies and labour found its way into the pockets of an economy that, until then, had been based largely on barter.

One immediate result of the railway's completion was soaring unemployment followed by emigration to the Eastern Seaboard, especially the "Boston States." A few small communities emerged along the line, but the large-scale economic development, which some proponents had predicted, proved elusive.

The railway, as one critic put it, "ran from nowhere, through nowhere, to nowhere." In the election of 1897, Whiteway's Liberal government was replaced by the Tories under James S. Winter. He and Receiver General A.B. Morine, negotiated with the railway baron a deal that provoked an unprecedented public outcry.

# HUMBER VALLEY TRAIL
### CORNER BROOK TO HOWLEY

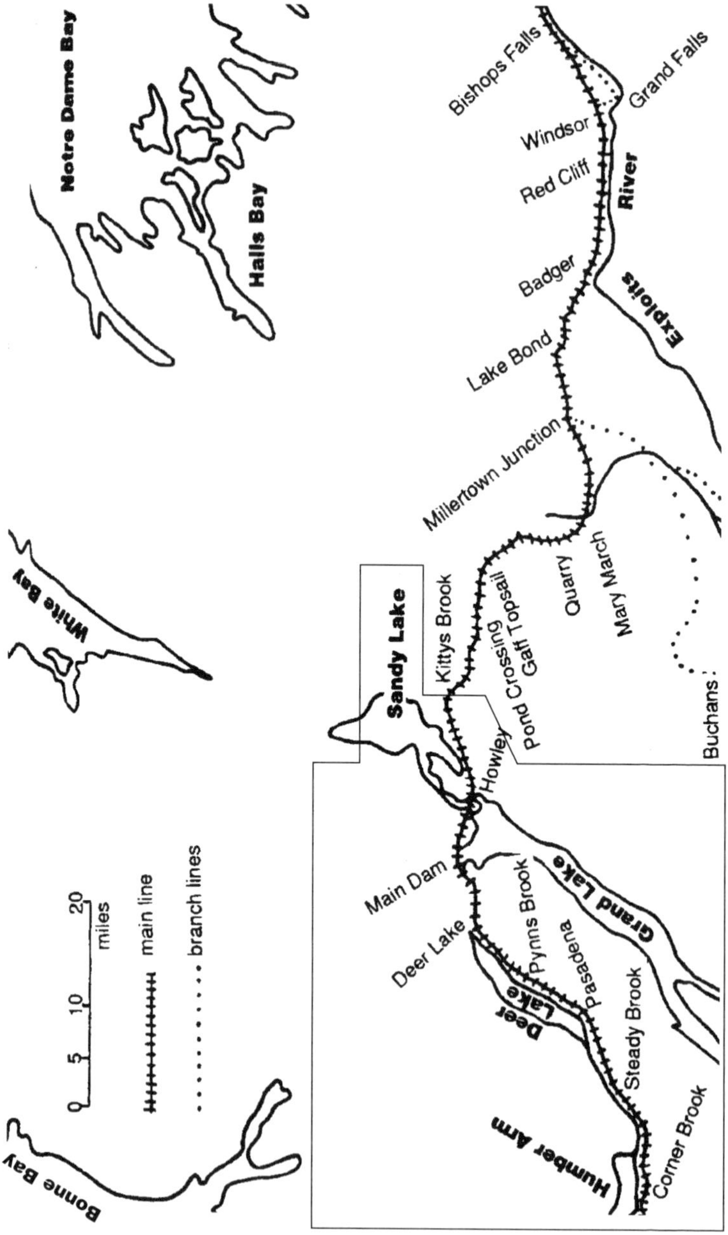

Notre Dame Bay
Halls Bay
White Bay
Bonne Bay
0
5
10
20
miles
main line
branch lines
Bishops Falls
Grand Falls
Windsor
Red Cliff
River
Exploits
Badger
Lake Bond
Millertown Junction
Sandy Lake
Kittys Brook
Pond Crossing
Gaff Topsail
Quarry
Mary March
Buchans
Howley
Main Dam
Grand Lake
Pynns Brook
Deer Lake
Deer Lake
Pasadena
Steady Brook
Humber Arm
Corner Brook

# HUMBER VALLEY TRAIL INTRODUCTION

We meet in the hotel restaurant. Otto Goulding has made the long drive from Pasadena to St. John's to attend a spring agricultural trade show. Except for his thinning hair, he hasn't changed: a ready laugh, a steady hand and that unfathomable look in his eyes. He's taken an hour out of his morning to chat with me about changes along the railbed since he and I worked together, as volunteers in 1993, to help protect the integrity of the rail line and encourage supporting provincial legislation.

Goulding begins with the big picture. The Trans-Canada Trail. This national initiative was launched in 1994, the year after I completed the walk. Goulding went to Calgary for the founding meeting. "I brought maps of Newfoundland's T'Railway with me," he says. "People looked at the maps and they said, 'you're lucky to have that trail right across the province,' and they were right," he says and slowly shakes his head. "But since then they've all moved ahead but we've moved backwards." Nowhere is that loss and the potential for proper development more evident than on the Humber Valley Trail.

The trail traces its way along Humber Mouth, along the Humber River and then inland past Grand Lake. This route is a hodge podge of development. The worst part is the huge gap from Corner Brook all the way north to Steady Brook at the foot of Marble Mountain. (The provincial government still has not made good on its promise to replace the T'Railway they buried when the Trans-Canada Highway was widened through that area almost two decades ago.)

In the Corner Brook area, including Curling and Petries, much of the T'Railway remains, but the many property access crossings create safety and liability concerns. The community may have to reroute the non-motorized path to follow Harbour Drive. And this in turn could link to the trails that fan out from the city centre through Margaret Bowater Park and on to places like the Gorge.

Farther up the valley beyond Steady Brook, towns like Pasadena have developed the walking trails within their boundaries. However, snowmobilers and ATVers have had to find their own way around these areas. Where the trail runs through Deer Lake, off-road traffic on the trail is blanketing local residents with dust. Experience has shown that there are only three possible solutions: pave the trouble spots, enforce strict regulation on speed and traffic, or ban motorized vehicles.

From Deer Lake the trail turns inland toward Howley. And, with no other communities along the way, not much has changed there. At the head of Grand Lake, Main Dam is still blocked to vehicular traffic by a chain-link fence which Deer Lake Power refuses to remove, citing safety and liability issues. This sounds reasonable, but there is no alternative route. That means off-road traffic continues to drive down through the river bed.

Goulding feels the Humber Valley has huge potential as an international tourism destination. It already is, with the Humber Valley Resort and Marble Mountain skiing. But he thinks it could be all the more attractive in the other seasons if there was a continuous biking trail down the valley. "That sort of thing appeals to the Europeans," he says. "But people need to speak out if they want to keep it. I think the executive of the T'Railway Council needs to be more forceful in protecting this resource. Municipalities and community-based groups need to challenge them. They need to realize that an opportunity may have been lost here and they need to speak out now and say, 'Why are we letting this resource disappear?'"

Author takes his best shot.

Photo by Otto Goulding

## CHAPTER 12
# UNLIKELY AMBASSADOR

**13 JULY, 9:30 P.M., MILE 405**

Dreams are tough. My stubbed, tired, straight-lipped face in the mirror, brown eyes staring back. A grin creeps across my face; two blissful days off. Sitting here at the writing table with the fan on, the evening rain plopping heavily on the eave outside my hotel window, I cannot recall ever being more tired. My shoulders and thighs and ankles and left knee are all so stiff that every way I lie is uncomfortable. My left leg looks like my right leg's poor cousin. One hundred and forty miles down, 400 and some to go.

I made it here to the Glynnmill Inn about 5:00 p.m. For the first time in over a week it is raining, and scheduled to rain for at least the next day. Here until Friday morning, then on to Pasadena.

Just like I felt the railbed sliding underneath me today, so this project keeps rolling along, growing as the miles add up. As media attention continues to grow, I stumble to keep up. Tonight one-third of a page in the Western Star is on my walk. And the local CBC morning show will be here tomorrow at 7:30 a.m. for a live interview.

*Things to do in Corner Brook*
Call Kathy and the girls
Doctor—get blisters and knee checked
Physiotherapist—get referral from Doc
Buy coverlet bandages and gauze bandage roll
Energy mix of nuts, raisins and M&Ms
Write, write, write
Do laundry
Buy Otto lunch
Visit Danny in hospital
Plan Gaff Topsails segment

## 14 July, Glynnmill Inn

Otto on the telephone with the latest news. Kathy called him two days ago to say there are two parcels on the way to him for me. One is socks and the other a pair of boots. She heard me on the news after Codroy Pond complaining about the boots so she went back to the retailers and they gave her a new pair. Otto says Danny Conway was admitted to hospital with pneumonia right after he dropped me off at Jim Collier's. When I call Danny he sounds fine. He is on penicillin and feeling much better after a day's rest. There are more baskets of fruit in his room than he could eat in a year. The doctor told him he could have him out by Thursday with an experimental drug. Danny signed the release forms and started on the medication.

Otto Goulding is like a coach, stage manager, and agent for me. As the chairperson of the T'Railway committee, he has done a great deal to help me make this trip work. It was Otto who alerted the rural development associations along the line to my intentions; Otto who encouraged them to set up transportation and accommodations for me as I make my way through. He and I discuss events every second day, sometimes daily if I am anywhere near a phone. He sets up the media "ops" and we discuss what to emphasize, what to play down, for each interview. Otto told me that he envies my freedom to say the things that he would like to say but cannot, because of his position as a volunteer with the NLRDC and as a government employee with the Department of Forestry and Agriculture.

We have our disagreements, but Otto is patient and encouraging, asking only that I listen to his views and then make up my own mind. After the CBC interview this morning he called to say it sounded good. Then he suggested that I make a publicized three-mile walk on Marine Drive when I start on Friday. I told him I have already walked that wretched distance and have no intention of walking it again. I also mentioned that I might take a five-mile ride as far east as Steady Brook, where the railbed picks up again. The widening of the Trans-Canada wiped out a section of the track and I have no interest in slogging along beside the rush of transport trucks. Otto told me I would be missing a nice walk. I emphasized to him that I am looking for ways to save my knee to get to the Gaff Topsails and beyond. I have to remember that Otto is a man with a larger vision. He sees a trailway across the Island along the abandoned railbed. So no matter how patient and helpful he may be, I'm a means to an end, or at least that is how I feel today.

When I was planning this journey I pictured myself wading across rivers, ferrying my supplies on makeshift rafts, days spent in the wilderness without human contact. Instead this is a journey through the backyard of the Island. And it has taken on a meaning that I did nothing to create. Because of the support of the rural development associations and their umbrella organization, the Newfoundland and Labrador Rural Development Council, my journey has been grafted onto their quest to save the T'Railway. So, when I make requests, Otto makes it happen. But what is it we are working to do?

Yes, let us keep the mythology of the railway alive. But the world is moving forward and if we are to preserve the route at all, then we must do so with an eye to the realities of the day. Tourism, mining, logging, new roads, municipal needs and rights, development association rights, individual rights, group rights, prior claim rights, the cost of maintenance—especially the large trestles—the necessity for co-ordination, the shrinking public purse. It is all a little overwhelming. All I set out to do was to hike across the rail line before it disappears. Now all of this, and me with way too much time to think about it all.

Up the Humber River.

# CHAPTER 13
# LOST IN NO MAN'S LAND

My hotel room looks like it's been ransacked. The tent hangs from the bathroom door, the flysheet drapes over the window, the sleeping bag is unrolled in front of the radiator. Maps, audio tapes, notebooks, dirty socks, cooking utensils, and a dozen other items, litter the bed and the floor.

How do you write it all down? Is it even possible? How do I pull the relevant bits from everything that I hear, say, see, smell, touch, remember. Often I wonder "Haven't I scribbled this before?" The pages and pages, the cassette tapes, my memories and the stories I've heard, everything merging and most of it I have to leave out of the book. So what is the point? I see my trail-hardened reflection and cannot see the end of this. And sometimes, when I look at the photo of Kathy, Sasha, and Julie, it feels like I will never get home. Other times, the scraps I have written seem so shallow and petty. I will never get anything out of it. I'll waste this chance.

Walking downstairs to the lobby my left leg almost collapses under me. I limp, yet it doesn't hurt. All along I've been saying that, if I made it to Corner Brook, then I could make it all the way. Now I am here and it is all just as uncertain as ever. The day I drag myself into St. John's is the day I'll know I can make it.

The doctor at Western Memorial Hospital, who does not identify himself, is so gruff he is amusing. After a minimum of poking and prodding he tells me there is fluid under the left kneecap and prescribes a drug to take the swelling down, then wraps a stretch bandage firmly around the knee. If the swelling continues, I will have to reconsider my journey. If it improves I can go on. But, he adds, other than the swelling, the leg seems fine. For the blisters he recommends soaking my feet two to three times a day in lightly salted water.

Wherever I go in town I watch people. There are so many ways of walking, knees bent, lift, down, lift, down. Young, old, slow, fast, stiff and loose. I feel trapped because there can be no leisurely strolls for me. Must preserve the cartilage, tendons and muscle for the business at hand. Or should I say at foot?

Janice Udell called today and invited me to a barbecue at Steve's place. He lives in a garage, a duck-your-head-to-enter, watch-out-for-the-loose-floorboards, lurking-aroma-of-cats sure enough garage. At thirty-four years old, Steve is the poor-artist-in-the-garret type—long hair, lots of great ideas. His thin one-eyed friend Gary and I have an intense conversation about the distance between intentions and actions. Janice stays out of the conversation, tending the barbecue.

Steve has a few stories about his family, some of them funny. Like his brother Frank's worm trick. Their father sent Frank out to dig worms for fishing. Frank was gone a long time so Steve went to see what was keeping him. "There was Frank hiding behind a tree. He was watching a robin that'd just landed on the lawn. Frank waited for the bird to pull a worm out, and then he chased the bird away and grabbed the worm. He only had three worms."

Steve's father, David, hosts a local open-line show and runs an antique shop. At Steve's suggestion, I went to see David in his Emporium. Loud accordion music blared on the sidewalk outside the shop (prevents loiterers). Inside was clean and bright with lots of wood and a selection of everything from old bottles to refinished antique furniture. David has a full close-cropped beard and neatly cut hair just long enough to cover his ears. He glares out at me through thick glasses when I introduce myself as a friend of Steve's. "Another starving artist I suppose," he snaps in a firm talk-first-think-later open-line host voice.

David is very outspoken on the uselessness of the roadbed without a rail line on it. He has tried to get the rights to the seven-mile section between the ski resort at Marble Mountain and Corner Brook. As manager of Marble Mountain in 1988 when the railway closed down, he wanted to link Marble Mountain Ski Resort and the railway as a special package to help make Corner Brook "the new Banff." He believes Premier Peckford sold the railway for a greater claim to the Hibernia oilfield offshore, over which the federal government claimed complete jurisdiction. David thinks the downgrading of CN service on the Island was a carefully calculated closure. He accuses "slippery bureaucrats" as the managers of that process. David's father walked the rail line from St. John's to Gander in the 1930s looking for work and almost died in the process. He's eighty-five years old now, but still has problems with his feet from the ordeal.

At lunch today Janice referred to the rail line as a "long, thin community." There is a common language, a common industry, a common style of living, a common mythology. So is the old railway now a roadbed or a trailway? Choose your reality. Otto is like a dog with a bone. To him this antique infrastructure has international potential as a tourism attraction. And it is a trailway. Pure and simple. I am attracted to this idea— have faith that it is right.

This thought brings me to the brink of changing the whole reason for my journey. Perhaps it has changed already. I sense the thing is big enough to chew me up and swallow me whole. It is easy to be skeptical. Much harder to be for something. But what am I for? Are we talking about a cross-Island, internationally marketed resource? Yet, as Steve told me, they have cruise ships coming into Corner Brook to be greeted by empty wharves. If we can't even get a few craftspeople to greet tourists on the dock, how can we coordinate and market something as vast as the T'Railway?

I feel as if I have unwittingly strolled into no man's land between two combating forces and I'm trying to say "Don't shoot me. International Press Corps, here's my badge of neutrality." But that won't work. I would be blown to bits anyway, so I may as well stand up for what I believe. Otto is exerting pressure on me, some subtle, some not so subtle, to choose the T'Railway vision and, though I hesitate, it seems that is the right direction. Other times it feels like Otto is slowly manoeuvring me into a straightjacket and it is already too late to wrestle my way out. My answer is this journey. It will be what it is and only I will know when I have completed it. That could be Corner Brook, Gander, Clarenville or St. John's.

The internal debate keeps me awake. Around midnight, as I sit quietly in bed listening to the rain through the open window I realize what troubles me about this whole "ambassador" thing. I am trying to protect what is for me the "artistic integrity" of this project. But what use is art if it serves no purpose? Even "art for art's sake" is a political statement.

### Postcard from the Holiday Inn

*A busload of them got in late, talking, laughing, doors slamming, people. Drag my hand across the blanket, little static sparks. The night drifts in on a light breeze.*

*I travel with a faceless companion through a flood. My calves ache. It is raining. Kathy and the girls are in an old house. Wading along the railroad, I finally reach Kathy and follow her up a dark stairway past a caribou head. The house is haunted, tingling at the base of my scalp. Pry open a closet door. No one. Then into the empty room where the girls are supposed to be. Wake.*

*Rain on the flysheet is the roar of a truck on the bypass. A wind through the trees becomes tires on a wet street. The heartbeat becomes the distant pounding of rock and roll music played too loud. The call of a crow becomes, "Go, go, go."*

*The memory of bird song from unseen birds lingers at night in my ear, like a lucky tune. And I see in black pools behind my eyes the reflection of the treetops and the sky behind it.*

Rhodie Hickey.

# CHAPTER 14
# AT HUMBERMOUTH

### 15 JULY, 10:30 A.M., MILE 403

The two trains on either side of him and his striped engineer's hat exaggerate Rhodie Hickey's height as he approaches up the grassy alley. His hand is firm but bony and his voice too is firm, with the slight waver of age. His gaze is steady and critical, his hair mostly grey. The sleeves of the brown sweater are pushed up, exposing his forearms.

We are just outside Corner Brook. Around us looms Rhodie's handiwork; two shining trains on 1,300 feet of track. At the front of the pre-1949 train to the right, the steam engine gleams black in the morning sun. Behind it on the track in succession is a passenger car, a dining car, a kitchen car and a caboose, all painted black on the outside and visually linked by white horizontal stripes at the top and bottom. The more modern train on the left has an orange plough, a diesel engine, several cars in various stages of renovation, then a bright orange caboose. Three young women in engineer's caps lead a group of Girl Guides into the last car in the older train. Despite very little publicity, there is a steady stream of visitors here. The guest book has over 4,500 signatures.

"I was an engineer for forty-four years," says Rhodie. Most of the volunteers working on this site are former railway people. "We're at it all the time, working, same as if we were still on the railway. You know there is a lot of work to do here yet," he sniffs proudly. "We got no grants, only what donations someone gives us, that's all we got. It's going to take a lot of work, but it passes the time away." Rhodie feels it is only the people who have worked with the railway who have the interest and the knowledge to do the kind of restoration they are doing here. "And one thing the workers do have is lots of time," he says with a half-smile.

Rhodie retired before the railway closed, but many of his friends took layoff packages. He leans against the newly painted blade of the snow plough and tips back his hat. "They were offered package deals and all this bull," he says. "They're sorry now for what they done, because half of them ... what they got they had to use right away, and by the time they paid the taxes, they had nothing left. The unions and management were telling the employees 'Don't worry we're gonna fix you up. We're gonna do this, we're gonna do that.' And then after a while these fellas said 'What the hell odds, let her go.' But they're sorry now."

When Joey Smallwood tried to organize the section men in the 1920s, he was engaged to be married. Rhodie says nothing ever came of the effort because "some say he used the money to go to New York and get married and did nothing for the railway workers."

Rhodie has a full head of steam now. So I figure the time is ripe to get his opinions on the events leading up to the closure of the railway. "A lot of people I've talked to say the railway wasn't shut down so much as undermined, because CN management were downgrading services so customers didn't feel like they could rely on the railroad any more. Do you buy that Rhodie?"

"Yeah, I buy that. I mean that's too big a thing for me to get into right now. When I was working I saw the service falling away. I could see them giving away business. I could see them setting up a force within the railway to go to other modes. I'd say they had a bunch working in the outfit going to business people and getting them to switch from freight trains to trucking. Not coming out in the public or stating what they were doing, but they were doing it. I know they were doing it for a fact. They even give the farmers boxcars for storage houses till the trucks could pick it up.

"I could name names, but there is no need of getting old sores going." He reckons the undermining of the railway was deliberate but adds that the narrow gauge was a headache. "You know, in '49 if they had gone to standard gauge, I'd say the railway'd be here now," says Rhodie, gesturing towards the metal wheels under the diesel engine. "It took three parts of a day to get a train off of the boat. By the time you jack her up, take out the standard gauge trucks [the wheels under the train cars] and put in the narrow gauge trucks on every car in an eighty-car train, the day was gone."

With the mention of the trucks Rhodie is back onto his favourite subject, the trains themselves. "For the diesel engineers you got a six-wheel truck and you got 200 horsepower on each wheel. That gives you 1,200 horsepower for each truck. One six-wheel truck weighs twenty-six ton. The diesel is 110 tons altogether but most of the weight is in the bottom. She holds 900 gallons of fuel."

*In the dining car white tablecloths are draped over the dozen or more tables. Each table has a vase with pink, white, and yellow plastic tulips.*

Rhodie leads me to the entrance to the snow plough where he gestures for me to enter. The low entrance leads to a cramped space about the size of a compact car. There are a few low sleeping benches around the side. In the front are a few simple levers to lift and drop the flange blades under the plough. Three rectangular windows look out over the front of the train. The cab of the plough feels like the inside of a metal coffin. I am glad to step back into the daylight.

Rhodie's wife Winnie joins us. She agrees that there are hard feelings about the closure of the railway. "It was a shame to see how they did it," she says as she leads us up the step and into the passenger car of the steam train. It is as well-preserved inside as outside. Rows of high-backed red vinyl chairs give a wide berth to the coal stove. The chairs, two per row on either side of the car, are aligned along the narrow aisle, their black armrests like the arms of otherwise invisible passengers. The wide square windows have pull-down blinds. Far down the narrow aisle through several cars, I can see the last of the Girl Guides disembarking.

"See, why would you change the name to TerraTransport from CN if it wasn't done for a purpose?" asks Rhodie, referring to how, in 1979, the Newfoundland Division of CN Railway changed its name to TerraTransport. "First when they come on they were going around shouting 'CN from Vancouver to St. John's.' Well they'd have to say that they were shutting down part of the CN when the time come."

In the dining car white tablecloths are draped over the dozen or more tables. Each table has a vase with pink, white, and yellow plastic tulips.

The dinnerware looks solid and ready. There is a large picture of a diesel train on the back wall, as if this steam train had a vision of its own future. Around the windows, red curtains frame the view of the diesel train to the west and large maples to the east.

When CN took over the Newfoundland Railway in 1949, one their first moves was to order signs on all the bridges. Rhodie remembers driving past section crews erecting signs at all the trestles and whitewashing rocks around the signs. "They were doing a big job. Dressing her right up."

When the passenger express was running, trains had to reach speeds of fifty mph to meet the timetable Rhodie says. That meant every twist and turn had to be ballasted with stone. But that all fell to the wayside after 1969 when passenger service was cut. "Soon as the express train went we had fifteen mile-per-hour orders on different parts of the track and ten mile-per-hour in parts that wasn't fit for anything more. That was the end of the paint too. No trouble to see the change of mind," says Rhodie with more than a hint of disgust.

"And once they shut her down the rails were taken up soon as the last train went around the curve. Pretty fast. I suppose they were frightened somebody would take a change of heart or a change of government and she wouldn't of went at all. So they had to hit while it was hot," says Rhodie.

"What do you think about the rail line now Rhodie? The roadbed itself: Do you think there is any use for it or do you think it is just as well to see the thing chopped up?"

"I'd say there's lots of use for it, but who's gonna pay? I mean if you're gonna pay to keep this up from Port aux Basques to St. John's, why close the railway? It's just as much money involved." He tugs at his engineer's cap. "Fighting the yearly damage from the beavers alone was costly for the railway. Beavers kept damming the culverts and they had trouble with washouts every spring. "We used to have to let the dams go. Who are you going to get to do that stuff now? And it's dangerous for people on the route today. You can be going along on one of these all-terrain machines and next thing you're down in a hole. But I can see different sections kept up. Sure. Nothing wrong with it."

Winnie has gone ahead and calls for us to join her in the cooking car. It is dominated by a big box-shaped stove with a silver front and the word Enterprise embossed on the door. The top is a solid black skillet. Rhodie points to the mantle. "I worked on one train where the cook used to keep an old-time alarm clock on the mantle over the stove. One day the engineer on duty gave a sudden stop and the alarm clock went down in the soup. The cook just fished it out with a spoon and kept stirring the pot. One of the stewards asked him 'What are you going to do with that cook?' He turned to the steward. 'Nothing,' he said, 'only call it alarm clock soup.'"

Jackman the pole climber.

## CHAPTER 15
# WHEN STORIES COME TUMBLING

Bathed in fluorescent light, surrounded by a larger semidarkness and the smell of brewing coffee, we begin the meeting in the basement conference room of the Driftwood Inn. More than a dozen people, including deputy mayor Charlie McCarthy, two councillors and two local writers, Jean Young and Marilyn Young. Glenda Garnier, coordinator for the Humber Valley Development Association, chairs the meeting. Otto is there, in his capacity as western director with the Rural Development Council, and chairperson of the T'Railway Committee. The guests of honour are the retired railway men, people like conductor Vern George, section man Saul Yetman and telegraph lineman Jackman White. Innkeeper Cybil Rogers listens from the back of the room.

The occasion is the second of several town hall meetings planned for my cross-Island trek. Glenda opens the meeting with introductions. Then Otto, after a few technical difficulties, plays a video on the "T'Railway" and talks briefly about the rails-to-trails proposal.

69

It is surprising that three Deer Lake council members are here. Gus Curran, the mayor, is a vocal opponent of the trail, which runs along the main street of town. His opposition can be traced back to the fall of 1992, when Otto invited mayors and development association representatives from Steady Brook to Howley to attend a meeting on the newly released $250,000 T'Railway Report. The report identified Deer Lake as a potential hub in the proposed cross-Island trail. Curran sat at the back of the room and left early, without any public comment. The next week Deer Lake council met on the report but neglected to call Otto or anyone else connected with the T'Railway initiative. Following the meeting, the local paper declared in bold red letters on the front page "Mayor Curran Opposed to T'Railway Report."

Otto's theory is that the town has other uses in mind for the rail line, in their new main street development plan.

Otto turns the floor over to me. I talk briefly about my trip and then start panning for stories. I discover that memories can be as real and well fingered as old nuggets; keepsakes like Vern George's pocket watch or Saul Yetman's old train schedule. Memories are the ties that bind these graying railroaders together now. The stories come tumbling out one after another until the line between storyteller and audience blurs. Some can even finish the stories begun by others. A word or a name is all it takes to invoke the subdued laughter of understanding, a name like Cyril Daniels.

"This lady going westward on a passenger train, she asks him 'Conductor does this train stop at Port aux Basques?' He turns to her straight as a whip, not a smile on his face 'Well I hope so ma'm, if she don't, there will be an awful splash!'"

"Another time they were waiting for the plough to come up. By and by one of the Yanks came up to find out what was the problem. 'Mr. Conductor, it's a beautiful blue sky up there, not a cloud.' 'Look, my son,' Cyril said, 'we're not going up there, we're going that way,' and pointed down the tracks. He looked straight at the Yank, never laughed or anything."

"At the station in Millertown Junction a woman on the platform said 'Conductor, what end of the coach do I get on?' 'Well, ma'm you get on either end, they're both moving!'"

"Another time the train left Corner Brook and passed the pulp and paper mill. There was an American on board who asked what the mill was and Cyril told him it was the biggest pulp and paper mill in North America. This American said 'My dad got a restaurant about the same size as that back home.' Showing unusual restraint Cyril said 'Well, he must have a fine restaurant.' When he was going through Curling just a few miles further down the track past the huge Imperial Oil storage tanks the American asked 'Conductor, what are those things out right here?' 'Salt and pepper shakers for your father's restaurant!' says Cyril, and he went on about his business."

"And he was always just as quick as that," fingers snap.

Charlie worked for CN for forty years. During his day the railway carried the pulp logs to the mills, hauled the paper from the Corner Brook mill to Port aux Basques during the winter, and year round from the Grand Falls mill to Botwood, transported the ore out of Buchans, and shipped airline fuel from Lewisporte to Gander. In 1955, twenty-six trains ran between Bishop's Falls and Corner Brook every day. "That was a lot of gear," recalls Charlie. "You get on a speeder and go out to work on the line, you had to know what you were doing, or else you were going to meet up with trouble in a very short time with that many trains on the tracks."

The railroaders agree that when CN introduced the passenger buses in 1968, they wanted to prove — one way or another — that the bus service was the best mode of passenger transportation. "On the last of it they downgraded the railway passenger service to the point...I seen right here in Deer Lake, they put #1, a passenger train, on the siding to wait two hours for a work train. They drove the passengers away with tricks like that," says Charlie emphatically.

"They told the car repair shop in St. John's on the last going off, 'Don't vacuum the sleeping cars no more. And no more paint to be used.' And that was it."

I am curious about the fact that when they wanted to downgrade the passenger service they cut back on expenditures, yet less than a year before they finally shut the railway down, CN installed all new ties and new crushed stone on many sections.

Bitter memories are sparked when the ghost of the railway management is invoked. And the voices tumbling over each other again, too fast to register who is speaking.

"You can see what they done over the years. They'd send a guy in from the mainland for to be the manager for a year and he'd take away service a little at a time. And when too much heat is on him they would send him back to the mainland and send another guy in. When they were just about ready to phase it out altogether, they took a local guy in there. Nothing left then, eh?" They all nod or murmur agreement.

"They'd send their undercover agents in pairs on the passenger trains to coax you to take whisky. I ran with Charlie Butler and Charlie said to me one day 'Saul old cock, you go back and have a double whisky,' I said 'No Charlie I'm not taking no chances on that guy.' We arrived in Bishop's Falls and Charlie was fired. Thirty-eight years' service and he was fired. If I had taken one drink off that bugger I would have been fired too."

Many of the railway workers believe that the slow strangulation of the Newfoundland railway is part of a much larger trend. Saul voices their concern. "You are going to see no trains east of the Diamond, in Quebec. They've started now, Canadian Pacific have already made application to Transport Canada to discontinue all freight services in New Brunswick."

"It's the historical part of it too, Saul. I mean it was there for 100 years, and we allowed them to tear it up and truck it away. What's next? Will it be carved up? Taken in as part of people's backyards? Doesn't seem fair to the history of the railway in Newfoundland."

"Well if we leave it up to CN, St. John's, to make the ... no don't wait for the decision. Make them give it to you."

This is Otto's cue. He smoothes back his thinning hair with a determined swipe of his hand. "Should we go and destroy something we already have? It might be left to the next generation, but it's also building on what you built. Okay, the trains are gone. Now we're moving into a new era of adventure tourism. And it is real," he says. The previous weekend he drove to Gros Morne Park and "there was a traffic jam going up the mountain."

Vern leans into the conversation. "I think that preserving the railbed is only part of it. If you can involve the people who worked on the railway, you're promoting it too. Tell the stories to people who visit. I mean that is going to make it a thousand times more effective than just having the T'Railway there for people to walk up and down."

To refocus the group on the topic at hand—future uses of the T'Railway—Otto jumps into the conversation again. "People say to me, 'You're against the quarry in the Gaff.' And I say 'No I am not! I am for this trailway.' So if the only access to the quarry is along the T'Railway then they have to work with us. It does take vision to say 'Wait now, look at the way the tourist industry is going. In ten years we could have a complete adventure tourism product.' Logging could still go on, so could the quarry in the Gaff Topsails, but do it with the T'Railway in mind."

Mention of the Gaff Topsails switches Vern into a whole new line of stories. "I was stuck up there for six days one time with a passenger train. Never moved a wheel. You couldn't see that far, look." He holds his hand six inches in front of his face. "When we had to go out, we'd pull a brim bag over our head with two eyeholes and tie a cord fast to the hand grip on the coach. That cord was the only way to find your way back." Voices come rushing in to share tales of winters on the Gaff. Again, I lose track of who is speaking in my efforts to capture the details.

"The train was stopped at Gaff Topsails, it was seven days. We hooked up a telegraph line and a call came that we were needed in Buchans. Immediately. What's immediately? We're here now seven days. I had to jump off the train and walk to Buchans, which was thirty-five miles. I know that well."

"One time they were stuck down to Quarry at the eastern base of the Gaff Topsails. One of the section men and a couple of other guys had to go in to Millertown Junction to get milk. A lot of people used to travel then with babies. The men walked twenty-four miles through the snow with snowshoes. You don't say no, you go. Twelve out and back with groceries."

"And when they are talking about trains being stuck in winter. I worked on the poles in the Gaff," says Jackman. "I used to walk along and step on the cross arm and do my work. That's about twenty-two feet of snow from the ground to where I was sitting down." Jackman explains that the state-of-the-art telegraph lines laid by the Americans in 1942-43 replaced the Newfoundland Railway's antiquated line. They laid telephone and telegraph lines along the railbed between their wartime bases in St. John's, Argentia, and Stephenville. "I worked with it from the start and I lived right through it. I put the lines there and I helped take them down forty years later," nods Jackman. Then, almost as an afterthought, "If all the poles I climbed were stacked end to end, I'd have been the first man on the moon."

## HISTORY SIDING FOUR
## THE REID DEAL

In the notorious Railway Contract of 1898, Robert Gillespie Reid, the man who built Newfoundland's rail line, exposed a degree of cunning and greed that startled many islanders. In the contract he agreed to pay the government of Newfoundland one million dollars and to operate the railway from St. John's to Port aux Basques for fifty years. He agreed to move the headquarters from Whitbourne to St. John's and to purchase the national dry dock. He agreed to operate the coastal steamer service for an annual $90,000 subsidy. And he agreed to operate and buy out the government's telegraph lines. The contract also obliged him to cobblestone Duckworth and Water streets in the capital and to operate streetcars on Water Street.

In return, the government granted Reid ownership of 5,000 acres more per mile of line, bringing his total ownership to five million acres—one sixth of the island! Additional clauses ensured that Reid's land entitlement included the Grand Lake coal area and that, at the end of his fifty-year contract, the railway reverted to his successors.

The uproar at this "abdication of public responsibility" grew to fever pitch when the opposition discovered that Morine, chief architect of the deal, was also on an annual $5,000 retainer as Reid's legal counsel.

When the Liberals returned to power in 1900, they were led by Robert Bond, Whiteway's successor and one of the most vociferous opponents of the "Reid Deal." As prime minister, Bond wanted to cancel the contract, but Reid supporters in his own party—among them Bond's lieutenant, Edward Patrick Morris—convinced Bond to settle for modified terms. In the contract of 1901, Newfoundland repaid Reid's fee plus interest, reclaimed 1.5 million acres, the telegraph lines, and ownership of the railway when the contract expired.

With renegotiations out of the way, Reid installed his three sons on the board of the new Reid Newfoundland Company and retired to Montreal.

# TOPSAILS TRAIL
### HOWLEY TO MILLERTOWN JUNCTION

76

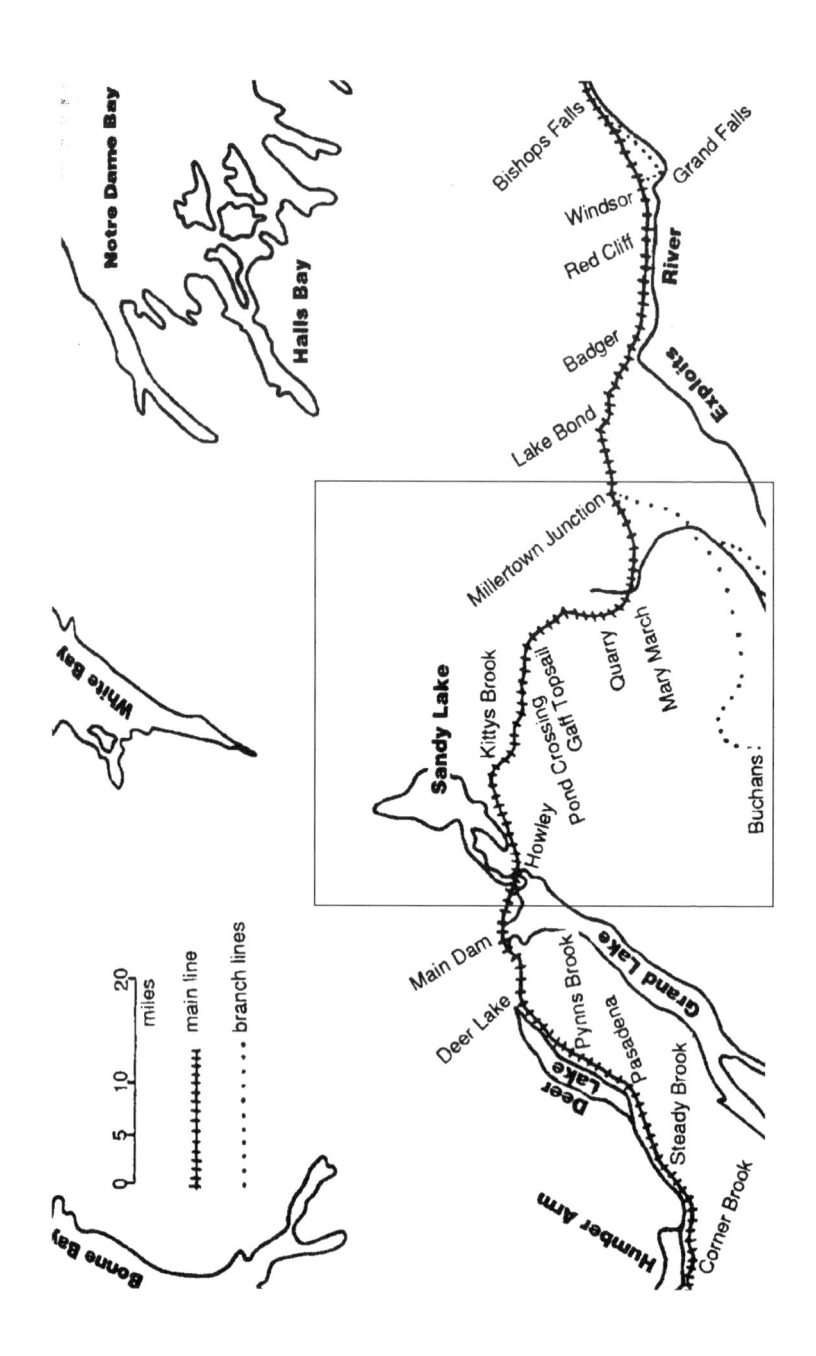

## TOPSAILS TRAIL INTRODUCTION

"They got it slaughtered up there," says Rod Kelly. He's talking about Kruger's logging operations on the once pristine slopes leading from Howley, along the banks of Kitty's Brook up to Pond Crossing in the Topsails. "Clear cut right to the track and roads everywhere," he says. "They'll do what they like. And don't expect to see any replanting up there." Kelly's voice is calm over the phone but he makes no secret of the fact that the winter logging by the pulp and paper industry has hurt his business and his favourite recreation. He also feels that the T'Railway Council should do more to keep that kind of activity as far away from the trail as possible.

Kelly is a member of the Junction Trailblazers Snowmobile Club and owner of Howley's grocery store and the tourist lodge (*www.howley-touristlodge.com*). Since 2004, logging operations have kept thirty-five kms of the T'Railway east to the Topsails ploughed all winter so they can truck out the logs to the mill in Corner Brook. This effectively eliminates what was a major snowmobile route through the area. And those people are the best kind of tourists says Kelly. "They're not like the people in the big mobile homes that drive across the province every summer," he explains. "People on their snowmobiles, and even ATVers, like to travel with their credit cards," and that is great for local business.

The trail itself on the west side of the Topsails is in relatively good shape according to the council's executive director Terry Morrison. Kruger has planked over the trestles and kept up the road so the trucks can get through. With the exception of the trestles on the Badger side, "there's really no point in us doing anything there until Kreuger moves on."

As far as life in Howley is concerned, Kelly says things are good. His father Rod Kelly Sr. retired a few years back and has returned to his first love, riding the rails. He managed to get 900 feet of original rails from CN and has set up a model rail line at Kelly's Point on Sandy Lake where he takes all comers on a ride. Kelly's two sons, and his brother Dean, work winters in Alberta where, Kelly says, the boys are making thirty-five dollars an hour and spending it as fast as they earn it. "They must have a bit of my blood in 'em," he laughs.

The granite quarry on the Gaff is no longer active, though several huge cubes of granite still sit there on the barren landscape like something dropped from outer space. Classic Stone has shut down and Fred Thorn lives in Fort McMurray, Alberta. His son Fred Jr. runs an outfitting business in Buchans and I managed to contact him by telephone. He'd rather not talk about how investors took over his father's company. But he is ready to talk about his three hunting lodges that keep him busy. Thorne says there's no spill-over from the Europeans in the Humber Valley. "No they're mainly into the soft tourism he says. It's the Americans who like to do the hunting," he explains. And hunting is good. One issue though is the growing presence of coyotes and the impact of their predation on the caribou herds. Some days when the caribou are on the move in October we can see 200 or 300 animals a day but the calf recruitment is way down from what it was even a few years ago."

Rod Kelly at Goose Brook.

# CHAPTER 16
# TRAPPER'S LOUNGE

### 17 JULY, 4:00 P.M., MILE 357

We are driving in reverse towards Howley aboard Dean Kelly's mufflerless van with the spider webbed windshield. Grand Lake on one side and a short drop to Sandy Pond on the other. The stench of creosote from the dozen or so railway ties in back is overpowering. It is a cool and misty afternoon and I am tired but exhilarated after two days' hike up the Humber Valley from Steady Brook.

Yesterday morning Sherry Hounsell, a development officer with the NLRDC, picked me up at the Holiday Inn where I spent my final night in Corner Brook. She drove me five miles to Steady Brook. There the rail line escapes from beneath the expanded Trans-Canada Highway. My new boots worked out great. For the mid-morning break I lay on the crushed stone in the rain. In the early afternoon I met Otto for lunch in a roadside restaurant. A small flock of women birders were there from Montreal. They were impressed with the birding on the Island and liked the idea of the railway as a bird-watching trail. Particularly the older women. Generally, they did not appreciate Newfoundland's rough terrain, but felt the railbed's grades were ideal for hiking.

The afternoon slog to Pynn's Brook was uneventful except for one trestle. Someone had removed all the ties and the town council had erected guardrails to keep ATVers and snowmobilers from plunging into the river. I had to balance on one of the side rails to get across.

At Bill's Cabins in Pasadena Otto introduced me to Ian Bell. He commandeered me for most of the afternoon to show me his huge collection of old movies and posters from the early days of cinema. He was very mysterious about how he'd managed to acquire the collection.

After dinner there was a small meeting in the Pasadena Town Hall. Councillor Jim Cheeseman presented me with a town pin. Ten or more other people were there, including former railway workers and people from several community groups interested in the T'Railway. Then Otto and I went to the local rod and gun club, which is right beside the track near the Deer Lake shoreline. The Provincial Skeet Shooting Competition was scheduled for the following day, and they had invited me back in the morning to officially open the event before I set out on the twenty-mile hike to Howley.

So next morning before I found myself yelling "Pull," four times into the wind and winging two of the four clay pigeons. Then I declared the competition open and set out along Deer Lake, through the town and inland over the Main Dam at the head of Grand Lake. The train actually ran over top of the dam, but that is fenced off now, and a sign warns trespassers to stay off. I managed to squeeze through. At one point I was ready to quit. "How much more of this forest and bog can I take?" But as I rounded the next curve an expanse of purple swamp orchids caught me off guard. Dozens of swallows darted back and forth just above the blossoms and the Mary Ann River meandered slowly among the grasses. The sight left me humbled and grateful.

When I finally spot the van ahead of me on the track, Dean, his friend Norm, and his twelve-year-old son Shane, are hauling old ties out of Sandy Lake less than half a mile west of Howley. They offer me a ride into town.

Dean drives and the other two sit on top of the ties so I can take the passenger seat. The rail line is so narrow there is no place to turn around, so Dean puts the van in reverse and back we go. Free of the muffler, the engine adds its complaints to the smell of creosote. Dean shouts to me that Rod Kelly, my contact in Howley, is his brother. When he learned that I was "that fella" walking across the rail line he "explains" his vanload of railway ties, assuring me the ties were only polluting the pond anyway and he needs them to secure the foundation of his house.

Backwards across the trestle at the edge of town, then swing around and forward through the small town to Trapper's Lounge, owned and operated by Rod.

Susie wipes the bar with brisk spare swipes. She is in her mid-fifties, five feet tall, glasses, short dark hair, and has a way of talking that is easy going and business-like at the same time. The only other person in the lounge is a young woman in a baggy sweat suit. She sits at the end of the bar smoking a cigarette. There is a pool table, several tables with hard bingo-style chairs, and a jukebox. Against one wall is a stuffed baby bear, a mounted moose head, and various stuffed owls. Rod is out and will not be back for an hour or more. Susie serves me a plate of French fries and a ginger ale while we chat. She hates French fries; she's been peeling potatoes all her life except for the few years when her husband was stationed overseas, first in Germany and later in Canada. He is retired now and does most of the cooking—pork chops mainly—fried, steamed, stewed and barbecued. Susie says he sometimes makes pork roast for a change, or pork sausages. "One of these days he's gonna turn into a pig," she laughs.

Susie remembers the trains fondly. Howley was founded as a logging town, after the railway went through the area. The railway was the only land route in or out. When she was young, people rushed to the station when a train came through. "There wasn't a lot to do for excitement in those days. A trip to Corner Brook meant an overnight stay, and only your best clothes would do."

A couple of customers come in so I move to a table by the window. The men joke with Susie and talk about the big celebrations this coming weekend. It is Come Home Year in Howley and every available bed in the community is taken, except for the cabins that belong to a failed tourism venture next door to the lounge. No one has seen the owner for a year or more.

An old, mostly green pickup pulls into the gravel parking lot and Susie calls to me that Rod is here. He is tall with reddish-blond hair, ruggedly handsome. I like Rod's easy manner and openness about his private life and his business. In addition to owning Howley's only lounge, he owns the only take-out, the only laundromat and the only tourist cabins that are not in receivership. His dad, Rod Sr., owns the local grocery store, and spent a lifetime working for the railway. Rod says he has arranged a meeting for me with his father tomorrow.

Forgotten cargo.

## CHAPTER 17
# ON PATROL IN THE GAFF

### 18 JULY, 2:00 P.M.

R od Kelly, my host while I am in Howley, drives me to the bungalow in the centre of town where his father lives, leads me in through the cluttered garage and up the carpeted steps to introduce me to his dad. Rod Sr. is a big man in his late sixties with thinning dark hair and eyes that seem to look beyond the walls to the horizon. Rod Jr. leaves on business. The father introduces me to his wife, their daughter Frances, and her boyfriend. The overstuffed chair where Rod collapses, and the couch where he gestures for me to sit, are centred around the television. Mrs. Kelly brings in tea and cookies and then retreats again.

Rod Kelly Sr. operates the only grocery store in town. He is a former railway worker who began as a plough operator's assistant and finished his career on the Gaff Topsails fire patrol. To this day he worries about the health effects from the spray they used to control the vegetation along the railway. And according to what Bud Hulan told me, he has reason to worry. But Rod would rather remember the adventures, like the time they derailed near Port aux Basques, and were hanging over the cliff. He fell asleep waiting for the crane to arrive. Or the time the plough went across

Main Dam, wings out, and cleaned out most of the ties. "The plough car was like a stone wall in front of the engineer so he couldn't see. My job would be to lift the flanges at crossings."

He once spent seventy-two hours straight, picking ice from the track where it runs close to Grand Lake, but most of the time the plough operators and assistants had to stay in the plough. It was their workplace and their berth. I flash back to the cold steel coffin at Humbermouth and shudder at the though of living in such a space. Rod says that in the morning everything inside the plough was covered in frost until the coal stove got enough heat to dry the place out. Perishables were stored under the hatch in the steel floor. As long as they weren't in a station they got paid. His biggest cheque was for eighty hours straight, 212 hours overtime. "Went in the bank and they looked at me," says Rod narrowing his eyes to imitate the teller's suspicious glance.

Before Rod's time the railway used a rotary plough with a circular blade to pitch the snow clear of the tracks in the Gaff. But it was too slow. The railway needed a better way for bashing its way through the awesome snowfalls on the Gaff Topsails. In the 1950s CN built snow fences and raised the railbed another four or five feet along the worst section in the Gaff. "They even had tractors up there in places where they needed to make cuts. Between storms those tractors would bull all the snow again."

Rod's fondest memories are of his last years with the railway. He worked alone on a speeder, though occasionally he would take one of his sons with him. "Fire patrol was pretty good. Just to patrol the Gaff Topsails, I would have paid them to let me do it," he smiles. When there was a train scheduled to come down over Kitty's Brook, Rod drove the speeder to Gaff Topsail Station and followed it down the grade towards Howley. The longest, steepest part of his patrol was the section twisting down out of the Gaffs along Kitty's Brook. Freight trains with up to 100 cars would twist around four or five curves at once. "The diesels would brake pretty hard coming down through those stretches, and whenever the engineer let go the brakes, red hot steel dropped onto the wooden ties. I put out as many as 100 fires a day in the track and on the roadbed. One got away from me, burned across the Howley Road," admits Rod. The crushed stone ballast laid in the 1970s' helped reduce the number of fires. Rod's eyes get that distant look again and I imagine him imagining himself again on his small trolley, with Dean or Rod Jr. beside him, speeding along the Gaff Topsails, a look of contentment on their faces.

*Mushroom in a railway tie.*

## CHAPTER 18
# TAKING UP THE RAILS

He may be sentimental about working on the railway, but Rod Kelly Sr. has no illusions about some of the people he worked with. According to him, railway people—both workers and management—helped destroy the industry. "They milked the railway. One night I saw bananas delivered and they were gone the next morning. I saw workers pour water over cartons of chips and candy." One supervisor was especially bold. The railway reclaimed CN tractors and snowmobiles from his property. He was fired.

As Howley's grocer, Rod was on the receiving end of such service. "I went to pick up a case of milk and one can in it was damaged. The agent says it's damaged goods and he can't release it. I needed the milk and I told him I'd sign for it, had to argue to get it released."

But Rod says there was a larger conspiracy at work, undermining the railway. "It was obvious the management wanted the railway to close." Rod recalls an incident with Sharp's Farm near Corner Brook. The farm had a siding where they filled eight to ten cars a day. The railway wanted to charge an extra $1000 for clearing snow on the points where the siding joins the main line. "It was no extra cost for the railway. Section men are on the job anyway, riding the rails. They just had to scoop out a little snow. Sharp's started trucking their produce." Rod slowly shakes his head.

Much of the maintenance work carried out in the last years of the railway was done simply to keep the red ink flowing and make the books look bad, says Rod. "In March of 1988 they put in 40,000 new ties; ditching and culverts were all done. That June the word came to close her down. The trains could have gone five years on that work before maintenance was needed."

When they took up the tracks in Howley many people went to watch the work crews. "It took two trains. One would go ahead and tie into two lines of fourteen or fifteen sections of rails each and haul them back to a burn-off crew, then go ahead to grab another section of rails," explains Rod. The crew from the second train would burn off the connecting bolts on these sections and load the disconnected rails on flatcars. Front-end loaders scooped up the ties and dumped them to one side where a crew would grade and tag them. Contractors trucked the ties to sorting yards.

Railway demolition crews felt the heat of the anger over the railway closure. "We used to call it the White Fleet—the cars and bunkhouse the railway demolition crews were staying in. One night one of the bunkhouses caught fire. Someone got up in the middle of the night and caught it afire to disrupt the job. They had the cops up but they couldn't pin it on anyone," says Rod nodding to himself.

"A welder from St. John's and another fella from Corner Brook were in young Rod's club one night. They cried like babies. They were part of the dismantling crew. Yes, devastating to them, hey, losing the railway and their jobs. I tried to pep talk 'em. I says: 'The qualifications you got, a welder, I knows now you got a good chance to get a job.' And he says 'Oh no, me ticket's only good for the railway.' 'Yes,' I said, 'you'll never get away with it anywhere else what you done with the railway,' so I guess it wasn't too much of a pep talk after all."

We finish our tea, shake hands and I head for the bunkhouse. On the way, I stop at the grocery store for a few supplies. Frances Kelly's boyfriend is in the store. He tells me he has hunted bears and I admit that I am concerned about encountering them in the bush. "You're not going to see any bears in there my son. They're too crafty. Did you ever hear of a bear attack in Newfoundland?"

"No."

"Of course, there's always a first time," he adds, wiping his mouth with the back of his hand to hide the grin.

Recalling that conversation, I prepare a bedtime cup of tea in the bunkhouse behind Trapper's Lounge. The kettle screams on the stove and

I feel a shovel turn in my gut. Since shortly after I began planning this trip I've had a vague premonition that I could die on the Topsails. Forty-seven miles of remote wilderness between Howley and Millertown Junction. I always dismissed that fear. But there's nothing to distract me now. The walls are unpainted gyproc and plaster, the floors uncovered aspenite, tinfoil on walls above the counter. Pubic hairs on the sheets. I leave my clothes on and climb in.

### Postcard from Howley

*I dream I'm a werewolf, wet and naked, curled in the fetal position on a small curbside bed of grass. Nearby the tent is flapping in the wind and my sleeping bag is torn and scattered on a rain-spattered sidewalk. From across the street bright shop windows hurt my eyes. I try to shake myself dry and enter the tent but the door is zippered. Tent poles are scattered around my feet. A bearded man in a college gown backs his pick-up truck and a glassed-in trailer towards me. I try to smash the windows, jabbing at them with the tent poles. The windows won't break and suddenly I am surrounded by tree trunks that whirl around me like a dizzy circus ride. It is time to go, time to go but I am feeling too sick to move. And then I'm on the outside looking through the glass at the pathetic creature I thought was me, his muzzled face hidden in his hands. Wild and needy. I climb aboard the truck and drive away. I am not the professor. I am not the wolf.*

*Denise, Jane and Maxine at Pond Crossing.*

## CHAPTER 19
# PYJAMAS WITH ROCKETS

**19 JULY, 7:20 A.M.**

Rain on the bunkhouse window wakes me. After a big, greasy breakfast I dial Rod's number. On the drive to Goose Brook Trestle, Mile 352, we spot a cow moose that is unphased by our presence. I haul my pack out of the back of the pick-up and Rod and I exchange gifts. He gives me a Howley Come-Home-Year tee shirt with a moose on it. I give him new hiking socks.

Tires have pushed the crushed stone aside, but it is a hard seven mile climb to Kitty's Brook Trestle and my first break of the day. The railbed traverses low, forested hills so steep that the tops of the telegraph poles, on the downward side of the slope, are barely higher than my head. Occasionally I shout or whistle—just in case there is a bear nearby. For the last mile before the trestle, the rapids run parallel to the trail, thrashing the boulders, crashing down off the Topsails plateau.

I drink tea on the porch of a caboose-cabin near Kitty's Brook. The rain has slacked to a light mist. The metal rungs of the ladder are cold. From the roof there is a clear view of the torrent beneath the trestle several hundred yards away. Through the window of the small room atop the caboose

I see a small bed with folded rocket-print pyjamas and a box full of dinkies. O, fortunate child!

All morning I have breathless waves of gratitude for being able to make this journey. Or is it fear? By one o'clock I reach Kitty's Brook East Trestle. On the near side is a four-inch galvanized funnel with water streaming out at the speed of a tap half open. I drink from the pipe and then fill my canteen. Just as I'm screwing on the cap, a blue and white four-wheel drive pulls up behind me and a woman with short blond hair jumps out the passenger side. "Wade?" she asks, hopefully.

The driver gets out and goes around to the back of the vehicle where he pulls out a large video camera.

"Boy you're really covering the miles. We thought we'd missed you." She is a CBC television reporter. They were supposed to do a story on a logging strike in Grand Falls, but the strike was postponed so her director said "find that railway fella."

I put on my pack and for the next hour trudge across the trestle, again and again, twirl Clara and do a general dog-and-pony show. The interview goes well and then they race off to meet a deadline, while I boot it for Pond Crossing.

When I estimate I'm at Mile 340 I stop. The forest is thinning, making way for the rising plateau that climbs up slowly beneath the shrubs to the south. This is where the end began. There is nothing to distinguish this remote place from any of a dozen or more miles of railbed. Yet it was here, in the fall of 1988, far from the maddened crowd, that the "White Fleet" began to rip up the rails. A quick cup of tea to ponder the situation and then on again.

An hour and a half later I lumber into Pond Crossing (a small collection of shacks), just as a family is locking up to leave: father, daughter and granddaughter. Six-year-old Jennifer and her grandfather come over to talk. "Too bad we're leaving, but there's been five days of rain and cold," he says. "If we were staying you could stay with us." With that cold comfort, they drive off and I'm alone in the cold mist.

While I scout for a place to pitch my tent among the thirty or so ramshackle cabins a pickup pulls up. Three women get out of the cab. Maxine, the driver, is the eldest. Her sister Jane, and Jane's daughter-in-law Denise are up to repair a broken window pane in their cabin and do some general carpentry work. "You'll even have lights tonight 'cause we got a generator," says Maxine.

"Great. I'll get my extension cord," I say, but I am a little sulky that my night of solitude is to be interrupted by the pattering of a gasoline generator. I decide to set up the tent on the other side of the track. Before I have unpacked the tent, the cabin chimney is spewing smoke. By the time I've battled the cold long enough to eat supper, I have a bad case of "poor me." So I deflate my pride and struggle through the bushes to the cabin. The window has been replaced—cracked the new one putting it in—and now they are going to "catch a few trout." Maxine is affixing bobbers and baiting the hooks on all three poles. I notice her right forefinger is cut off at the knuckle. "This is the life" Maxine sighs. The door is unlocked and Jane invites me to go in and have a cup of tea and a lassie bun, still half frozen from the deep freeze.

"If you need the lights before we get back, I'll show you how to turn on the generator," says Maxine and leads me to the small shed to demonstrate the appropriate switches. Then the women are gone, the bushes swishing around their rubber boots. I cut back to the tent, grab my journal and duck into the cabin for tea in the rosy warmth of the stove. My tent will be a frigid exile after this. They are back within forty-five minutes with half a dozen red-bellied trout.

We play cards. I have no money so they loan me five dollars, win that, loan it to me again and win it back. A lot of tea is drunk. That takes us up to 1:00 a.m. by which time my jaws are weak from laughter.

Maxine says her father, Charles, and his brother, were the first people to start coming to Pond Crossing in the 1930s to pick berries. In the fall partridgeberries lie thick as a red winter coat over the barrens. Maxine points to the hills beyond the cabin area, "No matter what time of the day in the fall you'll see people out there picking berries." Charlie first brought Maxine here more than forty years ago when she was a young girl. They stayed in canvas tents. There'd be twenty or thirty tents at a time, each with a wooden floor. Maxine tells me about her severed finger. A six-year-old cousin lopped it off with an axe when she was four, while they were making bows and arrows. Maxine's father had to carry her six miles through the country for medical help.

My own tent seems less than welcoming in the dark driving mist. The cold keeps its fingertips between my toes all night but I wake up fully only once, around 2:30 a.m. I have to get out and piss. I'm naked and the mist and wind are so bracing I almost burst a blood vessel trying to finish the tea-pee.

Next morning the fog is thick outside and it is so cold I can't think clearly. I haul on my thickest pants and race for the cabin. The trout are still out by the door, uncleaned. It is warm inside. Maxine was up an hour ago, at 6:15 a.m., and lit the fire. The others are still in bed. The distant hills emerge from the fog under patches of blue sky. Maxine has seen hundreds of caribou on these ridges. She recalls the spring of each year driving up to Pond Crossing and stopping for the cows on the railbed with newborn calves. Last year in July three caribou took over a section of the railbed. "When you'd drive past they'd move aside and as soon as you were gone they'd come back and lie on the road again. I imagine they're in somebody's freezer now."

Strange thing about Maxine—she's been coming up here since she was a child and she has never gone down the other side of the Gaff in all that time. Only over as far as the summit.

After breakfast I take down the tent, pack up and hit the trail. The three women have promised to drive out later today to see how I'm doing. An hour out of Pond Crossing I grow angrier with each step. Every fifty feet or so there is a pile of burned ties. Whoever was contracted to cart these ties out of here must have decided it was more convenient just to burn them where they lay. The old telegraph poles are sawn off and left where they fell. I have a vision: the fires burning as men tear up the track. Or are they ghosts of a work crew from 1896, burning brush and laying the bed?

Off to the right, clouds lift just enough to give me my first view of a rounded summit rising several hundred feet out of the bog. Gaff Topsail Siding, where the section crews once lived, is 333 miles from St. John's. As late as 1951 it boasted a total population of seventeen people. The place was abandoned in 1956 after CN made it an unmanned section. I can see the roof of an old cabin across the pond to the north and eight more ramshackle affairs closer to the track. There is a name painted on the stone nearby. "Tony Budgell, October, 87." Well that looks charming, Tony. Just charming.

The siding was named for the nearest of four isolated rocky masses that rise dramatically above the plateau, only three of which are visible from the rail line. In the early days the train stopped here so frequently due to drifting at Gaff Topsail that this whole stretch became known throughout Newfoundland as "the Gaff Topsails," rather than its geographic name, the Topsails. Ian Bell—Otto's pal with the movie and poster collection in Pasadena—apologized for his crudeness in describing The Topsails as "three tits all in a line." Of course I see them as three big blisters. There's a photocopied page in one of Joey's side pockets. It is from the Encyclopedia of Newfoundland and Labrador and describes these geological oddities. I wrestle with the wind to keep the page flat.

> *The Topsails, which include Main Topsail, Mizzen Topsail, Gaff Topsail and Fore Topsail, are geographically classified as monadnock. The Topsails rise 200-399 feet above the general surface of the Central Plateau of Newfoundland. Gaff Topsail itself takes its name from a distinctive granite crag among this rock mass which is entirely and colloquially referred to as "the lump."*

Glancing up I can see "the lump" about a mile to the east. The page tells me this is the highest section of the Newfoundland Railway, that it was both treacherous to build and difficult to maintain, with its high winds, steep grades and some of the heaviest accumulations of snow to blanket Newfoundland.

Of the Gaff Topsails settlement, the page says it was entirely dependent on the railway. Residents included section men, an agent, and a fire ranger. The settlement was recorded for the first time in the census of 1911 as "Topsails" with a population of ten in three families. By 1945, in response to wartime demands on the railway, the population peaked at forty-five. No one stayed long.

From the page I read:

> *"The railwaymen's cottages and shacks with their root cellars and wind generators, the railway water tower and coal shed make up all there is to the settlement. Men stay only two or three years because of the isolation, desolate surroundings, lack of any school facilities for the children, etc. It is twenty-three miles to the nearest permanent settlement to the east, at Millertown Junction ..."*

That is all I am to learn. The wind snatches the page from my hand and drives it across the clearing like a huge snowflake.

Looking across Wolf Brook to the Topsails.

## CHAPTER 20
# STONE ON WATER

To pass the time I holler scraps of songs for the new day, amazed at how limited my repertoire is when there is no music. One that keeps coming up is Cat Stevens' "Miles from Nowhere." It seems appropriate and I bellow variations from country to operatic, all a little more than slightly off-key. The horizon surrounds me with the Topsails' undulating bleakness. In a couple of hours I will begin the gradual descent down the eastern slopes and onto the long stretch into Millertown Junction. Every ten or fifteen minutes I spy nests of brazen yellowlegs. Their defense is always the same; a loud lancing cry, over and over, as they fly straight for me, veering off just as I start to feel uncomfortable, to circle at a safe distance, still shrieking. At first I find their defense irritating, and shout back as though at rude children. But as the morning wears on, the piercing calls and bad manners become familiar and humorous.

The map says there is a communications tower on the summit of the Gaff Topsail. There isn't. At the foot of the Gaff lie old cables and wires strewn over a sandpit. Small cloven hoof marks tattoo the sand. Further up among the stunted spruce lies a giant twisted metal X. To the north, five miles distant, the Main Topsail drifts above the fog like the tail-end of a giant duck diving for food. The scattered boulders are whale's backs.

Each new rise and dip reveals a new pod of boulders, some timid, hiding under the larch, others breaching red-stained from the pools. Lichen patterns on their granite hides trace almost-decipherable runes. Suddenly a grouse leaps from the alders and, for the first time in five days, the sun breaks through, torching the dark shrubs to brilliant green.

My new boots have rubbed the backs of my legs raw. I wrap a stretch bandage around each ankle and that allows me to walk without grimacing at each step. It is twenty miles to the nearest town. I am tired already. Missing lunch yesterday and then staying up so late last night playing cards is telling on me. The grade climbs ever upward, and no end in sight.

*Off to the left the green marsh stretches to the horizon. The pools ride the steep grade like terraced rice paddies in postcards from Asian foothills.*

From under the trestle at Wolf Brook, Mile 330.1, there is enough shelter from the wind to light the stove. At this low angle, looking north across the stepping stones in the wide rocky brook, I see the Main Topsail as a giant cairn, Gulliver's toe in Lilliput. Maxine, Jane and Denise stop on the trestle in their truck and call down a greeting. They saw two caribou and almost ran over a brood of grouse. The adult fled into a stunted tree but would not leave its chicks. Grinning down over the trestle at me Jane shouts they also saw a "troll fellow under the bridge." The scoffing mutter of the truck engine is swallowed by the wind and I am alone. My stomach tightens. I toss the rest of my tea into the stream.

Even on a mild day in July the wind is relentless. How overpowering it must be in the heavy drifting snow. During the winter train engines rammed through the drifts, like stubborn stags. Rod Kelly Sr. operated a plough through here. "Pieces of snow as big as houses go flying until the train brings up solid. Then you back up and make another run at it. Sometimes cutting through the deep snow," Rod told me, as his eyes lost their sparkle for a moment, "I used to be afraid that the snow rushing over the plough head and onto the window would burst through and smother me."

The descent is noticeable now. Off to the left the green marsh stretches to the horizon. The pools ride the steep grade like terraced rice paddies in postcards from Asian foothills. The wind and my pack push me limping onward. Noon comes and my feet will not stop. I am captive to the compulsion that keeps my legs moving long after the rest of me screams for a break.

Then I catch an acrid smell. It reminds me of the smell you get when you bang one stone on another. That smell is mixed with the visceral stench of a broken bog. Over the next rise in this grey-green world the bulldozer seems to glow yellow. Nearby is a compressor and a rock-blasting drill. Three grey blocks of granite, each the size of a cord of wood, lie side by side in the black ooze, their right angles at odds with the round irregular landscape of the Topsails. Not a person to be seen. I am transfixed for a moment, mouth agape. Then I turn my back on the site and see, on the opposite side of the track, a collapsed caribou skeleton bleached by the years. With Joey on my back I slip down the bank and kneel beside the bones. Then, with the feeling that I am stealing something from a church, I ply a molar from the jawbone.

For half an hour I watch a blue rectangular patch grow as I hike down from the quarry. I imagine it to be the tin roof of a huge warehouse. It turns out to be the blue tarpaulin roof a twenty-by-thirty-foot unpainted aspenite shack. There is a small trailer, two pickup trucks and, farther back, an outhouse. These must be the people operating the quarry. Anxious to talk to the quarrymen, I am half afraid to risk angering a work crew out here, so close the middle of nowhere. I hide my tape recorder and approach to ask how far to the next trestle. Two men lean out the window, the older man, about sixty years old with grey hair and black horned-rimmed glasses, invites me in for a meal of stew, homemade bread and black tea.

Inside the shack the filtered blue light alters the colours so I feel slightly disoriented. Four sets of bunks with crumpled sheets are gathered in a horseshoe at one end. There is one man asleep on a lower bunk. Three men sit at the other end of the shack at a picnic table. There's John Kieley, who invited me in, and two younger men. Their clothes are as rumpled as the beds. We chat about my trip and then I attempt to steer the conversation to the quarry. This is easier than I expected: granite is one of John's favourite topics. Despite a persistent cough he leans forward to bang the table and drive home his points. For half an hour after the others have driven back to the quarry, he outlines the history of quarrying granite: how the techniques used today are so similar to the techniques of Romans in the fifth century AD. Dimension stone, as they call it in the industry, has been rediscovered as a building material because it resists acid rain. "When you strip off the accumulated dirt on the ancient structures it looks just as good as when the Romans built them fourteen centuries ago," says John.

Most of the world's processing is done in Europe. At any given time the processors have "stone on water" in large ships from Brazil, South Africa, India, Scandinavia, Australia, China. From each twenty-tonne block they get ten tonnes of finished product such as floor, counter, and wall tiles. And headstones. The blocks I saw earlier have already been sold to a plant in Milan. John is enthusiastic about the potential of a Newfoundland dimension stone industry. At trade fairs all over the world, buyers tell him Newfoundland granite is as fine as anything on the market.

"It is worth pure gold. From each cubic meter of granite processors can make 400 twelve-inch tiles, three-eights of an inch thick. Each of those tiles is worth ten dollars at the wholesale level and can retail for thirty dollars each. That's $12,000 a metre, " he says his fist striking the table, "more than any metre of gold ore that was even taken out of Newfoundland and Labrador."

John is frustrated by the difficulty of getting government on side. "The mindset of the base-resource departments is that gold is the thing. And we try to get through to them that a metre of this rock is more valuable. But they don't hear us." John is hopeful that the processing will eventually be done at Buchans, forty miles from here, so instead of twenty-tonne blocks, it will be the value-added product that they ship.

Classic Stone Incorporated has applied to the Atlantic Canada Opportunities Agency, the Department of Development and others to share in the cost of developing the industry. Another bang on the table: "We've been fucking with them for a couple of years and we ran out of patience. So we're up here ourselves now taking it out and sending it overseas."

John reserves his greatest enthusiasm for the granite of the Topsails, where they have identified twenty-seven potential quarries. "To find within a short distance, in the same formation, one kilometer fields of reds, oranges, crimsons, browns, yellows, greens, you don't get it. This is very exceptional," he says, standing to limp towards the door. He caught his right foot in a cable at the quarry two days ago and "damn near crushed it."

John is anxious to assure me that the damage to the environment is minimal. They spent two years studying the movement of the caribou before opening a quarry. "In 100 years of quarrying we wouldn't remove as much material as the iron ore company takes out of Wabush in one day."

Just before I resume my trek, John shows me a rusty drill bit and chisel they found left in the rocks from a quarry operation that the Reid Newfoundland Company operated around the turn of the century. "No different than what we're using today," he says weighing the thumb-sized bit in his hand. He offers it to me and I put it in my coat pocket along with the caribou molar.

Gaff Topsails granite was used to pave Water Street in St. John's with cobblestones after the 1901 railway contract, and also in the building of the new Riverhead station. Scottish stonemason Charlie Henderson oversaw the quarrying. The Statue of Industry, mounted in front of the station, was also Henderson's handiwork. With Topsails granite as a base, he carved the statue itself out of sandstone originally intended as a gatepost for the Anglican Cathedral in St. John's. Using his housekeeper draped in a tablecloth as a model for the classical figure, Henderson sculpted the statue in his back yard.

It seems my education in the ways of granite is not complete. About two miles further east I spot a grey jeep parked on the roadbed. To the north three figures tromp over the bog. As I watch them zigzag around pools, stumble and leap from hummock to hummock, I realize that although I may be walking on the longest piece of sandpaper in the world—as I have come to think of this Island-wide ribbon of crushed stone—it could be worse. I could be slogging through the bog like those three. I reach the jeep first, then Andy, a senior geologist with the provincial government, then his partner Geoff, and finally Fred Thorne, president of Classic Stone.

Andy is tall and thin with close-cropped black hair and beard. In a British accent he tells me he and Geoff, who also sports the mandatory geologist's beard, are scouting the granite outcrops in the area to give Fred some advice about colour variation in the granite.

"They're making some pretty proud claims about the stone out this way," says Andy.

"It's a world-sought-after stone. It's attracting world attention," Fred says while his eyes are searching me for clues. He is short and stocky with a full head of blond hair and a clean-shaven but wind-burned face. Andy introduces him as the granite crew's boss.

"The stone does contain some very unusual materials," adds Andy.

At the turn of the century this area had a number of active quarries on both sides of the line, especially near Quarry Number One Trestle (Mile 325), just east of where we are standing. Reid brought over skilled quarrymen from Scotland. Andy points with his clipboard towards a raised section of shrubs. "See how the outcrops are fairly wide, low, sort of flat tables? What they did was remove those tables completely, remove the outcrop in blocks." I admit that I can't really tell what is natural and what had been quarried. Andy says he would never have spotted the old quarries until Fred showed him where to look. "It's mostly grown over, but there are drill holes left in the rock about finger depth," says Andy. "Keep an eye out when you get down to the Quarry Trestle. There's a white train car there on the side of the tracks opposite the old quarry."

The granite was used for railroad abutments across the Island, for cobblestones on Water and Duckworth streets in St. John's and for buildings. The main St. John's terminal, completed in 1903 as part of Reid's obligations under the 1898 contract, and the provincial courthouse were built from Newfoundland granite.

"People got quarrying mistaken for mining. With mining, the louder the bang and the more you destroy it the better it is. But in a quarry you have to keep the bang very low," Fred explains. If the rock is shattered it is useless for dimension stone. Fred says quarrying, by its very nature, is a delicate process. Andy nods.

"If you want to look for an environmental culprit on this Island the forestry industry is it," says Fred shaking his head slowly. My experience between Port aux Basques and here confirms what Fred says. "They really don't care. They cut down to the edge of lakes and right up to the railbed without any consideration for the environmental laws and the right of way. They'll tear the railroad up and won't really care," says Fred.

The conversation keeps shifting around to focus on the low-impact and environmentally friendly nature of the dimension stone industry. I get the impression Fred has been expecting me for some time and is mentally ticking off items he wants on the record. "When you say you're quarrying in the Gaff Topsails it sounds like you're going in to destroy a landmark, historical Gaff Topsails," he says hardly disguising his disdain for the uninformed. "That's not where we're going to at all. There's three basic hills. You got Gaff Topsail, your Main Topsail, and your Mizzen Topsail. Why touch them at all? They are the landmarks up here."

"There's a fourth Topsail as well," Andy pipes in. "It's called the Fore Topsail."

"Is that the one way the hell down there?" I ask looking northward to where the skies are now cloudless.

Fred does not miss a bet. "You can't touch those landmarks. But how're you gonna get to them if there's no road? Every cubic meter that comes out of this place helps to pay for the upkeep. Those bridges have to be maintained. A lot of them are breaking up," he says. "The Rails-to-Trails lobby are on the record as opposing this quarry operation. But we'll work together with them. They're going to need industry to upgrade roadbeds," Fred says and I can almost hear the mental tick as he crosses off another point.

Of the twenty-seven potential Topsails quarries the only one visible from the track is the one I saw. "The point about it," says Fred moving to the next item on his agenda "is this can work for tourism. In the States quarries are tourist attractions. People want to see how you cut out these massive cubes of rock and move them around. That will be a benefit to the T'Railway proposal rather than a disturbance."

Fred has convinced me of the relatively benign nature of the dimension stone industry, but I cannot help thinking it is the rounded boulders awash in this ancient plateau that the people would come here to see, not the stone cubes destined for the Atlantic shipping lanes and Milan.

"I was up here in '91 and it was very hard to get through because the road was washed out in several places. I came up from Howley and had to go back down that way," says Andy going to the jeep and opening the rear door to toss in his clipboard. "Now you can drive right through. But it's not good to walk on," he says and I am tempted to make a clever remark. Andy continues, "We met two people passing through here last week. They were taking four days to walk from Howley to Millertown Junction."

"That was Father Brophy from Bay de Verde and a friend from Port Union wasn't it?" Fred says, willing for once to be distracted from his checklist.

"Was it Father Brophy? I don't know. Never got their names," Andy admits. He says they were not in any hurry and told him they could not take their eyes of the roadbed for fear of stepping on a big rock and twisting an ankle.

Andy has seen a fair bit of the railbed over the past few years in the course of geological mapping and surveying work, and feels there's a lot of potential to develop some parts of it for tourism. "But I think realistically there's a need to be selective. The resources are not going to be there to do all of it." Alarms ring in my head. Another civil servant telling the world that something is impossible.

Mary March River.

## CHAPTER 21
# THE LAND SPEAKS

After three years quarrying the Topsails, Fred knows something of caribou behaviour. "Down in the low end, east of the Topsails, below the old quarry there are literally thousands of caribou," he says with a grand sweep of his arm to the east. "In the calving times of May and June they spend a lot of time in the valleys along the rivers and in the birch." Fred claims the big herds of caribou do not come onto the Gaff. In August the caribou herd south towards Buchans and scatter before herding back towards the valleys at the foot of the Topsails, and up onto the plateau.

Not to be outdone, Andy has his own caribou lore. He remembers Labrador field trips in summer. With blankets of blackflies and mosquitoes around, the caribou would retreat to the windy peaks and ridges. "I'm sure they do the same thing here," he says shading his eyes from the sun to glare at a distant ridge.

"You see a lot of carcasses and bones down through the rock faces where you get wide openings," Fred says. I have a vision of Beothuk chasing a herd of panic-stricken caribou over the edge, as prairie natives once herded the bison.

But like everything else Fred has told me this afternoon, there's an angle. The whole point is, if you allow 200 hunters to come in year after year and start shooting and throwing bullets all over the place," he pauses, "to me that's more devastating to the caribou than what we're going to do up there. In fifty years there won't even be any sign of the quarries." I finger the caribou molar I found this morning, but keep it in my pocket.

Back in Howley former plough operator Rod Kelly Sr. had described how, in the winter, herds of up to 100 animals would clamour into the fifteen-foot trough ploughed by the train and be trapped there. A train coming down the steep grade would sometimes kill or maim twenty or more animals before it could stop.

Reluctantly I leave the security of these people and their four-wheel drive. It is tempting to take a ride into Millertown Junction, but they have a half day of work to do yet. Once again I hoist Joey on my back and push on down towards the heavily birched valleys at the foot of the Topsails.

On the way down I pass the two forty-foot trestles marked on the map as Quarry Number Two and, by mid-afternoon, Quarry Number One. There is nothing to distinguish the countryside as the former site of a granite quarry. And I don't have the heart to go tromping through the alders and larch looking for the remaining stockpile of blocks. Instead I photograph the white railway car and keep going. There are a few birch mixed in with the undergrowth now, especially along the many small rivers. Sun rays through breaks in the fast moving clouds scan the landscape like spotlights.

Every step is agony now. The bandages protected my legs from the top edge of the boots for a while but the dragon is breathing fire around my ankles again. In the distance the Mary March River sweeps back and forth through forest and bog. If I can just make the seven miles to Mary March Trestle I'll camp there.

Though the day has been dappled with conversations and chance meetings, I've been alone on the trail for six of the seven hours and I am lonely, tired, hungry, and in pain. I collapse at the edge of the road and pull out the picture of Kathy and the girls. I kiss each of them and put the photo away. Cram the cheeks full of munchies, knock back a cup of water, lie down for a minute and then struggle up like an overladened mule to cover the last three miles. About two miles shy of Mary March I decide to risk a twisted ankle and pull on my sneakers. I leave the bandages on for support and because I am afraid to look at my legs where the boots were rubbing. My mind seeks distractions from the crushing monotony.

(In British accent) "Yes, Mr. Kearley do you mind if we interview you for a moment? It's four in the afternoon on the $20^{th}$ of July. You're a mile and half out of your campsite. How do you feel?"

'AAAAARRRRRGGGGhghghghghgh" echoes distantly—or is it just ringing in my head. And then silence.

"Thank you very much for that Mr. Kearley. Pleasant journey."

A surprise at West Brook Trestle, Mile 321.2. Through the trees I spot the roof of a cabin. Down the path, across a couple of narrow bridges to find a game warden's office. Locked tight. No sign of recent use. Through a gap in the closed curtains I can see a long couch against one wall. The air is thick with blue-ass flies. One dive bombs my tea. I can't camp here, so close and yet so far.

A large bull moose meanders across a nearby marsh, every now and then dipping his head, then on again until he disappears into the trees. I take this as a sign, pick up my pack and amble on. Within minutes I see a big cow moose strolling leisurely across the marsh at the side of West Brook. The landscape is heavily treed now, mostly deciduous, a lot of birch, all bog. Many rivers. And just as Fred predicted, there are caribou droppings and hoof prints all along the track—the size of a man's forefinger and ring finger clasped and pressed into the mud.

This country seems so alive, so ancient. Along these very marshes and rivers the extinct Beothuk tribe's last people hunted their last caribou. On the shore of Mary March River the corpse of Mary March, one of the last of her kind, was returned to the land. This shallow, fast-running river in the heart of the Island is the spiritual centre of my journey, in a country made sacred by its long human history. It is 6:00 p.m., I've walked for ten hours, yet I just stand here on the trestle, 320 miles from home, with forty pounds on my back, my ankles bound, and ten miles between me and Millertown Junction. Unsure how to react to a land that haunts me so, I do what any spooked tourist would; I take a few photographs, babble into my tape recorder, and stride on.

Before the song of the river has faded away a caribou steps out of the birch then freezes in its tracks. At least I hope it's a caribou and not a moose calf. Female moose do not take kindly to strangers who get too close to their young. I stop clicking my walking stick and the animal relaxes and galumphs out onto the trail, stands there 100 paces away looking at me, even takes a few steps towards me. A caribou. I keep my footsteps regular and rapid as I grope in the pockets of my knapsack for the apple I saved for just this purpose. Suddenly the caribou stops and turns side-on to me. Thirty paces separate us and I keep walking and finally dig out the apple. Twenty paces. The beast stands there looking at me, hooves apart as if it were bracing under a heavy load. Then it turns and lopes out into the bog, tail up. It stops, lowers its body to sit like a dog, watches me, then gallops away through the bog, water spraying from its hooves. It stops once more and looks back, then races off through the marsh. For a moment the head and back are visible through the trees before it disappears and leaves me with an apple in one hand, a tape recorder in the other, sweat rolling down the side of my face. The flies buzz me, my pack pulls down on me, my legs hurt and I feel great. Revived.

More and more signs of the outposts of civilization the deeper I go into the forest: ATV tracks through the bog, garbage and three cabins with moose antlers over the doors. A sign on a stake beside a path reads "Watering Hole (good water)." On one siding there's an old passenger car with a piece of plywood nailed over the door. A scrawl of black paint proclaims "No longer CN property."

After almost two days on the barrens the woods seem threatening. Where the caribou and I met was the last section of marshland, as if the spirit of the land came to greet me and size me up before I passed again into the land of pulpwood. I did not get a picture of the caribou. But maybe I just wanted, for that instant, to have an offering in my hand to give instead of take.

A sign to cut down on vandalism.

## CHAPTER 22
# LESSON OF THE MAP

Sometimes I wonder if I am on a suicide mission. It is 7:00 in the evening and I am standing with Joey on the ground beside me. Andy and Geoff's jeep just disappeared eastward, again, in the direction of Millertown Junction—which is still six miles away. Ten minutes ago I was a mile back, photographing the second caribou of the day and ignoring the long straight stretch of railbed that lay before me. I did not hear the engine and the crunch of crushed stone until Andy's vehicle pulled up beside me.

Within two minutes my pack was stowed in the back and I was staring through the window at the marshland and surrounding forest. Almost immediately I saw another moose, then another and, on the other side of the marsh, two caribou. The Garden of Eden. I can't drive through this. I have to walk. So I told Andy to stop. "It's at least seven kilometers to Millertown Junction," said Andy. I watched them go with a mixture of regret and relief.

There are so many moose and caribou I stop counting. A grouse and her brood waddle out onto the track. The adult sees me, shrieks to the four speckled chicks and flies into a small spruce tree at the edge of the trail. The young birds cannot fly very far and crash into the bushes where they lie motionless. The silence is broken only by the occasional crashing of the larger animals or the cooing of late birds.

For me the land is still haunted by the ghosts of a lost people. I know I can't camp here. Every stream whispers the name Shawnadithit, last of the Beothuk.

"Shawnadithit," I yell as loudly as I can and a faint echo answers me.

"Awnadithit," and then a long pause. The stream beside the road whispers. "Shhhhhhhhh."

Quietly I say her name one more time "Shawnadithit."

Now I know, as did the Beothuk, there is a price to pay for living in paradise. No wonder those "Red Indians" covered their skins with a mixture of grease and red ochre, believed to be an insect repellant. After five days with no mosquitoes or black flies I am surrounded by a ravenous hoard every time I stop. How can the moose and caribou thrive in this? At 8:30 p.m. I take what I swear is my last rest for the day and eat the apple that was supposed to be for breakfast tomorrow. Where the hell is Millertown Junction? Sandflies have infiltrated my netting. I am so exhausted my senses seem independent, each perception is distinct. Bite of apple. Bite of apple. Flies buzz my ear. Distant sound of robin song. A fly in my mouth. Spit. Trees merging in the deepening twilight. Weight of Joey on my shoulders. Itch of a fly bite. Smell of spruce and water. Stone crunching underfoot.

*Lying beneath the gentle clatter of an aspen grove I feel a serenity I have rarely felt before.*

I struggle into Millertown Junction just before twilight deepens into darkness. Actually I hear it before I see it. Voices in the treetops—the onset of delirium? Then I see two men standing on a rooftop of a bungalow. I hear them discussing the condition of the chimney. "How far to Millertown Junction boys?"

"You're in it," the shorter one calls back. His name is Roy Pennell, the unofficial mayor, as I learned later.

"Is there a bed and breakfast where I could stay for the night?" They laugh.

"No, nothing like that. No one lives here any more," Roy shouts.

"Oh," I say, trying to keep the quiver out of my voice. "Is there anywhere I could pitch my tent?"

The other man, Joe Bolus, suggests I camp in the meadow beside the cabin and then invites me in for coffee and what turns out to be my second supper. The cabin belonged to Joe's eccentric uncle, a trapper. When the uncle died in the 1970s he was the last person living year-round in the Junction. A lesson for sure: just because a place is marked by a dot on a map does not mean there is anyone living there.

Joe is a businessman and investor. He used to be the drummer for the Ducats, a popular sixtys band from the west coast of the province that enjoyed some popularity on the mainland and were even courted by Motown at one point. He lives in Stephenville now and plays in a band for recreation. Tonight Joe has a full house. There is his sister Pauline with her three kids, three-week-old Julia, Michael and Ethan. There is Joe and his spouse Roxanne, who is gamely trying to cook under difficult conditions, and there is Roxanne's sister and her seven-year-old daughter Brandy. So, despite the hospitality, it's a relief when I escape to the privacy of my tent. Roxanne's seventeen-year-old brother Jason comes out every twenty minutes or so for a smoke.

Lying beneath the gentle clatter of an aspen grove I feel a serenity I have rarely felt before. A dog barks in the distance. There is a mosquito buzzing me in the dark. More stars overhead than I have seen in a long time, including my first shooting star since boyhood. And every minute the earthbound blink of a jet trespasses on the starscape. Through a cabin window a dim light falls across a sagging clothesline of tiny shorts, shirts and diapers. Maybe, in some way, I did die on the trip across the Gaff, but not in the way I had expected. I look back over the past two days and realize I did not do it alone. The goading pride, the fear and the aches melt away. As I close my eyes a vaguely remembered quote from William Blake wafts through the tent like the smell of the new-mown hay beneath me. "I myself do nothing. Through me my higher power takes action."

### HISTORY SIDING FIVE
## OF THE PEOPLE, BY THE PEOPLE, FOR THE REIDS

In the summer of 1905, with no new railway construction in sight, the Reid Newfoundland Company offered to sell its holdings on the Island to the government for $9.5 million. The offer was declined.

The election of 1908—the year R.G. Reid died—was fought between Bond and former Justice Minister Morris, who resigned from the Liberals to form the "People's Party," financed by Reid's sons. The People's Party manifesto promised a new era of branch line construction. That election was a tie. But the People's Party won a runoff election the following year and soon after contracted with the Reid Newfoundland Company to construct five branch lines, totaling almost 300 miles. In return Reid Newfoundland was to be paid $15,000 in cash per mile completed, plus 4000 acres per mile for operation.

The railway was again the largest employer in Newfoundland. Gangs set to work slashing the brush, grading the rock and bog, and taming the distance with iron rails. They completed the eighty-eight-mile Bonavista branch in 1911 and the 105-mile Trepassey branch in 1914. In 1915 work gangs extended the Harbour Grace line thirty-seven miles to Bay de Verde and Grates Cove and lengthened the Blaketown branch by fifteen miles to Hearts Content. And forty-three miles of a proposed line to Fortune on the Burin Peninsula were completed before construction halted. The rails on the Fortune line were eventually taken up, while a proposed branch to Bonne Bay was merely cleared and graded before the Colony diverted its energies to the support of Great Britain in World War One.

# RED OCHRE TRAIL
MILLERTOWN JUNCTION TO BISHOP'S FALLS

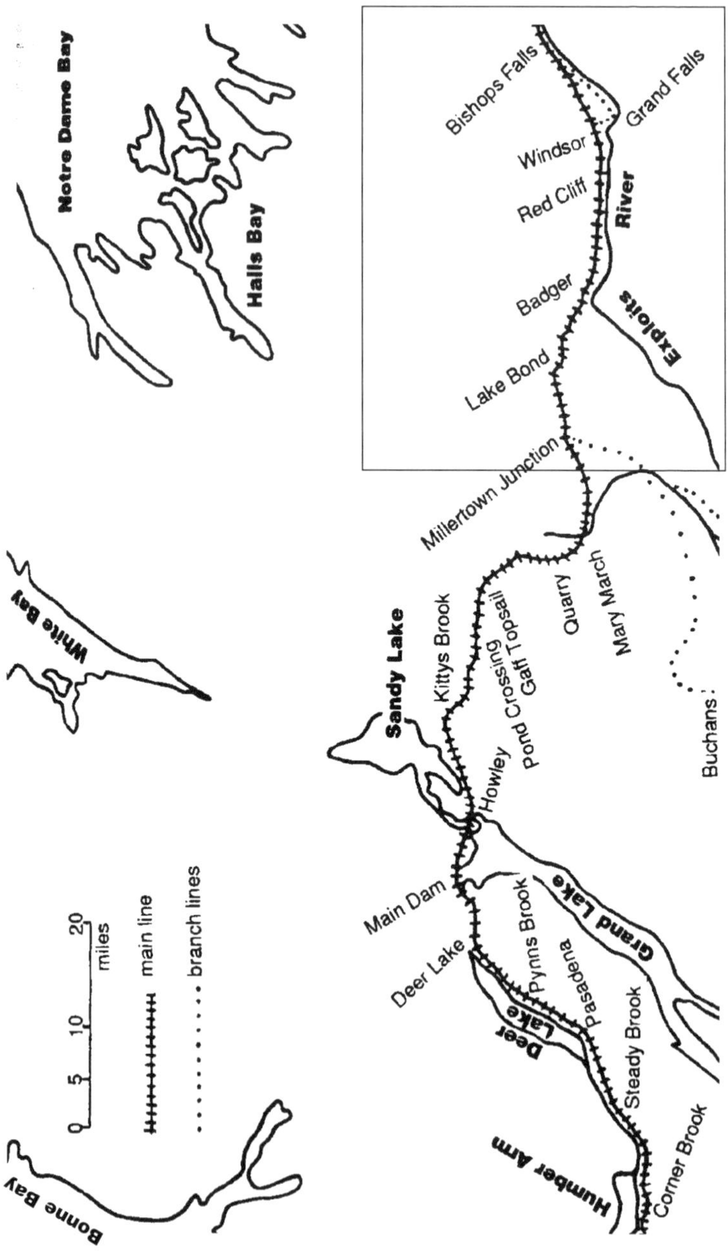
Notre Dame Bay
Halls Bay
White Bay
Bonne Bay
0 5 10 20
miles
main line
branch lines
Bishops Falls
Grand Falls
Windsor
Red Cliff
River
Badger
Exploits
Lake Bond
Millertown Junction
Quarry
Mary March
Buchans
Sandy Lake
Kittys Brook
Pond Crossing
Gaff Topsail
Howley
Main Dam
Grand Lake
Deer Lake
Pynns Brook
Pasadena
Deer Lake
Steady Brook
Humber Arm
Corner Brook

# RED OCHRE TRAIL INTRODUCTION

Pauline Lannon doesn't get up to Millertown Junction much since her brother Joe Bolus died a few years ago. Winter snow has pushed in the front wall of his cabin on Joe Glodes Pond. But what really gets Pauline is how the whole area has been cut to the ground by logging contractors. "I just don't like to go in there now to see what they have done to that beautiful area," she says with a heavy sigh into the receiver. But it didn't come as a complete surprise to her. Joe used to fly his own plane from Stephenville to Millertown Junction and had a bird's eye view of what the loggers were doing in the back-country. "He used to tell me that they had the interior mowed down," she says, "so I suppose there's nothing left in there to log." I can hear one of Pauline's five young children calling, "Mom, mom." Her husband John is in Fort McMurray looking for work and she's expecting good news any day.

That logging activity west of Badger is causing considerable grief for local snowmobilers as well. Apparently one contractor is ploughing snow off the trail so his logging trucks and skidders can more easily access the logs in winter.

But that is not the only cause for traffic in the area. Even with the logging activity, wildlife is abundant. Moose, caribou, coyotes, bear, and smaller animals like hares and game birds. Little wonder then, especially in the Fall, that the trail is a popular hunting route frequented by heavier than usual numbers of ATVs and pick-up trucks.

Despite the heavy traffic, or perhaps because of it, the trail is in relatively good condition, with some brush clearing needed between Millertown Junction and Badger and Badger and Grand Falls-Windsor in particular. A few of the trestles resurfaced by the T'Railway Council are in need of repairs. The decking was nailed too closely together so it holds the dirt which rots the wood.

Clear cutting through the Grand Falls-Windsor area is not as much of an issue as it was back in the 1990s.

Two people I met along this stretch are Dennis and Paula Flood. They have faced a lot since that evening back in 1993 when I visited their ranch to chat about their concerns with logging abuse along the T'Railway. In 1997 Paula was diagnosed with cancer. Then, in the middle of that struggle, one evening in the late 1990s, while the couple were away, their stable caught fire and all the horses were lost.

I contacted Paula in Whitbourne where she and Dennis have lived since 2002. He was away working on the Hibernia platform when I called.

Flood, now a cancer survivor of ten years, is enjoying their new home. She no longer owns horses but she still has them in her life. "When we first looked at this property I could smell the horses from the farm up the road. I knew then I could feel at home here," she says. Paula and Dennis still use the railbed near their home but these days it's for running and snowshoeing.

She has a couple of concerns about the T'Railway. In addition to the dust in the summer, she laments some people's lack of respect that manifests itself in, "litter and garbage dumped by the side of the trail." With the heavy traffic in this area there are also potholes. A new concern for her is the number of coyote tracks they see, so many in fact that Paula is no longer comfortable walking the dogs on the trail because she thinks the dogs might be in danger. "I'm not comfortable enough to go out in case I might happen on one of them on the trail."

Near Skull Hill.

## CHAPTER 23
# SKULL HILL

### 21 JULY, 3:30 P.M., MILE 294

The Badger Motel is a straight line of twenty or so white clapboard cabins on a gravel parking lot. Several tractor-trailers are parked to one side and the cars in front of every door have their windows open. The gas station and restaurant is a tacky bungalow hunched between the cabins and the Trans-Canada Highway, where the traffic whines past on the way to other accommodations. I wrestle Joey towards the blue door of cabin fifteen. Unlatching the door with the key, I don't so much push as fall into the room. Inside, the stained carpet, faded paint, and standard motel furniture tell of too many visitors and not a lot of care. Never mind, tonight this is the lap of luxury.

I dump the knapsack, strip on the way to the bathroom, punch the water on and droop under the hot steam, not caring if I ever take another step. There is nothing I need, or want, but to stay there with warm water pouring over my flesh.

In the steam-fogged bathroom I towel off and virtually fall onto the bed, barely revived enough to call home. Kathy wants to know if I have the flu, my voice sounds different, deeper—from all the shouting and singing I do out there on the trail? The girls have stopped asking me to come home.

Lying on the bed, I look into the dresser mirror and see, between the soles of my feet, a startled unfamiliar face. Walking over to the mirror I bend forward. No, it's me all right: bloodshot brown eyes, deeply tanned face, neck and hands, the rest of me fish-belly white and thinner. I have my first grey hair. Slight nausea and faintness, stinging boot-rubbed ankles, aching feet. I am very close to cashing in the whole thing. But this time there is more than just personal fatigue. The damage to the railroad right-of-way, and the despair of people I met today, anchors any buoyancy I might feel for having reached the 300 miles-from-St. John's marker.

After running a footbath, I perch on the edge of the tub and let the hot, salty water slowly drain away my discomfort. Leaning with my eyes closed I recall the dawn, wading into the cool of Joe Glode's Pond, scooping pond water to my face, handful after handful, cool on my chest and thighs, summoning goose bumps. One handful wriggles against my cheek. A witless minnow wriggles in my cupped hands.

It was 10:00 a.m. by the time I set out with a minimum of supplies in my day-pack, Clara clicking along and Badger on my mind. Joe Bolus has promised to drop my full pack at the motel. The first five miles, to Skull Hill Trestle, is thick crushed stone. Beyond that the railbed is hard packed. There is a fairly extensive area of private logging—200 feet wide—running parallel to the track for a quarter mile, the waste wood silvered with age. Then a larger logged-out area with a turnaround for large trucks. Then, on the breeze, the snarling of a chainsaw.

The rounded top of Skull Hill rises to the south as Skull Hill Brook drifts gently out the forest to approach the road and then back again into the woods. A mottled snipe leaps from the water and flies low along the track towards a huge ridge of crushed stone that towers to three times the height of the surrounding trees. It is a stockpile of railway stone near the Y-junction of the track and a wide, very well-used logging road. Atop the pile I gasp for breath and survey the landscape. The track is a long straight thread stretching to the west and east. An ATV carrying two men zooms up the track from the east like a low-flying bee and veers onto the logging road, past a parked yellow bus and on over the next ridge. A tail of dust spreads languidly into the air, drifts over the alders, pale as dirt.

Stones roll and tumble away from my boots as I race down the steep-sided pile (so crushed stone can yield to the feet!). Then back onto the trail where a pickup, with four workmen shoehorned into the cab, drives past. It stops. Backs up. There are chainsaws in the back. The men all look less than thirty years old, with torn sticky clothing and big grins. Apparently the television piece on my trip was broadcast the night before last. They want to know how it's going. Did I see many moose?

As the early afternoon clouds thicken, a large truck ladened with logs chugs up the track towards me. Chris Stuckless is a blond, sincere young man who drives a collector truck for the larger trailers. He tells me they are finished logging around Skull Hill. Chris admits they could not be logging this area if it were not for the track, or what's left of it. In several areas the rocks and bog are churned together. In other places gouges thirty feet long by four feet wide, full of mud and water, rip the edge of the forest into tatters. Heavy equipment groans. And clear-cut areas scream silently all around us. This is a walk through a pulpwood forest being strip-mined.

At Lake Bond I encounter the largest visible clear-cut for the day. The forest is slashed to the ground, right from the railbed to the shore of the lake, and even to the doorstep of a cabin, which stands out like a miraculous escapee from the destruction of a tornado.

Here come two big trucks, the first is an eighteen-wheel tractor-trailer with a crane lashed to it. The tractor is big and red with "Wild Bill" hand painted on one of those clear panels screwed to the hood. Apparently it has no brakes. I have to leap from the gravel and onto the bog that vibrates as the trailer rattles by. Next comes a tandem dump truck. Mcdonald's Trucking on the side. And again the bog shakes.

To dislodge these memories, I shake my head and am again in the bathroom of the Badger Motel. The headlights of a tractor-trailer fills cabin fifteen for an instant as if it was coming back to finish me. Then darkness. I rise stiffly to towel off my water-wrinkled feet and limp to the night table, counting again the miles on the map and making a few notes on the day.

Earlier this afternoon brothers Bill and Norm Pardy were waiting for me on the track, beside their small red pickup. They had seen the CBC spot and wanted to ask me to speak out on their behalf. Between them they had sixty years' experience working for the railway as section men. They are from Badger "less than 100 feet from the track" and grew up to love the sound of the whistle as the train braked down the grade from Millertown Junction. They had watched with regret as the rail line was stolen, and now they are desperate about the logging destruction.

Leaning against their truck, they grin widely at my approach and I realize that I must look pretty silly in my spandex and big boots, with my undershirt on my head to protect against sunstroke. After introductions and small talk, Bill gets down to it. "Men that worked and spent a lifetime around the railroad and then see this stuff going on, it hurts to see this area used like this." Bill jerks his thumb towards Norm. "He worked now forty-two years at the railroad on the section crew in this area from Badger to Gaff Topsails."

"Norm, what do you think when you see what they are doing here?"

"I don't know what to think of it," he says. "It's hard to believe what's happening."

"We were talking about it this morning. What they should do is leave it like it is right on through. A little pickup is not going to hurt it," Bill says, leaning on the fender of their little pickup, "but those big trucks…"

"They should know this in St. John's, all this stuff. I don't say they knows half of what's going on," says Norm.

"Yes, you wants to tell them west of Badger they ruined it hauling pulpwood over it," says Bill. "Shouldn't be allowed. We were around it since we were sixteen, seventeen years old. Now we're retired and have to see this. Why are they tearing up everything? And there's no need of it, that's the worst." He pauses and then gestures at the area around us. "If they tears up a place they don't fix it. There's places in there they got the stone and the bog all churned up just like it was a soup or something." Bill rubs his eyes with his right hand as if to dislodge the vision he has evoked.

Norm tells me about working with the railway before Confederation. "What a difference. You wouldn't think of opening a can and throwing it out. But now, sure there's bags of garbage." The desecration of this forest is a stark contrast to the wilderness of the previous two days coming over the Topsails, I say, trying to offer some comfort and to allay my feelings of frustration and powerlessness.

"Me and him was up to Pond Crossing one day last week and caribou, you couldn't count 'em. That was about three miles west of that railcar on the siding just the other side of Mary March River." I recall the hastily painted plywood sign.

"Oh yes, wonderful country in the spring of the year my son. You gotta tell them what is going on west of Badger," pleads Bill. I recall the massive logging at Cooks Pond and wonder aloud, since the railroad is public property, who is getting the benefit. That strikes a chord with Norm.

"You're damn right. We own this," he says. "The people of the Province."

"Keep it in shape you know. If a place washes out fix it. Keep it in shape," Bill adds and then asks about the rest of the line. I reassure them that most of the line is intact.

"That's the good thing. But we got to stop it now," he says as we say good-bye. Several pickups with loggers in the front and back head out the track. A pickup on the way in stops. There is a man behind the wheel, two women and a young girl as passengers. They are headed in to their cabin near Lake Bond, which luckily is on the side opposite the clear-cut. They shake their heads at the destruction and offer me a cold beer. Then they have to pull to one side quickly as an eighteen-wheeler loaded with logs lumbers around the turn.

Before shutting off the bedside lamp with Motel Badger engraved on it, I notice Clara's tip has worn down so it looks like a hoof. It even has a split in it, right where the cleft should be.

Furtive residents of the interior.

Photo courtesy of Terry Morrison

## CHAPTER 24
# WHAT'S IN A NAME

**22 JULY, 2:00 P.M., MILE 287, ASPEN BROOK**

A weird moan resounds through the aspen grove every couple of minutes. It is loud even above the raging traffic on the wet highway 200 yards through the trees to the left. I imagine a moose struck by a vehicle, disabled and lying unnoticed in the trees. After a short debate with myself, I decide to plunge into the dripping undergrowth, over fallen logs, through thickets of raspberry brambles. The moaning and the highway are closer. I burst through into the broad smell of clover and there is the object of my rescue, contentedly tethered in the midst of the roadside meadow: a damn cow.

This was supposed to be a day off, but the Badger Motel lost its charm overnight. Carl Budgell, coordinator with the Exploits Valley Development Association, and Bill Sterling of the Bishops Falls Development Association—the one set up with seven million dollars granted to Bishops Falls as compensation for the demise of the railway—visited me this morning. They arranged a couple of nights' accommodation for me at the Poplar Bed and Breakfast in Grand Falls. So I decided to make the trek partway to Grand Falls, hitch back to

Badger for the town hall meeting and then finish the last four miles to Grand Falls after the meeting.

For most of the walk between Badger and Grand Falls, the TCH is never out of earshot on the left, the Exploits River always visible to the right. A patch of ripe strawberries glistens and I scoop up a handful. All the way along this trip, I've preached about how important it is to take time to smell the wild roses, pretending to every one, including myself, that this trip across is my chance to do just that. But it's not a holiday. At least not anymore. It's a job.

Leach Brook Trestle is Mile 283.8 from St. John's. Very close to half way now. There are several ties missing, no way to drive over it. On the other side of the TCH is Thunder Brook, a new splash-and-putt park. On the newer maps the brook is renamed for the tourist attraction! A mile east from the brook the track passes under the TCH at Red Cliff. Here I climb up to the highway and try for twenty minutes to hitch a ride back to Badger. But it is useless, so I decide to finish the four miles into Grand Falls. Just beyond the underpass is the community of Red Cliff, a line of fifteen or twenty houses and one convenience store on a paved road. A helmetless kid on a motorcycle races down the road towing a boy on a bicycle with a twenty-foot length of yellow nylon rope.

Sandra Dyke, fifty, lets her slightly obese Labrador retriever out of the car. She grew up here and likes to drive out from Grand Falls to walk. She and her childhood friends used to make the hike up the track on hot summer days to swim at the place now called Thunder Brook. She resents that name change. When she grew up here it was called Leitch Brook. (Not Leach as my "official map" says.) Something in those three names for the one brook captures the different demands on the T'Railway: the give-the-tourists-what-you-think-they-want mentality, the officially misspelled designation, and the local name.

Reading the map and walking, I stumble and stagger to keep from falling where the crushed stone has been excavated. Someone has dropped a truckload of house construction refuse beside the track—boxes, empty five-gallon plaster buckets, paint cans, and old gyproc. Christmas-tree size spruce trees planted at regular intervals from each other are the only sign of reforestation I've seen since Port aux Basques.

Back in Badger just in the nick of time for the town hall meeting, I'm introduced to a more somber crowd than the storytellers who showed up at the Deer Lake Inn. Tonight there are ten former railroad workers, town councilors and media. Norm Pardy is here, Leonard Howell, Cliff Kirby, a tall guy Max, Pat and Harold. They asked the usual questions: who was

I doing this for? When did I start? What was the furthest I had walked in a day? What animals did I see? Jennifer Smith, a young reporter with the Grand Falls Advertiser wanted to know "if people want to make the railway into a road why do you object?"

"I don't."

"Then what are you talking about?"

"I'm talking about eighteen-wheelers with loads of logs driving over it, I'm talking about tandem dump trucks, I'm talking about skidders churning the roadbed up so that nobody can use it. I'm talking about people who are abusing the line. I'm not talking about people who are just using it for their own enjoyment. Does that make sense?" I sounded a little more impassioned than I had intended, and the reporter backed off.

Most men here are former railway section men, a few even inheriting their jobs from their fathers, apparently a common tradition among the families of the long thin community. And most started with the railway before Confederation. Leonard lived in the isolation of the Gaff for three years early in his career, but does not have much to say about it. He started when he was fourteen years old.

In contrast to the Gaff, Leonard remembers Millertown Junction, just fifteen miles from Quarry, as a busy place. "One time there was thirty-two trains in twenty-four hours passed through Millertown Junction." That included traffic shipping ore on the Buchans branch line.

I notice, for the first time, resentment among the railroaders against the encroachment of the highroads after Confederation; roads which helped erode the railway's passenger and freight service.

"At the Main Gut in Stephenville Crossing you couldn't get through the small bridge. It was only a piece built on the railway bridge for the cars and small trucks to go through, then they put in the new road and the bigger trucks could get by into town fine then," says Leonard, slouching as deep as it is possible to slouch in a bingo chair, arms crossed over his generous belly. "That was the end of the railway." There is general agreement around the table, heads nod, chairs scrape.

Another resentment. It's Norm. "In the 'early years' they wanted every bit of freight they could get to haul. And the 'later years' they was trying to get clear of freight. The railway management was doing everything they could to make the books look bad."

Another man whose name I'd already lost: "Between here and Bishop's Falls, it was all new crushed stone and rails and everything. Then three years later they tears it all up and puts in all new again. They must be trying to get clear of their money."

"And once they hauled up the first rail at Mile 340 that was it. That was about seven miles west of Pond Crossing. And that wasn't long after the last train. When they closes a line on the mainland, they waits five years before they takes the rail off. But here they said 'Get a start and then it's too late.'"

I wondered if anyone had worked on the demolition. "Yes sir. I helped take up the first rail, in October 1988 I believe," says Leonard. There is resignation in his voice.

"So you were there? How did that feel?"

"It felt hard at the time. But you know, what can you do?" he says looking me straight in the eyes and holding up his hands as if they were scrubbed for surgery. "It was September third when the last train went over." Judging by the faces around the table it's time to change the topic.

"So, now we've got this track... What should we do with it?"

"It should be used for trails."

"It's not what should be done with it, who is going to maintain it?" This from one of the Badger town councillors, speaking up for the first time in the meeting. He repeats the chorus from what the municipal song book on the T'Railway, "Who will pay?"

"Let's decide what our dreams are first. Then let's worry about accomplishing them," I say. I'd learned that from Otto. "What do you think should be done?"

Norm was waiting for this. He leans forward with his skinny elbows on the table. "I figure it should be for trails. For people. On Gaff Topsails, it's a good tourist area. All kinds of caribou. Good scenery. Good fishing." Then just like in Deer Lake, a tumble of voices.

"Good people up there."

"Yeah. Lots of berries, lots of cabins."

"Good place for skidooing in the winter."

"Oh, I imagine it must be pretty scary up there in the winter storms. There's still caribou bones you know up there along the tracks."

"Oh yes, from where the trains killed them. Used to kill a lot of caribou up there every winter."

"It seems there's more caribou hanging around the track these days."

"More moose too. Train used to mangle fifty or sixty of them every winter. Some wouldn't be so badly hurt and would walk off."

"My brother come down with a plough special one night from West Brook when a moose jumped in the track and the plough scooped it up. That's all they thought. Figured they had him killed. When they got down to the Junction and stopped on the siding, the old moose jumped off the front of the plough and beat it across the bogs." The hall echoes the laughter.

"You take holidays, first and second of September, and get on that Express, she'd be packed. You couldn't get a seat. I often come right from Port aux Basques like that on a holiday, couldn't get a seat. Anywhere. Blocked right through."

And then the talk swings around again to the destruction west of Badger, to calls for the need to do something, anything. But what? No answers. After the meeting we mill about for a few moments, shake hands. An interview with a radio reporter. The hall empties.

Supper is with the Badger Walker, Joe Roberts, his wife Ivy, and son Michael. Joe is soft-spoken and gentle, a tall man with a full head of grey hair. He has walked across the Province along the TCH three times raising money for the children's hospital. His advice to me was to soak my feet every day and never think about the final destination, just about the place I want to reach that night.

## CHAPTER 25
# HALFWAY TO NOWHERE

**21 JULY, 10:15 P.M.,
POPLAR BED AND BREAKFAST, GRAND FALLS**

Hosea just put the moves on me. I should have known when he said he would like to drop by to talk, but I agreed without thinking. It was only back in my room that I realized I had been propositioned. So I left the door wide open, put the picture of Kathy and the girls on the bed beside me, made sure my wedding ring was on the right finger and then put my feet in the foot bath. They weren't there for long when Hosea came knocking.

He is five foot four, close-cut dark brown hair, tight jeans, tee shirt and a Miami accent. He closed the door and sat down on the bed picking up the photo as he did, asked if they were my family. Chat chat chat. Touched a scar on my leg, asked about the strength of my legs, asked if I wanted to have my feet massaged.

"No thanks, I do it myself. Learned by doing my wife's feet." Chat chat, married thirteen years. He picked up the photo again.

"You have a beautiful family," he said and placed the photo back on the bed beside me, then hurried towards the door. "See you later," and he was gone.

At 11:00 p.m. a phone call. Standing in the plush carpeted downstairs hall, I listen as Kathy tells me a friend's baby has died. After less than a year struggling with a chronic illness, baby Kevin Walbourne faded away. Suddenly my aches and pains seem so petty.

The morning of July 23 is a flurry of interviews for the local and provincial news. Between 8:30 a.m. and 11:00 a.m I talk with five different reporters giving all but one of them the same pat answers to the same simplistic questions. One, a young anthropologist-turned-reporter, the same Jennifer Smith from the town hall yesterday, delves into my motivations for the trip, asks how they changed from one of seeking a wilderness trek to being an ambassador for the trail and its cross-Island integrity.

> *It is an easy two-hour stroll past horse tracks, a long garland of plump wild strawberries, and grassy ponds, to the outskirts of Bishop's Falls.*

Jennifer's is the final interview before I set out on the eight-mile hike to Bishop's Falls, so she gives me a lift to the start-off point. The map shows a branch line ran from the paper mill along the Exploits River to Bishop's Falls. It belonged to the old Anglo-Newfoundland Development Company when the company shipped paper thirty miles from the mill to the port of Botwood. The main Newfoundland Railway line is on the other side of the TCH in Windsor. That is on her way, so Jennifer drops me there near what is now a bus station. The terminal is still in sight as I cross the halfway mark of my journey (273.5 miles from both Port aux Basques and St. John's).

An older man, slightly stooped, eyes shaded under a red baseball cap, walks steadily towards me across a huge expanse of pavement behind a large warehouse. There are no trucks or trailers in sight. Frank Jackman is interested in anyone who walks across the Province. "Did you meet Joe Roberts in Badger? The biggest mistake he made when he started walking first was wearing two pairs of socks. The doctors told him it would kill him," says Frank. I do not tell him I started the same way.

"Joe gave me a few hints. He said wear one pair of socks and soak your feet in salty water at night," I say, then change the subject. "Did you work with the rail line Frank?"

He used to work in the freight shed until he "took the package" five years ago. "There was sixty-seven of us here, night shift and everything. Only three truck drivers here now." Frank says CN spent over $1.5 million to build and pave the site where we are standing "a few years before they closed the railway." He gestures towards the high-tech amber lights drooping over the pavement like colossal eyes. "When they turned them on first the people over there started complaining," he says, pointing to a row of houses a quarter mile away. "You could paint your house in the night time by those lights. CN turned them down and then they turned them off in late 1992."

Frank wonders why this paved expanse was built at all. The entire area, as big as three football fields, was dug out to a depth of thirty feet and filled in with Class A gravel. Pavement twelve inches thick was laid over that. "This is supposed to be for heavy container traffic. I used to say to the boys when they were laying it, 'this ain't no trucking outfit; it's a goddamned airstrip, that's what it is.'" And Frank wonders what the point was. "They got three truck drivers there now all controlled from St. John's. They only go out when they're called." But the place hasn't been totally abandoned. "They used this place for the salmon festival last week. They had all the trailers parked here. And there was room to spare."

It is an easy two-hour stroll past horse tracks, a long garland of plump wild strawberries, and grassy ponds, to the outskirts of Bishop's Falls. The intersection where the trains once passed under the TCH is now part of a highway cloverleaf. A jeep drives out through the underpass and the driver pulls in, throws open the passenger door.

"You Wade? Hop in. I'm George Saunders."

He is solid looking with graying hair, and he grips the wheel like a racecar driver. After our introductions and a handshake he passes me a town pin, a brochure and a town flag, then spins the car around in the road and heads back into Bishop's Falls for the official tour.

"You have a lot of admirers out in Stephenville Crossing" I tell him. "They were telling me about George Saunders and how he got seven million dollars for Bishop's Falls when the railway shut down."

"We got the seven million dollars. We're still working on that. We've converted the station into a development corporation centre," says George. I'd already met Bill Sterling, director of the corporation, when he visited me at the Badger Motel two days before.

George takes me past industrial buildings, past Diamond Crossing (where the AND rail line from the mill in Grand Falls and the Newfoundland Railway intersected). The pole line to the mill runs along the AND track and is a popular route along the Exploits River for ATVs and dirt bikes. In the 1940s Abitibi-Price used the track to run a pipeline for pulp from the Bishop's Falls plant to the Grand Falls paper mill.

Once across the tracks, George drives through the oldest section of town. One old-style bungalow has the whistle marker from Mile 333, Gaff Topsails, plunked proudly in the middle of the lawn while a figurine of a black boy in a straw hat commiserates on the concrete steps.

At the centre of town is a half-mile-long expanse of crushed stone and weeds beside the Exploits River. Here the freight yard once reverberated with the shunting to and fro of the Newfoundland Railway's steam engines, passenger and freight cars, and, later, diesels and the orange cabooses of the CN line. Beginning in 1919 Bishop's was the headquarters for the Western Division of the railway. Gone now from this half mile stretch are the seven "levels" of rails, a roundhouse, repair shops and a railway station; an industry large enough to help sustain this town of several thousand. The echoes of metal pounding metal, the screech of wheels on rails belong to history. The future looks silent.

In the distance the Exploits Trestle, the longest in the Province, looks like a zipper stretching across the river's grey expanse. Robert Reid's railway construction crews reached the opposite bank of this formidable river in 1893. It was then that Reid signed a new contract, at the request of the government, to divert the main line from its original intended terminus at Halls Bay to push on west and finally south to Port aux Basques, by way of the Topsails. The trestle is one more testament to Reid's engineering skills.

Near the western end of the train yard, farthest from the trestle, is the former station, well preserved but virtually silent. At the far end of the yard, several neglected train cars huddle on a brief length of track "to be developed later," says George apologetically. "You have to come inside to put it into perspective. We have a lot of photographs in there." But I have to forego the tour when Carl Budgell, coordinator for the local development association, arrives to drive me back to Grand Falls.

### HISTORY SIDING SIX
# THE HEART OF THE MATTER

In 1920, a year after Bishop's Falls became the headquarters for the Western Division of the railway, there were 2,000 people on the annual $700,000 payroll of the Reid Newfoundland Company. During the construction phase it employed up to five per cent of the Island's work force. Towns with a railway terminus prospered. Nor was the island any longer a "husk without a kernel." Since 1908 the Anglo-Newfoundland Development Company operated a large pulp and paper mill on the Exploits River, establishing the town of Grand Falls. Other forest industry towns along the line included Deer Lake, Howley, Badger, Bishop's Falls, Glenwood, Benton and Terra Nova. Investors were slowly beginning to endorse a pulp and paper deal for Corner Brook.

Nevertheless, the Reid Newfoundland Company continually operated at a loss and owed $1 million to the banks. Reid had recognized this early when he tried to limit the amount of time for which his company was obliged to operate the railway business. Now his sons were dealing with the consequences. In June of 1920, they approached the Liberal Reform government of Sir Richard Squires for help. Squires' alternatives were to take over the railway or to close it down. He decided to loan the company $1.5 million, accept responsibility for yearly losses in excess of $100,000 and assume joint management of the railway.

They appointed a commissioner, Sir George Bury, a former vice-president of the CPR. In his final report Bury identified systemic problems: small engines traveling on narrow gauge lines over heavy grades could not pull enough cars to be profitable; and freight rates were low considering the increasing labour and material costs. The branch lines had apparently been built for political reasons, with no hope of operating in the black.

In May 1922, under increasing pressure from creditors, Reid Newfoundland closed for a week. This was likely a bluff. The Reids were closing a deal for a paper mill on the Humber River. Good news for the government. But the other investors might refuse the deal if a shareholder, and owner of vast tracts of forest, was insolvent. The Squires government, plagued by unemployment, paid the company $2 million to settle all claims and cancelled the 1898 and 1901 contracts. Effective 1 July 1923, they reclaimed the railway, the dockyard and the steamships. In 1926 the railway was officially renamed the Newfoundland Railway.

# TWO RIVERS TRAIL
## BISHOP'S FALLS TO GANDER

128

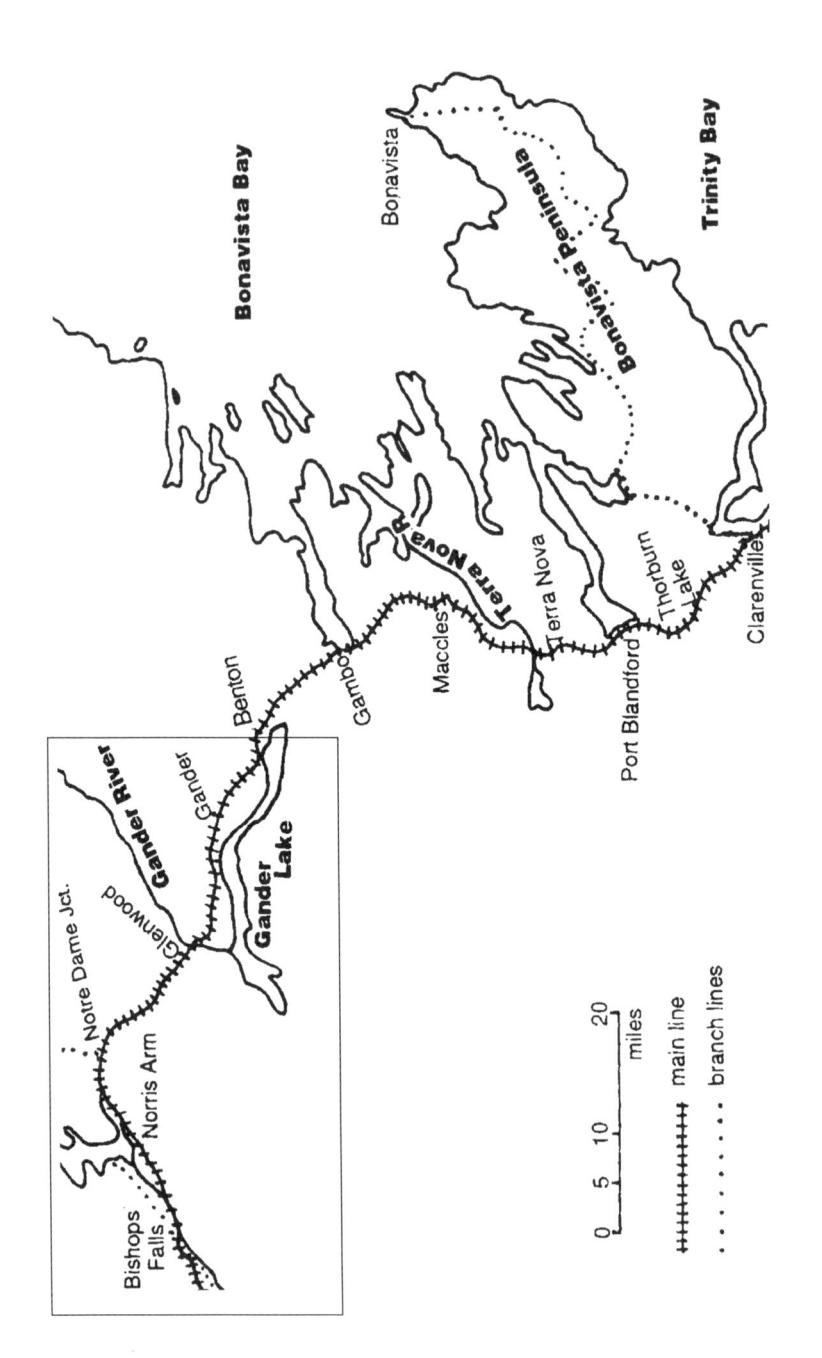

# TWO RIVERS TRAIL INTRODUCTION

The Exploits River Trestle at Bishop's Falls is a source of pride for the town. And George Saunders doesn't mind boasting about it. Retired from the public service, latterly as the commissioner of the Petroleum Products Pricing Commission, Saunders is enjoying an active retired life as a consultant in the town. "For come home year in 2004 the town partnered with Newfoundland Power and had 25,000 lights strung along the trestle. It was something to see I can tell you," says Saunders. He says the T'Railway Council resurfaced the entire 927 feet of the trestle so that it is easy and safe to walk or drive.

An enthusiastic ATVer, Saunders enjoys the freedom that his central location gives him. "I can follow the trail in any direction," he says. To go west he follows the T'Railway back towards Grand Falls Windsor. To go east, north or south he crosses the Exploits Trestle. To go north or east he then follows the main line towards Norris Arm and beyond. Or turning right at the far side of the trestle he can follow the river past the Max Simms Memorial Park and on south into the interior following old logging roads.

"Trail use here in Central is strong but the railbed is getting chopped up in the towns," he says. Bishop's Falls itself had to get tough with ATVers who used to speed through town blanketing residents in a fine coat of dust. These were short areas adjacent to homes where residents were complaining about dust. The town was very proactive in solving these problems, installing a series of gates that slowed traffic. They also partnered with the T'Railway Council, over three years to pave the more troublesome spots within the town.

Farther east, in Norris Arm, dust from speeding ATVs plagued residents and Council attempted to control the problem by spreading a special calcium dust control material. It was expensive and ineffective. According to residents, all it took was one heavy rain to wash that material away and they were back in the thick of it again. So, around 2001, the Council experimented with used paving scraped up during local road upgrades in the Norris Arm area. According to Terry Morrison, the Council's executive director, "This solved the problem although it wasn't pretty—bumpy, cracked in places, bare spots. We learned from this that it's just as well to apply it properly with a spreader and roll it in while still warm. It lasts longer and is much more pleasing to the eye."

At the Gander River the resurfaced trestle between Glenwood and Appleton is a popular community feature that many local residents include in their evening strolls.

In 2006, the town of Gander worked with the T'Railway Council to reroute and pave a small section around an industrial park as part of a multi-year initiative to pave the entire route through town.

The Two Rivers Trail is well used, both summer and winter, and is in relatively good shape, perhaps because this is the section where the T'Railway Council's head office is located.

## CHAPTER 26
# NEW PANTS FOR JOEY

**24 JULY, MILE 266**

From the Exploits Trestle the water is a long way down—spit and count, "One, two, three, four, five, six, sev…" and it joins the river. There is a community of ten or twelve bungalows on the south bank and the people there use the trestle as their main route into Bishop's Falls. I concentrate on the surface of the ties instead of looking through to the water. Two-thirds of the way across I am really concentrating, because of occasional foot-wide gaps. I do not look around very much, except once when I step onto one of the several "stand-asides," a retreat for people caught on the trestle by an oncoming train. Yesterday Carl Budgell told me how a boy, on his way to the store across the trestle, was caught by the train, lost an arm. "When they found the severed limb, the stiffened hand still clutched a nickel. He works in Glenwood as a welder now. Best welder in Central Newfoundland," he said.

In the background a crow yells, "Walk, walk." Finally, solid ground. Around the first bend is a long stretch through the forest with another turn at the far end. Entering this straight section I am stopped in my tracks by the sound of a train approaching from beyond the far turn. The earth shakes under me, the bushes swish. The wind from the ghost train sweeps back my hair, blows right through me. Frozen for a moment, I shake my head to dislodge the sensation. It is as if this place is imbued with the spirit of the train. For a few moments I grapple with the experience, make a few notes in my journal. But there's nothing more to be done, so I hike on over the abandoned railbed, away from the river.

The many clear-cut areas and ATV tracks cutting into the forest are stark confirmation that the rail line itself may become a ghost. Every step drives that impression home: beer bottles, little piles of sawdust. Yet in the midst of this destruction are places where the alders grow so close that spider webs tug at my face. Tall, silky-green larch shade the track and purple swamp orchids blink along the banks of countless small streams.

*The salt air feels good. I am on the coast again for the first time since Corner Brook.*

Suddenly, above the treetops I see the flick of speeding automobiles. I glance at the two inches I have covered on the map, frustration welling up. I felt this way before, between Deer Lake and Howley, when the small planes on the way into the airport passed low overhead. In two minutes they were in the airport, I still had hours on the trail. I swallow my resentment and push on.

Ahead is a tunnel beneath the TCH. Inside the eight-foot-high culvert my voice sounds like a call over a cheap phone. Underfoot is pavement and there are handrails on either side. What does this say? It is recognition of the right-of-way! The ghost train must get through.

The remains of an old moose hide putrefying on the stones, the stink of death rising. More swatches of hide, fragments of bone.

I am learning to appreciate the granite "crush" under every step—despite the torturous feeling of walking on it. Most of the stones in any stretch of several miles are identical in colour and dimensions, but every now and then is a stone of pink or green, or white, or orange, that stands out like an open eye in a room of sleepers. I always stop to pick up the newest discovery, cradle its roughness in my hand.

North of the TCH is the most destructive private cutting yet, though it is dwarfed by the scale of the commercial devastation at Cooks Brook. Here the 200-yard-wide logged area runs with small interruptions of bog and tamarack, from the TCH twelve miles to Norris Arm. Stacked along the roadbed are forty-foot logs of aspen, leaves still green on the few untrimmed branches. A pair of greasy black gloves hangs in the crook of two branches. One glove dangles by the middle finger mocking me. "Here's what you can do with your judgements." In light of this destruction, it seems fitting that it was in this area, at the Jumpers Brook Trestle, Mile 261.9, on 16 November 1990, that demolition crews loaded the last rails onto a flatbed truck.

"Pete" Barrett is waiting in her car on the outskirts of Norris Arm, just above the powerhouse. She has agreed to let me stay at her place tonight. She takes my pack and tells me I have a thirty-minute walk to the fairground where, despite the intermittent rain, Norris Arm Day is in full swing. Then she's gone and Clara and I click along. A pickup blocks the track. The branches of the alders hang over the back of the truck on either side. Three men shovel the crushed stone into five-gallon buckets and load them onto the truck. "It'll soon be grown over anyway," the biggest one says to me.

The salt air feels good. I am on the coast again for the first time since Corner Brook. There is a row of houses on either side of the main road at the approach to the waterfront of Norris Arm. The track runs close enough to the road to be another lane and there are places where all signs that this had been a railway are ploughed under.

Then change comes with the suddenness I have come to accept but can never anticipate. Twenty kids from the local Boys and Girls Club have come out to welcome me, present me with a tee shirt and walk ahead of me for the last quarter mile to the fairground. In one driveway a fire burns under a large barrel from which swirls black smoke. Next to the drum is a pile of black-edged asphalt pieces. At the other end of the driveway several men stand on a black strip of newly recycled asphalt to stare at our little parade.

The whine of an accordion greets us at the fairground and Pete takes me to meet Mayor Fred Budgell. I must look as tired as I feel, because the first thing he does is usher me to a picnic table. "We got cold plates, fish and brewis, hamburgers, hot dogs. What would you like?"

Pete introduces me to the family at the next table. Their two-year old boy is screaming along with the accordion on the P.A. system. Fred returns with a cold plate. Unlike many local councillors I have spoken to, he's convinced of the importance of the T'Railway and places its value as a resource ahead of the cost of maintaining it. "The T'Railway would be a great asset in our town too. Where it goes right through the centre of town. A lot of things can be developed," Fred says.

A snowmobiler himself, Fred is enthusiastic about that potential for a backwoods trail across the Province. "I do a lot of skidooing. So I like the railway track. We get a lot of them through here in the winter," he says, then adds, "It's too bad about the logging, because the country's being crucified. But what can you do?"

Later, on the drive to Pete's house in Sandy Point, she tells me this is her daughter's twenty-first birthday, and her son Tom and his wife will arrive home on a visit from Ontario this evening.

The aroma of turkey dinner floods the house that Pete and her husband have built. It is a large cottage-like home with narrow stairs and odd-shaped rooms. The picture window looks out across a wide lawn, through a low stand of shrubs beneath the tall aspen and past a boathouse to the wind-chopped waters of Norris Arm.

Soon the family begins to arrive, brothers, sisters, spouses, children, Pete's parents, her two sons and her husband and other guests. I have grown used to eating with strangers, but I do feel like an intruder here and do my best to speak only when spoken to. The table is spread and the feast begins. After the meal the adults linger over coffee and there is some reminiscing about the railway. Three kids run crazy and a chatty two-year-old wants to sit in my lap. I start to relax a little.

When Joey Smallwood passed through here on his 1925 trek to organize the section men, he stayed overnight in the Norris Arm hotel near the railway station. It was owned at the time by Saunders and Howell and run by the grandfather of Pete's brother-in-law Calvin. "Joey straggled in with his suitcase and a pair of pants that you could see through in places," laughs Calvin. "Joey and grandfather were around the same size and he was sympathetic with Joey's efforts so he offered him a pair of his trousers. Next morning Joey headed off down the tracks in a much newer pair of pants."

Another story which is common currency in this family is of the young man from Norris Arm who struck up a conversation from the station platform with a gentleman who leaned out the window of a St. John's-bound train. When the train began to pull away the young man snatched the passenger's pipe and hat, then waved generously to the departing man with his own hat as the train accelerated eastward.

After the homecoming, guitar strumming, and family chitchat, I climb the narrow stairs to the bedroom of the absent daughter. She is celebrating her birthday away from home. Her teddy bears and knickknacks still litter the small space under the sloping ceiling, but tonight a stranger, in need of more than new pants, sleeps there.

## Postcard from Norris Arm

*The physical sensation of walking all day has seeped into my pores. I start fresh, my mind dark with details. Then fatigue sets in. So I stop, adjust straps, laces and socks, drink water, eat trail mix and let the legs walk away with me again. Then there's looking at the map and saying, "Is that all the far I am?" Or, "Wow am I that far already?" That is followed by periods of euphoria at being able to make the trip. Followed again by exhaustion and another rest. More walking and, often, periods of nausea. More rest. Throughout the day strings of thought, sometimes gentle as the small streams that run beneath the track, sometimes raging like a train through a tunnel. At other times realizing suddenly that, for I don't know how long, my thoughts have been still, like waking from a dreamless but restful sleep. Towards the end of the day comes the straining around each turn, looking for the landmark that I know means rest. And finally the sacred moment when I slide Joey off my back, feel the buoyancy and freedom of being out of harness, and slip my feet out of the boots.*

The province's first private underpass.

## CHAPTER 27
# THE SIGN ON MY FOREHEAD

### 25 JULY, MILE 248

A grove of tall aspen evokes a feeling of nostalgia so potent it stops me in my tracks. But I'm not sure why. A robin bursts out of the bush, chides me for lingering so close to its nest, and then dives into the greenery. Just ahead a squirrel darts across the trail, tail curled into a question mark.

George Barrett Jr., Pete's youngest son, volunteered to drop my back pack Joey in Glenwood at Marina Pritchett's. It is still sixteen miles to Salmon River, the trestle nearest that town. Marina works with the NLRDC in Gander, and when she heard yesterday that I was going to stop overnight she invited me to her place. Tomorrow it is Gander or bust and a four-day break to be with Kathy and the girls, and to visit with my grandparents.

Four miles out on the trail I grasp for my canteen and realize it's still on Pete's kitchen counter. Thirst drives me down the bank to put my lips to a small (and what I hope is pristine) stream. The water is cool and has a soft trace of sweetness. I've just scrambled back up over the bank when a

136

pickup pulls onto the track at an intersection ahead. It's Pete and her husband George. She holds the canteen triumphantly out the window. They tried driving on the track to catch me but after a few miles they took the highway and drove back to meet me. It is a relief to have the water and after thank you's and best wishes it's back to the business at hand. Trudging.

Sign nailed to a tree:

> NOTICE TO PUBLIC
> *Corner Brook Pulp and Paper Ltd. wishes to inform the public that cabin development is strictly prohibited on the company's freehold land. This includes all lands in the western, northern, and central areas of the province. All cabins constructed on company freehold land, except those with prior written authorization must be removed to avoid court action.*
> *Corner Brook Pulp and Paper Ltd.*

Lunchtime comes and goes but my legs will not stop. The weather is misty and cool, perfect for walking. I promise myself I will finish off the turkey sandwiches Pete made from last night's dinner when I get to the Neyles Brook Trestle, three miles distant. Instead I eat the sandwiches as I walk and reach Salmon River Trestle (Mile 232.8) two hours early. The TCH is just a gunshot away so I break my way through the brush and raise my frustration level in a fruitless effort to hitch a ride into Glenwood. This is the third time this trip I've tried to thumb down a ride and the message finally starts to sink in. No one in their right mind would stop for someone who looks the way I do after a day on the trail. So it looks like a two-mile hike to the gas station where I can phone for my ride.

A mile west of Glenwood, the site where the rail line passed under the TCH, is a major construction site. The department of transportation is building a cloverleaf intersection leading nowhere. It is a joke in the community that the logging company A.L. Stuckless, near the construction site, is the only sawmill in the Province with its own overpass. Closer to Glenwood there's a small grey railway station, with doors and windows boarded over.

Just before I reach the gas station a car pulls up on the other side of the road. It is Hayward and Audrey Seymour, neighbours from my childhood in Neil's Line. They are returning to Conception Bay after a weekend in Grand Falls. They'd heard me "at least ten times" on the radio and wanted to know if there was anything they could do for me. Hayward seems particularly delighted with my call for one level of government or another to stand up and take charge of the railbed. He tweaks my cheek, a sparkle in his eye.

As they pull away, Audrey turns to wave, and I know every time they see me from now on they'll think "T'Railway," like a sign on my forehead, "In the name of the steam, the diesels and the railway ghost." Will I ever be able to live this down? Am I destined to talk about the railbed for the rest of my days? My identity is somehow merging with the politics that rumbles along that route.

Finally I reach the station just outside Glenwood. Marina's spouse, Roger John, comes to fetch me. He's a soft-spoken man who enjoys his work as a salmon protection officer, but wishes he could do more to help the dwindling stocks. Every year, in the off-season, Roger cuts enough trees for thirty cords of wood: fifteen for his place and fifteen for his mom. When I asked him where he gets it he said "Anywhere I can find a stick."

Marina's home is an older, two-storey house. The kitchen windows are steamed over as a basted chicken browns in the oven and vegetables bubble on the stove. The chrome table is set for three. Outside the cool rain continues.

When asked, some people from Glenwood will say they are from Appleton, on the opposite bank of the Gander River. But not Marina. Despite a nagging health problem, Marina loves to go fishing, takes ten-mile "walks" and embraces the relaxed life they have in Glenwood, even if it is considered to be "on the wrong side of the river."

After supper I spread the map out on the kitchen table. Tomorrow morning I'll cross the Gander River Trestle, Mile 230.2, then on to Gander where John Lannon has offered his basement apartment as a base for my stopover. When I called John tonight he said I already know his wife ... we met at the cottage in Millertown Junction. She's Pauline, Joe Bolus's sister with the three young kids.

I telephoned my grandfather, George Legrow, to say I would be in town for the next few days. He didn't sound very well and he certainly didn't want to talk about his recent operation. "It's not something you boast about," he told me.

Rolling over the ghost of the railway.

# CHAPTER 28
# GANDHI IN GANDER

### 26 JULY, MILE 220

One of the dilemmas of meeting people who are stealing the stone or ties and cutting the timber along the rail line is that, although I don't like what they are doing, there's nothing I can say. Is there? The whole premise of this trip is about finding out about what people along the route want to do with the resource. It is not about imposing my judgments, no mater how self-righteous. I mull that over for a while but there are no answers.

About six miles west of Gander the rail line sweeps within twenty yards of the highway. Every two minutes or less a transport truck punches past, sometimes two or three at a time. And yet the railway couldn't make it work?

The sun mocks me, glinting off the cars at my finishing point for the day on the other side of a five-mile-long straight stretch across the marsh. I am fading like a plucked weed at the outskirts of Gander. It's Newfoundland Railway's longest section of straight track in a route where one-third of all the rails laid are on curves.

The Gander stopover is not really a vacation. There are radio interviews and contacts with interest groups. Bob Green, representing a "loose association of cabin owners in the Placentia Junction area," calls about his concerns with the ATVs. "The bogs in the area are torn to rat shit," he says. John Lannon and I collar Gander's Mayor Doug Sheppard in the parking lot behind the town council office. We ask him to commit a member of council to the steering committee for the T'Railway. He says he is supportive, boasts about the Cobbs Pond Trail, then mentions that council is interested in the four miles of T'Railway passing through Gander. But he hedges on naming a member to the T'Railway steering committee because "there would be a lot of infighting no matter which councillor was named."

At the coffee shop John introduces me to councilor Gerald Saunders from Gambo. He is noncommittal on the trail, but he has stories. A man he called Uncle Jim Saunders died three months ago. Uncle Jim used to tell of how the section men transported Joey Smallwood by speeder when he was organizing their union, a trip which Joey later claimed he made on foot.

After two weeks on the trail it is difficult to let go of the walk and relax. My mind keeps trudging on to Gambo, my next overnight stop, and beyond ... a mirage with Clarenville hovering small but distinct in the distance, marking three quarters of the journey complete. I love having the family around me, but how quickly I'd forgotten the little things about being patient with children! With my family here I feel vulnerable and the demands of the kids are wearing me down. Kate must be having quite a summer managing them herself. And, on the other hand, there are so many people I should meet, so much to be coordinated. Maybe I should just start carrying my full knapsack all the time, avoid people, except when I need supplies. Seems simpler. No more interviews, no more town halls, no more "coordinating." Just walk.

Called Janice Udell today. She's leaving Wednesday from Bottle Cove on her cross-Island walkabout. She has caches in place right across, and she's taking a dog. Her trip will be lower key than mine. She is concerned about being a woman alone on the trail. Janice told me she was proud of me, said I'm like a Gandhi of the T'Railway. Thank God I laughed it off.

I'm trying to meet John Lannon's father Clar here in Gander. He was track supervisor from Gambo to just west of the Gaff. He confirmed for John this morning that the section men did in fact transport Joey. They would sign up with him and then carry him halfway to the next section. There the next crew would pick Joey up and carry him to their section house, and then halfway to the next stop and so on. There's also a ninety-two-year-old former railway man from Appleton, Jack Wall, who walked the rail line in the late 1970s. I hope to meet with him too. He divides his time between here and his daughter's home on the banks of the Gander River.

Denis Flood on the outskirts of Grand Falls-Windsor.

# CHAPTER 29
# OF HORSES AND FLOODS

The protest against unregulated logging is gathering some momentum. A riding school owner in Grand Falls is featured in the Grand Falls *Advertiser* today. Denis and Paula Flood applied to the provincial government for permission to use the railbed as a trail for their riding school. They were turned down because the horses might pollute water along the railbed. Then, last week, Denis discovered that Abitibi-Price was churning up the same section of railbed with heavy trucks and skidders, as they prepared to clear-cut the area. Denis objected to the company and to the newspaper, wondering how a few horses could be more of a threat to the environment than a logging operation. Kathy and I decide to drive back to Grand Falls so I can interview the Floods.

Denis and Paula live on the outskirts of Grand Falls. Tall with a trimmed beard and a receding hairline, Denis takes us on a tour of the stables. He speaks slowly, mulling over each thought before he voices it. Among their horses is a Newfoundland pony. There is little practical use for these animals nowadays, he tells us, but they once hauled wood out the low, thick forest all over the Island. Modern machinery has long since supplanted them. An apt metaphor for the trains.

After the stables, Denis takes us inside to meet his wife. Laying her pen on the ledger, Paula stands to shake hands. She is medium height with long blond hair. The little office also holds a cage with two lovebirds, and beneath that is a cage with an aged rabbit. A white kitten skitters between my legs and Julie and Sasha disappear through the doorway in pursuit. Paula's hand is strong and carries a distinct aroma of horse.

Was it coincidence that Abitibi only began their work along the trail after I walked through the area? she wonders. When Denis learned about the cutting he called Don Brain, an employee of Abitibi, who told Denis it was all a misunderstanding. "He told me that they are just cutting a road. He said they're going to use the railbed to cut a road into the woods. I said "Well, the foreman on the project doesn't know that.' I went down talking to the foreman on the project and he's cutting everything right to the road," says Denis.

"I talked to the reporter from the *Advertiser*, Jennifer Smith. She told me that Roger Pike, the public relations officer for Abitibi, said it was their wood and they would cut it if they wanted to cut it." Paula too is disgusted by Abitibi's response. "That's their attitude. And I hope that's what the newspaper prints. They're getting a lot of phone calls. The bit of wood they're going to get is not worth the bad press."

Denis is particularly aggravated by the provincial government's secrecy about the ownership of the rail line. Just yesterday the Province declared they were in possession of the railbed, though they have actually had possession since early June. Denis shakes his head slowly, "It was on CBC Radio this morning. A guy from the Department of Environment admitted their ownership. I mean that makes it worse. All my questions before were 'How come something is not done to preserve it?' And they always said 'We don't own it, there's nothing we can do.' So now they own it. Why aren't they protecting it?"

Denis tried another angle. He phoned Environment and told them he would like to report people cutting inside the thirty-metre buffer to the water supply. "The fellow who answered said "The guy who handles that is out today. I'll give him the message and he'll get back to you Monday,'" says Denis shaking his head slowly in amazement. "So I said 'Excuse me, I'm reporting somebody breaking the law. I want action taken now. What about the RCMP? Can't they be notified?' He said, 'I don't know what they can do about it.'" Denis points at me, "If Abitibi reported you, see how quick the RCMP would be there."

"What I can't stand is when one industry is infringing on the possibility of a new, growing industry," says Paula thumping the ledger closed and shoving it on a shelf above the desk.

## HISTORY SIDING SEVEN
# STRETCHED TO THE LIMIT

In 1927, a new branch line was built from Millertown Junction to Buchans to serve a mine. Traffic on the main line increased each year until, by 1930, the operating deficit of $380,000 was less than half that of 1925. In 1931, to continue reducing the operating deficit, the Railway Commission shut the Bay de Verde and Trepassey lines and reduced main line traffic. Snow clearing was suspended on the remaining branches, effectively closing them in winter.

For many Newfoundlanders 1934 marked the beginning of the end of nationhood when, unable to service a public debt of $100 million, Newfoundland forfeited its right to responsible government in favour of a commission government by Great Britain. The cost of constructing and maintaining the railway—once touted as the road to economic independence and nationhood—accounted for about thirty-five percent of that debt.

At the start of World War II the Newfoundland Railway, still staggering from the effects of the Depression, suspended its ten-year bridge replacement program and its gradual conversion from coal to oil-driven steam locomotives. It's main focus was on transporting troops and shipping guns, munitions, and supplies. The railway was a key link between the American military bases in St. John's, Argentia, Gander and Stephenville.

To deliver this service, rail crews and rolling stock were stretched to the limit. Cars loaded in St. John's increased from 150 to 228 a week. Freight tonnage grew by fifty percent between 1938 and 1944. The United States government supplied locomotives, cars, and two and a half million in financing to the railway. They erected communication lines between bases, giving the railway access to modern communication links. Not surprisingly, for the years 1941-45, the railway recorded an annual operating surplus. In fact, the decade ending in 1946 was the most profitable ten years in the history of the railway—a total operating surplus of more than $300,000.

But there was a cost that had yet to be paid. The heavy traffic and the lack of maintenance left the railway in deplorable condition. The railbed, for example, needed 750,000 ties replaced immediately.

# CROSSROADS TRAIL
## GANDER TO TERRA NOVA VILLAGE

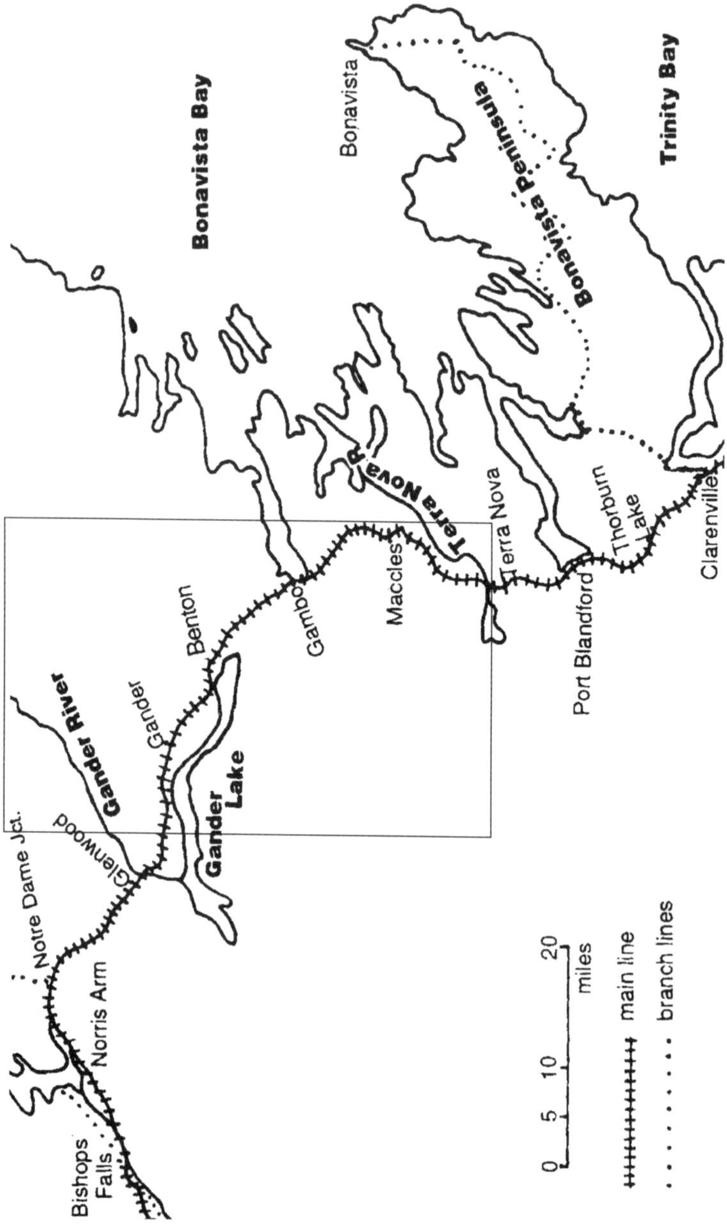
Bonavista Bay
Bonavista
Bonavista Peninsula
Trinity Bay
Terra Nova R.
Terra Nova
Clarenville
Thorburn Lake
Port Blandford
Maccles
Gambo
Benton
Gander
Gander River
Gander Lake
Glenwood
Notre Dame Jct.
Norris Arm
Bishops Falls
0 5 10 20
miles
main line
branch lines

# CROSSROADS INTRODUCTION

Even though they were building their family home when they hosted me in 1993, Burness and Cindy Taylor have moved on. When I called the only Taylor I could find in the Gambo phone book, Sylvia Taylor answered. She is Burness's mother. It was her home I stayed in on my night in Gambo. She and her husband were on the mainland at the time, visiting a son who'd moved away.

Taylor tells me that Burness and Cindy moved to Alberta seven years ago and then to northern British Columbia. A year later they were home briefly for the funeral of her husband of forty-seven years, Burness Taylor Senior. Taylor met him in Gander where he was stationed with the American air force. Before they could get married they had to take the train to St. John's so Taylor could be "examined by American doctors" at the Fort Pepperell base. "We got married in there then. There was no ceremony, just a few of his friends he knew from when he was stationed there before." After that she followed Burness Sr. to Africa with Burness Jr., where the second of their four children was born, and then into the United States. "He always liked Newfoundland, so after he retired we moved back home." Now all four of her children have moved away to the mainland looking for work. "Sure they have to, there's no opportunity here in Newfoundland," she laments.

Although she's willing to share the facts of her life, Taylor doesn't use the trails in her area so she's not able to share anything about the state of the T'Railway in the region.

If I could have found Edgar Keats I know he would have told me the traffic past his cabin on the T'Railway is "very discouraging." From Chain Lake, north of Terra Nova Village, logging trucks rumble along a two-mile logging road and onto the railbed. Throughout the spring, summer and fall they haul those logs north on the main line for about fifteen miles, through the section known as Welsh's camp where Edgar and Mabel have their cabin, and on to Norm Smart's sawmill right on the T'Railway.

This section is heavily used by snowmobiles in winter. In the spring, summer, and fall, in addition to the logging trucks, there are ATVs and local cabin owners using the entire length of the Crossroads Trail. According to the T'Railway Council, the local snowmobile club does clear the brush but the alders are a persistent problem.

Where the Terra Nova River skirts the north side of Terra Nova Village, the large trestle has become dangerous and unsightly. It was so bad a few years ago that the 200 seasonal residents and twelve to fifteen permanent families banded together to get something done. It was becoming a safety concern for the Council too, being one of the larger trestles in an area. The MHA for the area was able to find money under a "forestry program" to cover the costs and the T'Railway Council sanctioned the improvements.

And it looks like Walter Calloway turns after his father after all. When I walked through the village in 1993 there were many agricultural acres, owned by the late Ralph Calloway, lying fallow for a number of years. Walter was just a boy when Ralph died, too young to take on the formidable task of managing an operation that employed thirty or so people on a seasonal basis. Now Walter, in his forties, has made the land green again, and red. "He's moved out of the root vegetables and taken to growing sods and farming cranberries. And he seems to be doing very well at it," according to former Terra Nova Village resident, Eugene Dyke.

Daughters Sasha and Julie with the author in Benton.

Photo by Katharine Kearley

# CHAPTER 30
# WALKING BACKWARDS

### 30 JULY, BENTON

This was supposed to be my last day of rest in Gander. But I thought better of it. Tomorrow the scheduled walk is twenty-four miles from Gander to Gambo and, based on my experience, I don't want to face that distance after four days off. So today Kathy dropped me at Benton and I'm walking the ten miles back to Gander. Tomorrow I'll start at Benton and walk east to cover the remaining fourteen miles to Gambo.

"I want to take a picture," Sasha says snatching at the camera with her eager four-year-old hands. She points the camera up at me. Whir of the winding mechanism and she is ready to click off another but I manage to grab the camera back.

"Bye dad."

"Bye Sasha." Meanwhile, Julie has been searching the trail around the car for a pretty stone. She knows I have been collecting one piece of crushed stone daily. Now she hands me a stone she found, my memento for the day.

A blue pickup turns off the main road and rolls towards us barmping its horn. The driver stops beside Kathy and leans out the window. He is

Edison Osmond, come to warn us not to leave our car where it is parked on the railbed or "it may not be there for very long. There's several outfits actively logging along the rail line between here and Gander and they wouldn't take too kindly to a vehicle parked across their access road." Edison is on the Lakeland Rural Development Association, which has been fighting the logging along the railbed. "Barry Keats, Eli Humby, and Walsh, I think, in Gander. They should be all shot. And you think this is bad? Wait till you goes out there," he says pointing east. "They're still logging down by Butts Pond. They're not supposed to touch fifty feet on either side of the track. Well they're coming closer than that."

"When you get part way up," he says, pointing east towards Gambo, "there's an old quarry where Reid hauled stone to the track. There's still a big pile of the quarried stone there by the roadbed. Well the loggers got that area skinned." Edison shakes his head. He is going out to the quarry cutover in the fall to pick up the felled trees left on the ground. "I can use it for firewood. Maybe clean some of it up. They smashed off two beams in the trestle there." He's guessed who I am. With the media coverage I seldom have to introduce myself anymore, except as a courtesy, or to learn the other person's name. Kathy and the girls, sensing that I've pulled on my business mask, are in the car now and pulling away. Goodbye again.

"I've walked the ten miles to Gander many times," says Edison.

"A girlfriend in Gander was it?" I say, nudging his arm.

"No I used to go up hunting ducks and rabbits. I might be driving out that way later today to see if there's any bake apples." He jerks his thumb over his shoulder. "They digs worms up there to the quarry too."

He tells me I am in for a real treat tomorrow when I start east from Benton to Gambo. "Out towards Butts Pond you got the Wilkinsons logging the area, and they're worse than the people along here. If you leave your car on the side of the road when you come back it'll probably be in the ditch. They won't slow down with the tractor trailers."

Refreshed after the three days off, these tales of fresh disaster are bringing me down. So when Edison starts in about the fibre-optics cable trench, I bid him good day and set out walking backwards to Gander.

Before long the landscape confirms the worst. It's a mess. And to compound the logging damage, the fresh scar from Newfoundland Telephone's fibre-optics cable runs along the railbed, uprooting trees and displacing boulders, like the path from some huge underground monster. Blasting wire litters the track, along with bits of trees. The road is potholed, with water running in the wheel ruts and across the railbed.

Must anger be the motivation for me for the rest of this journey? This could be the walking backwards—walking from a feeling of obligation and anger, instead of caring and joy. But what is more infuriating to me is whenever someone blames this on "stupid Newfoundlanders." This is not about Newfoundlanders. This is the work of a few damn pirates, and it doesn't matter what their nationality.

In the distance to the south, broken by the branches and leaves, blue glimpses of Gander Lake. The telegraph poles remain intact for miles along the trail, strung with a wire that suddenly veers off on tripods across the bog and into the forest with no sign of what it is connected to. By mid-morning I reach Mile 207, Burnt Brook Trestle. Undisturbed bog and ponds—except for the fibre-optics scar. Crushed stone underfoot again. Sun coming through every now and then. The frogs croaking sound like hammers striking metal in the distance.

Not far past the trestle fresh scats, large as a pig's, with berry seeds and twigs and who knows what else. I cannot identify what animal left these but I assume they were dropped by a bear. Then I hear branches rustle close by. The trees are fairly low and I can't see a moose, so I make lots of noise and hasten westward.

A yellowlegs springs into the air, chastising me as its cousins did in the Topsails. I realize the destruction that I have seen is not enough to make me want to stop, but rather it is all the more reason to go on.

Don Gosse "gunnin' 'er" across Butts Pond.

## CHAPTER 31
# FIBRE-OPTICS DARKLY

**31 JULY, 8:20 A.M. BENTON (AGAIN)**

Two tractor-trailers loaded with logs are the gateway to the track headed east from Benton. Kathy and the girls are on the way back to St. John's and I have to re-adjust to life on the people's road. It is ten days to Whitbourne and my next two-day break. But there are miles to go before I sleep.

Edison told me yesterday that the Newfoundland Telephone slash for the fibre-optics cable runs the twenty miles from Gander to Butts Pond before it veers off towards a distant pole line. The damage is as bad as the clear-cut left by woods contractors. The rip may only be forty feet wide but it goes on unbroken for so long, smashing through rocks, pushing up boulders, destroying small and large trees alike. At one point there's a twenty-foot-high larch ripped out by the roots and tossed on the bank opposite. It reminds me of the trails left by the giant sandworms in Frank Herbert's science fiction novel, *Dune*.

By mid-morning I've passed the clear-cutting and entered undisturbed forest. Occasional knots or orange surveyors' tape mark trails back into the forest. For a while I cut away every tag I see, hoping that will delay the logging which I assume will follow. Then I pull up a surveyor's stake along the trail left in the wake of the Newfoundland Telephone sandworm. But, as tempting as it is, I cannot allow myself to continue that deceit. It is not the way to fight this destruction.

Then into another clear-cut dead zone. A flock of crows yells invisibly from the distant wall of trees on the far side of a graying tangle where the forest once stood. A bullfrog croaks in the ditch. If I tell myself I am on a logging road my mind can make more sense of this. It seems less an atrocity. One bullfrog in the middle of this desolation. Nearby several loads of logs, some two feet in diameter, birch and softwood mixed, stacked for a final journey.

Several miles east of Benton is the former granite quarry Edison Osmond told me about yesterday. There, right beside the track, is a tumbled pile of four-foot-by-two-foot granite blocks, each a foot or more thick. The blocks are scrambled as if two or three flatcar loads were spilled from a train. The once-fresh cuts are now lichen covered. Small trees have pushed their way up among the stones. Surely this is a historical site?

*My winged buddies, the stouts, are back hungrier than ever and the weather plays games with me all morning.*

Not according to Newfoundland Telephone. Immediately behind this old stockpile the sandworm has churned up whiter granite, and further back is a large clear-cut area. The section I am walking through this morning may be fine for snowmobiles and skiers in the winter, but as far as summertime hiking goes it's a write off.

My winged buddies, the stouts, are back hungrier than ever and the weather plays games with me all morning. It rains long enough to make me put on the rain clothes and then stops.

In the cabin area around Butts Pond a man on an ATV approaches up the track, passes me and turns back to haul up along side and shout over the noise of the engine "You the guy walking across the railway?"

"Yeah, that's me."

"Oh well," he says with a smile and switches off the engine. We shake hands. His name is Don Gosse. "I'm from Gander. I got a cabin there to Butts Pond. Heard about you on the radio. I grew up in a railway town. Whitbourne." I can tell from the glazed look in his blue eyes that he has summoned powerful memories. "My wife and I were just on a little trip down through the Maritimes. You see trains in the morning and in the afternoon and it brings a lot of memories."

Don invites me back to his cabin for lunch. The he accelerates back towards his cabin and within fifteen minutes returns in a pickup. Don still goes back to Whitbourne occasionally to visit his mother. He says ATVs in that area have the bogs "tore to bits."

On the way to his cabin we pass a small clutch of camper-trailers on the shore of Butts Pond. The people who have built cabins in the area don't like the campers so close to the lake. "The cottage owners have to have sewage systems, but you know damn well where the campers' sewage is going. Right?" says Don. "But it is not the people, it's the system. The bunch of us here tried to move them out of it. But the system wasn't working for us. You have a meeting and you get the Department of Environment, the Department of Forestry, the Department of something else, and nothing gets done. So we decided 'why bother?'"

About a mile out a dirt road off the track, Don pulls into a short grassy driveway among the spruce. Down a short path from his three-room cabin there is a small aluminum boat tied to the wharf. Don's very concerned about logging in the area. The loggers did not even leave a stick standing around the last pond they came to. "They cut it right to the pond, so you can't even go out and enjoy a boat ride." He blames some of it on the fishermen displaced by The Moratorium. They are people with a lot of energy and not much to do. "Give them a chainsaw and look out." But Don won't complain to the authorities. Cabins have burned to the ground in the area before. He doesn't want to add his to the list.

We cross a deck and enter the cabin's large kitchen. The couch and chairs look worn but comfortable. Don and his wife come here for a quiet time since their children grew up. He fills the kettle and places it on the propane stove. Every time I call his place a cabin Don responds by referring to it as a "cottage."

Don doesn't know where the snacks are, but when his wife and her friend return from a stroll, she puts a generous share of cookies and fruitcake in front of us.

Their next-door neighbour, and a member of the "bunch" is Dick Carroll. He's a senior employee with the Department of Forestry in Gander. While the kettle is heating, Don strolls over to invite Dick in for a cup of tea. Dick fills the door when he enters, smile at the ready. Another neighbour drops by and then another. They all want to hear about the trip.

I ask if anyone knows about the quarried stone beside the track near Benton. Dick speaks up "They're cut granite. There's a man in Gander, an old man. Larry Lannon, he's still there. He was telling me that was done by hand around the end of the last century. Not out of quarry as much as rocks that were there, and they used hand tools to square them up. They hauled the blocks out to the railway using big tackle with the horses hooked on. And they would load the blocks on flatcars. Moved them all to the railway bridges," says Dick.

"Seems strange they'd go to all that trouble to square off a rock, I mean that must take a lot of work. And then just to leave it there. It looks like there's a couple of train car loads," I say.

"There's some blocks back in the woods too, and metal wedges are still in the rocks," adds Dick. "I suppose the government owns that now since they inherited the right of way across the Province. The Newfoundland Railway used to own that quarry," he says.

"Yeah, fifty feet from the centre line. But that's being violated right and left," I add.

"Oh, I know. I know, it's too late now in most cases."

"Look what Newfoundland Telephone… As far as I'm concerned, they've got more damage done than the loggers," I say.

"They cross brooks and that's a real environmental disaster, that," says Don.

The conversation drifts to other issues like the weather and who is in their cottages this weekend. I finish my tea and cake. Since Dick is with Forestry I ask about the private woodlots I saw marked and cut down to the rail line around Howley. Is Corner Brook Pulp and Paper issuing private licenses?

"They want new growth there. I suspect that's what they're trying to do with the property, get an unorganized cut. And when it's finished it will be pretty well clear-cut. Then they replant. Besides, issuing permits in that area keeps people out of their good woods. So they allow private people to go in where the railway gives them easy access. But they should tell the people they issue permits to about the right of way. People are cutting right to the track," says Dick.

With the last of the tea cold, the cake eaten, and the conversation starting to repeat itself, we shake hands and Don leads me down the short path to the boat. One pull of the motor cord and we are splashing across the pond, the forested perimeter echoing the engines putter back to us.

Coyote-eye view.

## CHAPTER 32
# COYOTE WARNING

### 31 JULY, 8:30 P.M., GAMBO

I am spending the night with Burness and Cindy Taylor. They live with his parents while they build a house across the street. He is thirty-five and thin, with blond hair and a thin moustache. He has an intense stare that makes me slightly uncomfortable. Cindy is shorter, attractive, with hair cut just shy of shoulder length. She is open and welcoming, helps to ease my discomfort at yet another night of crashing in a stranger's home. Because the parents are away, the couple will sleep in that bed and give theirs to me.

Burness is an outdoors type, a park officer with Square Pond Provincial Park. In his spare time he traps. He has definite ideas on the need for conservation and does not mind sharing them. According to him the coyote is on the Island and should be stopped now before it gets a toehold. "I don't care how many times Wildlife's denied it, the coyote is here. I saw one in the park this summer," claims Burness. He does not have much tolerance for salmon poachers either, has seen illegal nets set underneath the trestle at Butts Pond.

He sees "Greenpeacers" as out of touch when it comes to trapping beavers. "They see it as wrong that an animal suffers two minutes in a trap when the alternative might be months of hunger, starvation, disease, and eventual death," explains Burness. The signs of a beaver colony in trouble are easy to read he says. "When they begin to gnaw at softwoods, like spruce and fir, that means they've used up all the deciduous trees in the area and the time is up for that colony." But he agrees that trappers should be better regulated, and licensed, and is pushing for that requirement. To him, trapping is a source of pride. He spends three and a half hours on each beaver pelt and gets twenty-nine dollars each, whereas untrained trappers might spend thirty minutes and get ten dollars.

Burness inherited the first cabin on Butts Pond. It was a caboose the Newfoundland Railway gave to his grandfather when he operated a sawmill in that area. The grandfather in turn willed it to Burness. It mysteriously burned down one fall.

About a fifteen-minute walk from the Taylor's bungalow is a salmon-counting ladder on Middle Brook. After supper Cindy, Burness and their young children Sean and Sara take me there. The counting is over for the day but no one has told the salmon, so they continue to swim up the ladder as far as the holding pen where at least twenty or more big fish hold their place in the stream, occasionally thrashing against the gate and each other.

With Woody at the washout.

Photo by Don Collins

## CHAPTER 33
# JUST THE WIND

Woody Mullett and Don Collins are at the Taylor's door early. They'll take me out to the trail in Woody's old, battered pickup. Woody is the volunteer president of the Newfoundland and Labrador Rural Development Council. Don is affiliated with a group working for the preservation of the Newfoundland pony. This cloudy morning we are clanking over the railbed before 8:00 a.m. on our way to Maccles Lake, where I pick up the trail again. Woody will drive Joey on to Clarenville, three days' walk away. With only my day pack, I must trust to fortune and the generosity of people I hope to meet along the trail.

We reach Maccles Lake Trestle, Mile 178.2, in less than an hour. This is a popular area for cabins. Woody tells me that people used carts with train wheels to transport their building material into the area while the trains were still running. In the 1980s there were only two trains a day, one in either direction, so the cabin builders had plenty of time to use the line. A wave of sadness sweeps over me as I remember how, in the last years, trains were such a rarity I would pull off the road just to watch one go by.

The trail climbs slowly away from Maccles Lake. Hills in the distance bristle with communication towers. It is hot and muggy. The ditches are full of water. To the north Alexander Bay looks like a large steel lake between the hills. The terrain is much hillier than the Gander plateau.

Around mid-morning I encounter the first full-grown bull moose of the trek. He is grazing the tops of tall shrubs in a clearing about twenty yards off the track. I feel a jolt like an electric current. "Holy Jesus! What if he charges me?" Clara feels flimsy in my hand. This guy would not even notice a whack from a walking stick. When he sees me he gives a start, galumphs about 100 yards back and then stands up to have a final look before the forest swallows him. At least twenty points on his antlers.

Just as I was starting to enjoy the solitude and undisturbed forest again, the Newfoundland Telephone sandworm sweeps in and follows me like a stray. The only other sign of life is two older men and a boy in a pickup truck. They overtake me and pause long enough to say that "a fisherman who doesn't lie" told them there is a great place to go fishing in here.

The loggers have chewed up the forest pretty badly in several areas. The debris blocks streams that swell to stagnant teas of bog and boughs. Somewhere in the middle of one quagmire a single frog calls and gets no reply. Calls again. Cords and cords of fresh logs are stacked along the track, their sawn ends staring like ashen faces. Then I am back in the undisturbed forest again, stopping at the largest patch of strawberries I've seen yet, to stuff my face. Within minutes the flies envelop me. I splash on the Deep Woods Off and the flies bug off into the deep woods.

Far down to the left a pole line follows the broad Terra Nova River. Beyond the river a thick forest climbs the steep hills and rolls to the east. Not one man-made sound. My mind invents engines in the wind, and of course there is the hum of the tape recorder. But that's the loudest thing. Then it occurs to me; no bird sounds. I stop talking, switch off the recorder. Just the wind. In all the gullies I have passed this morning there was not a single splash or ripple of fish feeding. Where is the wildlife?

Edger Keals and his bear-proof cabin.

# CHAPTER 34
# WELSH'S CAMP

### 1 AUGUST, MILE 169

A little shack sits half hidden behind a small rise at the back of a meadow surrounded by tall spruce and birch. From the track only the roof is visible and the chimney which, despite the heat of midday, spews wood smoke. There is a pickup truck parked in the gravel beside the shack and Edgar Keats is walking down the driveway greeting me like I am a lost friend. "We expected you'll be going through this morning. Come in for a spell," he says in a high voice with the hint of a rattle.

From the small square porch a low door enters into a ten-foot by fifteen-foot cabin. The heat is remarkable. A grey-haired woman with a soft-looking face welcomes me from her wheelchair. She introduces herself as Mabel. A double bed dominates one side of the room. A rifle hangs from a nail beside the bed. There is a small table under the window at the foot of the bed which overlooks the back meadow and the outhouse. Against the right-hand wall the wood stove spits and crackles under a bubbling pot. Another window looks out front towards the track. All the windows are barred over on the outside with sections of chain link fence. Close overhead are the open beams of the roof trusses. When I comment on the cozy cabin, Edgar says it is just the right size. They come out here to be alone.

"Any bigger than this see and people come to stay overnight. Now they just come to visit," says Mabel.

Edgar knows quite a bit about the site. "This was called Welsh's Camp, Section twenty-two from St. John's. The first section foreman here was Ned Welsh… So father Keats, he took over from Ned Welsh. We lived there in the two-storey house. But after they shortened up the sections in … in …" Edgar searches his memory.

"… 1955," says Mabel.

"… yes, 1955. The section was cut out here, and they tore down the house in 1968."

"It was pretty run down by then I suppose?"

"Oh no. Because it was kept up good. Painted every second or third year and kept up good."

"So you grew up in these woods?"

"I grew up here. I remember as a young fella, not much more than two or three, getting off in a strange place," says Edgar as he flicks open the fire chamber with a split, pokes at the fire and shoves in a few more junks. I wipe the sweat from my eyebrows.

"So what do you think about what's going on around here now," I ask Edgar as I soothe my face with a damp cloth he's retrieved for me.

"To tell you the truth I'm very discouraged because it was a lovely wilderness area all through the track and now they got it just tore up. Destroyed. My heart is more or less broke. After being here for so many years.

"We come up here last fall, we usually come up here moose hunting and rabbit catching… "

"Birding, duck hunting," says Mabel, lightly but insistent.

"Any excuse you can get?"

"Today we come up to cook a Jiggs dinner. That's a good excuse," she announces.

Edgar continues, "We come up here last fall and the season opened on a Saturday on the rabbits. Well, I tied up me trail of snares in there. And there was no sign of anybody around. I didn't check the slips on Sunday but I did look at a few slips along side here for a rabbit to cook for Sunday dinner. But we didn't get any which was unusual. So anyhow, I went in Monday morning and went down through and I couldn't find my trail. Everything was just mowed right down, oh gee." Edgar pauses here wiping his mouth with the back of his hand, re-living the experience. "I heard the power saws down below. There was eight or ten fellas there. I was down talking to them. They said they never seen any slips, but they had to. And one day after the other they just destroyed me trail. I had to move on out of it and pretty soon there'll be nothing left. Oh it's very discouraging after being here for years."

"The loggers are coming this way are they?"

"Well they come this way on this side of the track. They come so far, you see where that birch and stuff is to, back the trail, and then gone farther back again and coming on the opposite side. They're just destroying it."

"Something should be done," I add helplessly.

"Yes, but it don't seem like there's anything that..." The fire spits and crackles, devouring Edgar's words.

"Well what do you think should be done with the trail, with the old track?"

"I think it should be kept up more for a tourist trail like for cars and trucks and skidoos wintertime. I think it should be kept up for that. But I mean I don't know. That's my mind on it. It should be kept up for these reasons, hey. But it's not so much scenery now as what it was."

"And look at that ditch Newfoundland Telephone dug," I say.

"They just tore up everything too them fellas. There was no regard for nothing." But apparently this train of discussion holds much Edgar would rather avoid, for he switches without explanation into tales of bears.

"... I has a bear permit now, I shot two bears there the year. I was here the year before last and I was in the bunk. It was after daylight and I had me rifle laid there on the bunk with four shells and I heard someone out to the door trying to get in. They tears into cabins, hey. Bears tore into the porch five or six times," says Edgar pointing to a low window. "And in this one too," he says fingering rough scratches in the windowsill. "There's he's toenail marks there in the sill where he used to go back and forth. We had to put the wire on the window. But anyhow, I said I must see who's there so I got up and I went to see who was there before I lets him in. I opened the inside door and there was a 500-pound bear at the door." The fire makes a crack like the report of a gun. "So anyhow I took me rifle, loaded it, and when I opened the latch there he hauled back from the cabin and went around the corner. See that mark there?" He points to a loony-sized hole in the screen over the window at the back of the cabin. "That's from the rifle."

"He shot through the screen at it," Mabel titters.

"He was coming pretty bold at the door. So when he went around back I dropped en right there. Anyhow he was playing dead for awhile. I shot him again. His head was forty-two pounds."

"So what do you do with a bear when you get him?"

"I give one to a fella for fox bait. We used to eat them years ago when there was no garbage dumps or nothing. But we wouldn't eat them now. And you aren't allowed to mount it because I got en on a permit not a license. He would have been a nice head to get done. You talk about the size of a bear ... he was huge."

Edgar continues; "My brother come in last year and he stopped the truck and went and unlocked his door. And when he come out and looked, there was a bear in the back of the truck at the bacon, even cracked the eggs and ate them. My brother tired to drive him away but the bear wouldn't go."

Edgar comes in from the truck with bread, a can of milk and teabags. "Sugar, forks and knives," Mabel says to him and he obediently turns and heads to the truck again. "I got rheumatoid arthritis see, and my privilege is to order him around," she confides. Mabel asks if I would like to have a cup of tea. Edgar suggests I have a beer instead. I decline and Mabel's eyebrows raise slightly. A pleased smile. "You don't drink beer?" she asks.

"You're a buddy for me then," says Edgar clapping his knee. "I have had one, no, two bottles of beer since Christmas. I usually has whisky here. Cause the doctor told me that's good for to thin out the blood." He stands and heads out through the porch. "So I has a drink of whisky." His voice receding. "Sometimes one, sometimes two."

Mabel calls after him "We need some bread." A light, dancing laugh.

It was only after I was back on the trail again that I realized something about Edgar. When he talked about bears there was no fear in his voice, more like awe for their cleverness, agility and daring. There is something less tangible in the forests that he fears more.

There's not a fish left in the ponds. Used to be a few until the railway dam for the water chute broke. No fish for the last three to five years. The lakes are dead. And no birds.

About three miles west of Terra Nova Village, yellow splashes of colour nailed to the trees every hundred yards or so with "No Cutting" printed in black.

And finally, around 4:00 p.m., comes that sacred time of day when the houses of the community where I'll stay the night show their roofs through the treetops. For the last half mile I walk on a wide sandy shoulder, as grateful for its softness as a man who is given an electric fan partway through a sweltering night. The dragonfly patrol is on guard but that doesn't deter the stouts and mosquitoes every time I slacken my pace.

The low sun presses on the right side of my face and on my neck and through my clothing. Pick up a stone and it is hot in my hand. Thick, sticky smell of alders. Small white and yellow butterflies. The slosh of my canteen. To the west across a small marsh is Terra Nova Lake. The rush of a cool wind off the lake whistles through the trestle. Mile 164.8.

## HISTORY SIDING EIGHT
## DEATH OF A THOUSAND CUTS

When Newfoundland joined Canada in 1949, the Canadian National Railway assumed responsibility for the "ribbon of rust." Over the next decade CN erected signs along the route, widened the roadbed for crushed stone ballast, laid millions of standard creosote ties, upgraded the poles and increased the number of communications circuits. Along one ten-mile section through the Topsails, the roadbed was raised four feet to lessen drifting in winter. CN upgraded rolling stock, increasing the number and type of freight cars, and, during the 1950s, replaced steam engines with diesel.

Other sectors of the province's transportation network were also growing. Liberal Premier Joseph R. Smallwood presided over an unprecedented period of prosperity. Regularly scheduled air flights increased to a growing number of modern airports, and in 1965 the Trans-Canada Highway was paved across the island, providing a faster means of overland transportation for both passengers and freight. Unable or unwilling to meet the competition, CN dropped its main line passenger service, replacing it in 1969 with a bus line.

The quality of freight service dropped. In 1971, railway employees blocked the TCH to halt transport trucks and buses, focusing attention on the railway crisis. Regional authority was shifted from St. John's to Moncton, New Brunswick, and between 1972 and 1976 the railway's share of the Island's freight traffic dropped from eighty-seven per cent to sixty-one per cent. CN called for a provincial inquiry into the state of the transportation system.

The unions blamed CN for the drop. CN claimed the loss of customers came first. The railway's inferior service was irrefutable. Frustration on both sides mounted as the share of freight slipped below forty per cent.

CN pointed to increased highway competition, and subsidized shipping from Montreal and Halifax to St. John's. They blamed the narrow gauge line with its many curves and steep gradients for the restriction of train length and speed.

Newfoundland Railway supporters, including the railway employee unions, attributed the decline in freight and passenger traffic to CN management, high rates and a policy of downgrading services that amounted to sabotage.

# EASTERN EDGE TRAIL
## TERRA NOVA VILLAGE TO GOOBIES

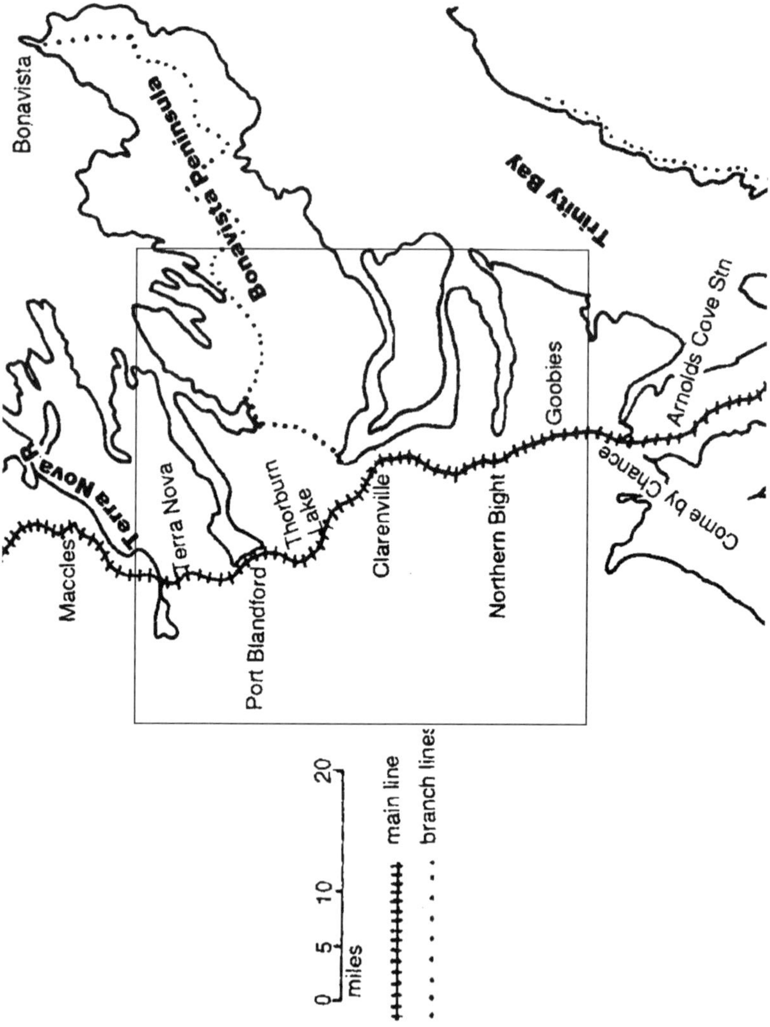
Bonavista
Bonavista Peninsula
Trinity Bay
Terra Nova R.
Maccles
Terra Nova
Port Blandford
Thorburn Lake
Clarenville
Northern Bight
Goobies
Arnolds Cove Stn
Come by Chance
0 5 10 20
miles
main line
branch lines

# EASTERN EDGE TRAIL INTRODUCTION

On the morning of May 19, 2007, Clyde Penny and his friend Lindo Palmer witnessed something these former railroaders thought they'd never see again: the #900—the first diesel locomotive to work Newfoundland's narrow gauge line—followed by a dining car rolling to a stop at the former railway yard.

But, this time, the train came from Pippy Park in St. John's. It was carried by two tractor trailers, accompanied by a boom truck, two cranes, several escort vehicles and a team of more than a dozen people. By the time the train reached the outskirts of Clarenville, the streets were lined with spectators, cameras and camcorders at the ready, to record the moment for posterity.

Now in his eighties, Clyde Penney says the event didn't really have any effect on him, although he admitted he was heartened by the fact that the local heritage society cared enough to make the effort. "It is a step forward but we lost our opportunity after the railway closed down," he says, and there is an undercurrent of resentment in his voice. "This is a railway area. It was the lifeblood of this town. And when they closed her down we had a full train coupled together down there on a siding."

Penney recalls that although there were those who lobbied to keep the railway assets it wasn't enough. "There are not too many of us left now," he says referring to the former railway workers and their families. "And there were many against us. They were talking about pollution from servicing the diesels," he explains. "And when you don't have the interest from the town council," he pauses as if he's tasted something disagreeable, "to preserve your heritage, well then there isn't much you can do. All the council is interested in is sports."

Now, twenty years later, what do they have to remind them of their heritage he asks: "A derelict that the Heritage Society will have a lot of work to restore." Despite his anger over what he sees as the town's short-sightedness, Penney is optimistic about the future of the railway heritage. "In a matter of time, that diesel and the dining car will be a landmark in this area," he says. "And I think the Heritage Society president, Carmilla O'Shea, and her group deserve a lot of credit for going full speed ahead on this."

The Society is not the only community association actively working to preserve what remains of the railway. The East Coast Snowmobile Club (*www.eastcoastsnow.com*) has proven to be an ally of the T'Railway Association. According to T'Railway director Terry Morrison, "The snowmobile club has been very active. They've carried out upgrading and repairs over the years. That helps us considerably," he says. Included in their co-operative efforts was the resurfacing of four trestles in the fall of 2005—including Lower Shoal River, Frost's Mill, Black Brook and Little Come By Chance. "They helped with logistical support and labour. "We just supplied the materials," says Morrison. "This is a good example of how you can get more done when everyone pulls together."

Before finishing this section I should also include mention of Eugene and Phyllis Dyke. Their store in Terra Nova Village is closed now. They haven't lived there since 1995 when, after thirty years, they sold the house and store to Don Stanley from Clarenville and moved twenty miles out the road to Traytown and a house Phyllis owned from a previous marriage. "We weren't getting any younger," Phyllis told me, "so when we had the opportunity to sell the property we took it."

Eugene has been back to the village occasionally but he told me he uses the highway, not the trail, so he can't speak to the condition of it. But he tells me there are still people building summer homes around the lake. "There's thirty or forty more of them since we left. People call them cottages but they are more like mansions to me," he says with a trace of wonder in his laugh.

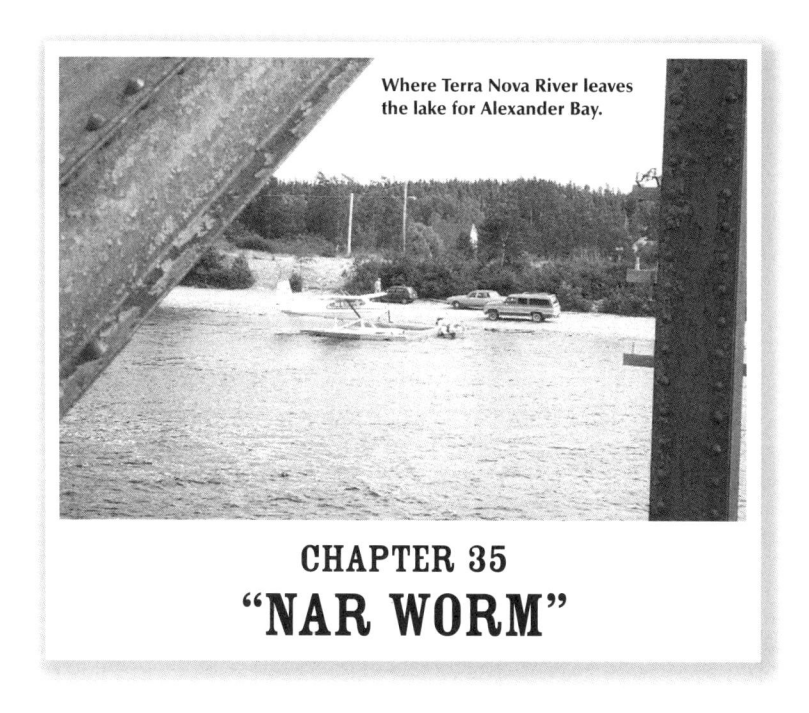

*Where Terra Nova River leaves the lake for Alexander Bay.*

# CHAPTER 35
# "NAR WORM"

### 1 AUGUST, MILE 164, TERRA NOVA VILLAGE, DECK OF PHYLLIS AND EUGENE DYKE'S HOUSE

Next to the veranda white cabbage roses and lupins grow in profusion. Bees slake their thirst in the cool moist depths of the flowers. Tall aspen on one side and even taller birch out back. I am showered and clean and my feet are up. Phyllis says it'll be an hour before the Jiggs dinner is cooked. Just met Tom Lush, provincial minister of Social Services, and his wife Lily. The Lushes have a cottage on Terra Nova Lake. He was very interested in how much damage has been done, and in what people are telling me. We did not really have a discussion so much as he was pumping me for information. And I was giving it as fast as my lips would move. And then the minister was gone. The deck is quiet again, except for the occasional car on the road, and the kids returning home from the swimming hole just up the road.

After the Jiggs dinner, Eugene and Phyllis offer to drive me on a tour of the village. I agree "provided we don't walk a step." We climb into their touring van and their black cat leaps in with us just before the door slides shut. The main road is a circular route of about a mile in circumference.

The rail line cuts that circle into two uneven sections and there are several side roads in the immediate area. It's a ten-mile drive out a winding access road to reach the TCH.

"I'll be serious with you now," says Eugene adopting the tone of a tour guide and pointing to the white two-storey house we just exited. "That is my house there." Next door is Dyke's General store which he and Phyllis own and operate. They bought it from Steers in 1965, when the Anglo-Newfoundland Development Company (AND) shut down logging operations in the area.

Eugene backs slowly into the road and we are off. Although there are close to sixty houses in Terra Nova, only fourteen families live there year round. And most of those are older couples. The last school in Terra Nova closed in 1967. "We are about one of the younger families here and we're no spring chickens," he says. Phyllis laughs.

Eugene turns the van onto an old logging road. He says there are eighty-one summer homes in the next seven miles along the shore of Terra Nova. "You got them up there with indoor swimming pools, paved tennis courts. Money people mostly. The Tootons got a place out there had a $250,000 contract. For a summer cottage!" Beyond Eight Mile, to what they call New Pond, twenty-six miles up, there are another forty more summer homes. Those are more remote and you have to get in there on ATVs. Beyond that to lakes Kepenkeck and Kaegudeck, about halfway through the wilderness towards Bay d'Espoir, are the cabins that people fly in to reach, says Eugene as he weaves the van among the potholes.

"We got people with cabins up here I wouldn't say they miss four weekends a year, winter or summer. More of them only comes periodically summer time. They spend Christmas here, New Year's and every other holiday." He brakes the van as the first ruts appear in the road. "But I'm not going out there. The road is too bad."

For more than fifty years Terra Nova was a bustling logging town, logs being loaded from the Terra Nova River onto trains twenty-four hours a day. The AND Company operated seventeen camps up-country, laying the roads now used by the cabin owners.

In the village the AND Company's long bunkhouse and a large workshop are still standing. Eugene's father worked there building boats in the winter time. Today it is the Pine Ridge Lodge office. They are outfitters for backcountry horseback tours. The garage remains too, where all the heavy equipment was repaired. The windows in all these buildings are intact but the wood is faded and the walls lean on themselves.

"When AND was operating up here, all the wood was driven by water. Out there," says Eugene pointing towards the wide lake, "was the booms holding the wood. They were loaded on the train just up here where the Terra Nova River leaves the lake for Alexander Bay. It was worth seeing. And those trains out there day and night. The trains going and the boats going." From the main rail line two sidings ran downstream on the east bank of the Terra Nova. A tractor shunted the empty cars down the riverside track past the cranes which operated on the sidings, downstream to a quiet pool called Comfort Cove. As the cars were loaded, the full ones were shunted back up the outside track. Then a train would push another line of empty flatcars down on the inside track. "Go down empty and come back full," as Eugene puts it. The old shunting road now leads to summer cottages along the river. The former sidings are overgrown with alders.

"They had big piers built up in the river and parts of the cribwork is still visible," says Eugene hauling up at a break in the riverside vegetation and pointing to the river. All I see is dark, flowing water. "They had pontoons, big watertight plank boxes with high sides sunk about four feet from shore. You had two men in each one, with picks or pulls, just picking the wood to fill the cable. The crane'd put it right over on a flat car."

Eugene has the van slowly rolling again and westward through the trestle we watch the sun as it settles into the lake. "In the meantime now, out there about half way across the lake, they had more boats going over there twenty-four hours a day. The tide from the propellers would drive the wood in underneath the trestle to the men."

AND tried loading the logs from the lake side of the trestle using a jack ladder—revolving chains like tractor wheels—"pushing the wood in stick after stick after stick. It was too slow. The cranes were much faster, loading two trainloads every twenty-four hours," explains Eugene. The limiting factor seems to have been how much the trains could pull. Two steam engines would haul twenty to twenty-five cars and three steam engines could take thirty to forty. The diesel engines were in place by the late 1950s but by then much of the area had been logged. The last year they loaded logs at Terra Nova was 1964.

Another industry to prosper here was driven by the initiative of one man. The road into the village skirts acres of a meadow, now overgrown with wild grasses and weeds. It belonged to Ralph Calloway. There is a memorial park named after him just outside the village. Ralph operated a successful farm. "He had a barn that held 20,000 hens and he got 114 acres of land and he used to have all that sowed in root crops. But he died a young man with cancer and Walter, his son, wasn't old enough at that time to take an interest in it," explains Eugene. "Walter's mother, she couldn't look after it. She hired a fella to operate the farm for three years but he made a piss-poor job of it....

"That's another permanent residence there. Max Holloway," says Eugene without missing a breath as he points to a man raking the lawn in front of an older home. "This is my son's house here. He's never home. It was dad's home, but when mother died he give it to my son. He was out this weekend. Don't know when he'll be out again, it could be this weekend, it could be three months time." Eugene and Phyllis exchange glances.

Past the town hall, named after local hero Eddie Eastman, who made a small splash on the country music circuits on the mainland. Past the small "double church" with pivoting seats. One end United Church, the other end Anglican.

"This is the cemetery."

"How many are dead in there?"

"They're all dead," he quips and Phyllis laughs gleefully. My ears burn.

"See that stone over there with the kind of curly chop on it? That's my first wife. Right next to her is my mother."

"Oh dear, what happened to your wife?"

"Cancer. She died in '46."

"It was either cancer, a heart attack, or aneurism," says Phyllis. Eugene steps on the accelerator.

Outside the village he pulls off onto the shoulder on a hill overlooking the neglected Calloway meadows. Beyond are the trees and the rooftops of a few large "cottages," then more forest and then the lake.

"So this was the farm?"

"This was one third of it."

"And he worked it all himself?"

"Calloway had all kinds of equipment, several tractors, all kinds of ploughs, manure spreaders, he had it all. From the middle of July to the last of September, middle of October, he had twenty-five or thirty people employed. I was truck driving for him for eleven years. He had everything sowed. He never had a square inch that he never had sowed."

"What was his secret? Why was he able to come here to Terra Nova and make a business like that work?"

"I'm not able to answer you boy. But I can say this much, he was a worker and he pushed his men.... And he probably got government help."

"The soil seems awful sandy for farming."

"And that's what it is. Sure you can't find nar worm in it to save your life. I'll take you up to the sandpit now, where all the ATVers goes."

After the sandpit we drive around the back of the village's round-about road towards the Dykes' home. As we pass a low brown bungalow with a real estate sign pegged in front, Eugene stops. The windows are dark and the grass has grown to three or four feet high. "That place there has been in the news. Mount Cashel Orphanage bought it in the late years. It's for sale now. Some of the damage to the Mount Cashel boys was done there," says Eugene. "I looked after the building. I did all the supplies and I'd be back and forth there quite a lot with the Brothers, and my youngest fellow. He's in the navy now. He spent three weeks for three summers in at the Mount Cashel building in St. John's with the Brothers, with the boys. Friends of theirs. And he swears he never seen one thing. But then again, the dorm he was in and the Brothers he was with, there has never been nothing about them. But this is where some of the damage was done." All Newfoundland was deeply shocked several years ago when orphans who had formerly lived at Mount Cashel revealed that certain Christian Brothers had sexually abused them in the 1960s and 1970s. The cat leaps into Eugene's lap and rubs its head luxuriously against the steering wheel.

Back at the store Eugene and Phyllis retire to the living room, tune their shortwave radio to the police band, and marvel at the "goings on." I retreat to my second-story bedroom, stifle in the heat to write a few pages, then rejoin my hosts. Phyllis is crocheting on the couch and Eugene has a drink on the coffee table beside his recliner. The radio still on—a doctor assaulting his girlfriend, a moose killed on the Burgeo highway, a fisheries officer leaves his truck on a wharf, comes back to find the tires slashed. Each of these incidents is dissected by Phyllis and Eugene, who know several of the protagonists even though the area covered includes several hundred square miles.

Phyllis has the table set for my breakfast. They will not be up until hours after I am on the trail. I thank them for their hospitality, bid them good-bye, and head upstairs to sleep, the static of their police band radio crackling faintly behind me.

The bridge over Northwest Brook.

## CHAPTER 36
# RABBITS' HOTEL

### 2 AUGUST, JUST EAST OF TERRA NOVA VILLAGE

Each day I slip into the long thin world of the rail line as easily as I slip into my clothing. But how will it be settling down in the world of people again, instead of channeling through it, with no schedule except to get up and walk, talk, eat, and rest?

At 8:00 a.m. sharp, the crushed stone is crunching underfoot again as Clara taps out a coded message to the moose and bears of my determination to complete this walk. Pine trees grow tall along the sandy ridges. The Newfoundland Telephone sandworm and countless chickadees keep me company. My arms and the back of my neck sting from yesterday's sun. My right knee hints of its need for rest and the west coast blister resurrects itself in my left boot.

Just before mid-morning a Newfoundland Telephone van drives into sight and stops 200 yards up the track. A man in a white hard hat gets out and walks along the destructive slash that is the wake of the fibre-optics cable. He is tying orange tags to strands of tangled wire that loop over the scar of earth.

"Good morning. What're you up to? Out tying up metal?"

"No, all this stuff has to be removed from the right-of-way. Because most likely this trail is going to be used by skidooers or something like that," says the hard-hatted man. He is Neil Flynn, an inspector with Newfoundland Telephone for the fibre-optic project. His job is to "make sure we get the land back so it will re-grow again. Take that approach rather than the other options of grassing it and all that. If we can get the natural vegetation back it would be much better."

Neil obviously expected he might meet "that fella" walking across the rail line. He's making his points, calling to mind Fred Thorne and his dimension stone checklist on the Gaff. I ask him if he thinks it is possible for the natural vegetation to reclaim this destruction in two years, as Newfoundland Telephone claims.

"Oh, yeah. If you smooth it down it will come back. It's starting to come back in the Port aux Basques area, where we started two years ago," he says. As I recall, the cable path through the bogs was grown over, but the vegetation did not match the vegetation on either side. And in places they had chain-sawed their way through centuries-old clumps of tuckamore. Is that supposed to grow back in two years? Neil gestures to the barren, bouldered strip of dirt along the track. "This is less than a year."

"Where you blasted through bluffs and cliffs, what do you do there?" I ask.

"Well, later this morning you'll see Northwest Brook. It was all blasted rock, rock piled on rock. That can't be a restoration. It never looked like that. What we want to do is kind of spread out the rock and then throw some soil on it. And try to get something to grow on top of it.

"With the boulders, we'd try to bury them but if you cut the land all you'd see is more boulders. But to speed up the re-growth process, rather then have boulders sitting around, the decision was made to bury them. Go back and do the whole works again."

"So that's going to delay the growth another year then. Won't it?"

"Not really, it'll speed it up because now you've got topsoil on top of the boulders, right?" he explains, but I do not see the good news.

"We got a backhoe guy up there now. Name's Frank Reid. He's with us since Port aux Basques, crawling across the Island in his tractor. We call him the Easter Bunny because he hides the boulders so well. When you get to him he'll probably be turning his head away. He's shy. Wave him down," encourages Neil. "But the whole idea is restoration. And that means bringing back the environment, rather than hydroseed. We figure that in two years you won't recognize where the cable is."

We both turn at the sound of scrunching gravel. A pickup hauls in behind Neil's van and two men, both looking about retirement age, climb out. The one on the passenger side bends down to pick up a metal tie plate left from the railway demolition. He tosses it casually into the back of the truck and there is a clink of metal on metal.

"On a salvage hunt are you boys?" I call to them.

"Yeah, we're on a salvage hunt. We're starting a railway," Norm Keats says. He and his partner, a guy Peddle, have a good laugh at that. Both are former railway men. Then they walk up to where Neil and I are standing. "I've picked up a scattered splice bar and tie plate because years down the road somebody's going to say 'Boy, I should have picked up a souvenir of that railroad.'"

"You notice some of those spikes got CN embossed on em, if you can find one. They are special spikes," Neil tells us. That's news to me but the boys already knew it.

"I was up the other day and picked up some shimming spikes, that's the longer ones. He knew where they were to," says Peddle jerking his thumb towards Norm. "It's twenty-something years since I worked on the railway but he only give it up a little while ago."

"Fourteen years ago I give it up. I worked thirty-five years at the rails with sections right from Clarenville to Notre Dame Junction. I worked so far as Bishop's but I was never stationed there."

Time for me to pump for information. "They tell me every curve got a name?"

"A lot of 'em. This here is what they calls Rabbits' Hotel," says Norm, gesturing expansively.

Peddle continues, "There used to be a lot of rabbits up here one time and there used to be a lot of rabbit-catchers come up here and camp."

"It's going to be seven more years before you get any more rabbits around here. They say it's every seven years but I'll tell you it's longer than that," says Norm. "Because when they went down before, I figure it was about or eleven years, nine for sure before they peaked again. But I'm sure the moose don't have a cycle. Did you see many moose coming across? Norm asks.

"Yeah I saw quite a few. I saw a bull yesterday. Boy, he had twenty points or more."

"Norm, you were telling me yesterday you saw a caribou out here," says Neil.

"Where's the herd from here?"

"Oh in on the back," says Peddle. "You don't have to go in very far to see caribou."

"Boy, I'll tell you, just down in on the back of Port Blandford," Norm brushes away a stout that has pitched on his face, "there's no such thing as not getting your caribou, especially a doe and the young ones. You're dodging up the bog and don't see a thing. Not minutes later there'll be packs of small caribou coming behind you, small ones, or maybe a small doe. They're too curious for their own good.

"Fellows that's used to caribou they don't just shoot the first animal they see," says Norm. "They want to get the big stag. You don't get that many big stags out in sight because they're hiding away and keeping an eye on everything. You got to flush them out. A scattered one will take over a mound like a mountain. And he'll stay around that area and watch it. But they hide a lot, the stags do."

More wild game talk, then Peddle tells Neil that during their scavenging they noticed one of the drainage culverts under the railbed was blocked with stones from the fibre-optic trail. He says if Neil will give them a length of surveying tape he will mark it so Neil's crew can fix it. Neil enthusiastically peels off a strip of tape about twenty feet long. And, Peddle wonders what they are doing with the remains of all the trees they've uprooted, and whether anyone can take those logs. Neil tells him sure, help yourself. And I think "That's generous, giving away material that belongs to the Province. Better that than letting it rot beside the trail I suppose." As I bid the three good luck and head off through Rabbits' Hotel, I can't help wondering how many more culverts were blocked that no one has spotted. How ironic—the retired railroaders still out taking care of the route, even after their railway is taken from them and dozens of competing interests are chipping away at what is left.

The sun bores into my head all morning. I stop occasionally at a stream or pond to dunk my hat, but fifteen minutes later the hat is dry again. The sandy landscape around Terra Nova surprises me. Sand and large rounded boulders. Glacial till. Good for spruce and pine. It is unusual to see pine trees in the wild in Newfoundland. But by noon I've walked out of the sandy zone and back into the more familiar boreal forests of spruce, fir, birch and alders growing from the thin veneer of turf over rocks and clay.

Northwest Brook—Mile 155.7. I hear the river, like the roar of a busy highway, long before I see it. The black water and white foam sweep towards me from around a steep turn, swirling, about to boil. The falls pour over cliffs which blink and twitch through the watery curtain, like animated faces, as the river churns down into brown-white foam ten feet below, and on, still boiling beneath the spectacular trestle, through a high gorge and on towards Clode Sound five miles to the north. Here the sandworm thrashed about in the forest, cutting and blasting a 100-foot swath down through the forest and rock to the riverbed, upstream from the falls, disappearing into the black boiling water and escaping up the other side, veering off towards the pole line and away, finally, from the track. The noon sun is my signal so I stop for a brief lunch and marvel at the power of the river, wonder how salmon can possibly compete against such power to gain the upper spawning grounds. Lying there on the hot ledge, I dissolve into the white noise of the falls. It occurs to me then that, as my body has adapted to the trail, I am focusing less on myself, more on the people I meet, watching lives unfold.

On the trail once more I turn as a green pickup with a huge tractor tire in the back, ambles up from behind, headed to Port Blandford. The driver has a mop of grizzled hair. There's a large black Labrador retriever perched on the seat beside him. "That's some size of a spare you got there," I say. The truck stops. The dog slaps its tail off the dash, the back of the seat, the dash, the seat, the dash, and climbs across the man to sniff at me.

The driver leans his sunburned face out the window. He hasn't shaved for several days. "Are you going that way or just walking?" he says.

I introduce myself over the noise of the engine and strain to hear his reply. He's from Jamestown, Bernard Fry. He raises his bushy eyebrows when I ask what he thinks of the railbed.

"Right now it's a public road. I think it could be used to haul wood so you can get it out. But with regard to it being a public road for anybody? Well, one thing, you're going to get a lot of traffic on it and it is not wide enough."

"What about if they promote it as a trailway? Where people ... well you'd get the ATVs on it and the snowmobiles, like you do in the winter. But you'd get people on mountain bikes or people skiing on it, stuff like that?"

"We got a big old country up there that is better than this for skiing because you can go where you want to go. You put skiing on this, you'd have to bar everybody else. Once you gets a track with a skidoo you gets this rut that's no good for anything else."

"Do you do any skiing yourself?"

"No."

"Eugene, who owns the General Store in Terra Nova right beside the track, he was telling me that one day last winter he had forty-three snowmobiles parked in front of the store. And they all came by the track."

"I'd say that is about where the government is going to make the most money," says Bernard. Then he offers me a lift and when I decline he shrugs and puts the truck in low gear.

Half an hour later I meet the light-fingered Easter Bunny driving his crane towards me on the track. As I approach the crane, camera in hand, Frank keeps the crane bucket balanced just a few feet from my face, as deftly as if he were holding his hand there. I cannot see him or get a photo until he finally clanks past; at the last second I get a flash of him, barechested, shorts on, behind the dusty windows. He glares at me and clanks steadily by at a tortoise pace, the wide metal tracks screeching as they leave a corduroy track in the gravel.

Around 2:00 p.m., in a heat-blurred stupor, I almost stumble past Terra Nova Park Lodge. But patches of a large green roof blink at me between the treetops and I streel up to the front desk, sweaty and dirty. With the reservation confirmed, I trip over my gear, fall into the elevator, drag myself to my third floor room, switch the air conditioning to "burst" and collapse onto the bed.

This trip is so unlike the wilderness trek I expected. What is it? A journey through the scattered backyards and neighbourhoods of Newfoundland? A hike down the main street of a long thin community? A back road?

I wake to the pasteurized bleep of the telephone. It is Brent Meade calling from Clarenville. He is a development worker with the NLRDC, the east coast counterpart of Sherry Hounsell who drove me to Steady Brook the morning I left Corner Brook. Brent is helping coordinate this section of my trip. He's coming down tonight to dinner. Before we ring off I ask if he has a long-sleeve shirt I can borrow, then find myself apologizing to him. "People have been giving me so much I've lost perspective on what is okay to ask for and what is crossing the line."

In the homes where I've stayed this month, the men often help themselves to food or treats without offering anything to me. The women immediately notice and offer the same to me. This holds true with the exception of one refreshment: alcohol. It is the men who offer this. And when I decline, they always minimize the amount they drink, careful to explain that they drink one, or at most two, a day.

Brent brings the shirt.

Jawbone of an ungulate.

# CHAPTER 37
# "DO NOT DISTROY"

### 3 AUGUST, 9:00 A.M., MILE 148.8

A strong wind whips the waves beneath the Clode Sound Trestle at the east end of Port Blandford, throwing sea froth north towards the open water. Once across the trestle and into the woods, aspen trees slow the wind to a steady rattle in the treetops. Crushed stone on the eastern side of the trestle has been "harvested" and a sign advertises a construction company from Port Blandford. Can they really be unaware that this is theft? Heavy clouds threaten rain.

The grade climbs upward steadily for two hours, above but closely paralleling the TCH. Transport trucks roar through the swish of leaves and birdsong. With its axle broken, a pickup truck lies like a dead packhorse at the mouth of a woods trail. There are frequent moose tracks and scat, several moose hocks left by hunters, even a skull, from which I pry a molar to go along the one I extracted from the caribou in the Topsails.

A stream, its culvert blocked by debris, spills across the roadbed. I wrestle with a large branch until I have hauled it clear of the stream, scrape out the sticks and leaves, and roll away a few rocks so that the culvert is free again. Circumstances argue that I'm hiking on a road, a road with certain restrictions, but nevertheless a road. "Look back to Port aux Basques," I tell myself. "How many hikers have I met in over 400 miles of walking? The Turtle Man near Cooks Brook. And the two priests I just missed in the Topsails. How many ATVs, cars, pickups, tractors, dump trucks? More than I could easily count."

Two hours out of Port Blandford the track crests the spine of the Bonavista Peninsula and levels out before passing under the TCH on its approach to Thorburn Lake and the slow descent into Shoal Harbour and Clarenville. The morning's clouds have fled and the underpass is a shelter from the heat. Overhead, protruding from the massive concrete wall, rusty metal arms that once held the old telegraph wires. The teenage graffiti keeps my eyes scanning the lower third of the walls. "Guns n Roses" "Pink Floyd" "Fuck Police" "Don't walk on the grass—smoke it" "Support the youth—throw a party" "Mega death" "school sucks" around a one-foot square hole and someone has scrawled "insert dick" "Randy + Kim" "raining August 24."

East of the TCH a dirt road curves in from the highway and joins the railbed along the shore of Thorburn Lake. Every hundred yards there is a cabin under construction, or already built. None of them look very old. The sound of hammering. A sign nailed to a tree advertises a landscaping and equipment rentals company in Deep Bight. Dozens of gates where driveways leave the road and curve into the woods towards Thorburn Lake where cabins are hidden by clumps of spruce.

There is a sawmill on the opposite side of the track. The buzz of the chainsaws. The mill is back 300 yards or so and all around it, for a quarter mile nothing is standing except shrubs of alder and birch, not a stick of spruce or balsam fir. For half a mile they have cut right to the railbed.

At one point the track passes within forty yards of the water and the trees there are cut down to the shore. The bottom of the lake is covered with sawmill slabs. Water lilies grow on the other side of the inlet. Close to the rail line, where the woods begins again, a small cabin nestles close to the shore. A man in his late sixties, with short graying hair and red braces over his green flannel shirt waves and walks out the driveway wiping paint from his hands. His name is Hedley. He has a long association with Thorburn Lake though he's only had this cabin since the road crew put in a new intersection to the railbed, while they were upgrading the TCH three years ago. With a slight stutter he says the improvements to the intersection opened up the area. Traffic around the lake has really picked up since then. He offers me water or a bite to eat, but I've just struck my stride for the day and I'm reluctant to stop for long. Hedley is eager to talk. He is discouraged by the increase in the number of cabins around the lake.

"And the government put a road in up around the hangar," he says pointing to the other side of the lake where a couple of float planes are tied to the dock. "There's something around thirty-two lots up there. Mostly people from out around Mount Pearl. Neil Windsor—the MHA from Mount Pearl—got something to do with it I think. And there's another place out here to Clarence's Pond. When them lots went on sale most of them went to people from Norman's Cove."

"Who's out there?"

"Some Member I suppose." Hedley says this not with bitterness, but with a kind of cheerful resignation. "There's good fish here, but they're on the bottom. There was a fella there the spring he got seven, all a foot long or more in eighty-five feet of water. One was seven pounds. You'll get them there eleven or twelve inches off The Anchor they calls it. When the ice goes. They got every colour of the rainbow on 'em and they got a big V tail. There's a fella down here got a depth sounder that goes down 180 feet and when he was over there the light goes out it's so deep."

Hedley and his father kept a dory on Thorburn Lake half a century ago. "I was born here, almost," he says, but before I can find out what that means he continues. "I lived into Milton and we worked in the woods all our lifetime. We had our horses and everything here. We was going across the lake over there one time and we see this trout floating on its side, about a pound and a half. Father thought he was dead and he went to catch the fish but, when he touched him, the fish swam away.

"Another time we rowed ashore over here, myself and another fella. Two of us used to get aboard the express in Clarenville, midnight, or come in on the freight train. Clar Lannon would put you off anywhere at all. They'd put you off right about here where we're to. We used to row across over there to what they call Horse Barn Cove, handy over by where Tucker's is now. We rowed ashore one time in November, and there was three big trout, over there on the beach, two or three pounds each. Dead. They says what happens to them, the fish goes into the small rivers to spawn and when they comes out into the lake they dives in water that's too deep and they dies."

"We used to drive the logs out Shoal Harbour River. After you get up here now," says Hedley, waving in the direction I'm headed, "you'll come to Camp Pond and then you go down to Tucks Pond and eight or nine miles from here you'll cross a trestle over Shoal Harbour River. He goes right on up the country. There'd be ten or twelve people and we'd all stay in the woods all the winter. Keep the horses in the woods. I had a team of six big dogs, and they were all eighty or ninety pound each. I used to wear out two pairs of logans a winter scuffing behind those dogs, hauling the wood out when the snow was too deep for the horses."

"What did you feed the dogs?"

"Used to get the herring. Years ago there used to be a fella putting up herring. And they cut up the heads and everything and they'd freeze it and bring it in bags. And I used to buy beach-dried capelin down to New Bonaventure for three cents a pound." He has a friendly bubbling laugh. "Three dollars a hundred pound of dried capelin. So I'd feed em that. And I used to save me scraps from the camp and the pot liquor and you heave your potato scraps and that in, put it on the stove, heave a baking powder can full of corn meal into it and mix it all up, and give them all so much each of that. And that would keep them good." The buzz of chainsaws drifts to us occasionally on the wind. "Them working dogs won't eat in the day. They only eats evening time."

*Dragonflies patrol the air above faded pink wild roses, their season almost finished.*

Hedley recalls that long before TCH went through, there was a forest fire in the area. For years after that people from Bonavista, where "the crows have to bring their own stick to pitch on" used to come to Thorburn Lake in the winter and cut the burned wood—smuts they used to call it—and load up a flatcar to be hauled back the Bonavista Branch for firewood.

One time Hedley and his father came out of the woods and stopped for a drink of water at a cabin where Bonavista people were staying. His father asked for a drink. The woman gave him a cup and told him to go out and get it in the gully. Hedley chuckles as he recalls the expression on his father's face. "Father knew the land pretty well and he says "Sure there's no gully around here.' And the woman laughed at him and pointed to the water barrel 'gully' out on the back step."

On the east side of Thorburn Lake is a man and his three sons, with water floats in their hands and wet towels around their necks. Roland Temple is a local resource officer with the Department of Forestry and Agriculture. A few weeks ago he and all his co-workers received a department-wide memo from his minister telling them that the railway was now Crown Land. Prior to that Roland says his department didn't have jurisdiction along the railbed because it belonged to CN. I'm encouraged by this news until Roland explains his new position on jurisdiction.

He understands that domestic cutters can't cut within fifty feet of the railbed and he has the right to charge anyone he catches. But commercial loggers, according to Roland, can cut right down to the track, as Don Smith has done on his block of land immediately to the south of us. The smell of spruce sap and mud is strong.

Just half a mile past the eastern edge of Don Smith's forest block is a huge gravel pit right down to the sides of the track and the guy who's digging it stuck a sign in the dirt. Who issued the permit for him to come in here and do the like of this? Most likely, it was the Reid Newfoundland Company, which retains mineral rights to the granted lands although surface rights have since been bought back by the Province. The Reid Newfoundland Company remains in business almost entirely to lease gravel pits. And who issued the permit to use the railroad for commercial access?

After Camp Pond, where I discover a beaver dam someone has recently destroyed, the grade flows down beside the Shoal Harbour River towards Clarenville. The river is waist deep in the pools. At the intersection of track and river is Shoal Harbour River Trestle, Mile 138. It has hip-high metal sides and is about forty very chewed-up ties wide. Dragonflies patrol the air above faded pink wild roses, their season almost finished. The blueberries are greenish white and small. The country is getting much more hilly. I imagine how different this scene must have been years ago, at the height of the spring flood, when Hedley and his fellows drove their harvest of winter logs down the stone-cold waters towards Shoal Harbour and whatever profit they could glean from a long winter's work.

A pickup drives past, headed up-country with a man, woman and two children in light clothes, all grins. An inflated inner tube in the back of the truck. There is a bird claw print, almost as big as my hand, in the mud at the edge of a puddle and I wonder if it was made by one of the eagles nesting in the cliffs of the nearby twin peaks.

August $3^{rd}$, 2:00 p.m. under the TCH overpass two or three miles shy of Shoal Harbour. Muffled sound of traffic overhead every ten seconds or less. My voice has a hollow cavern-like ambience. These underpasses are real hangouts for the kids. This one has all the usual graffiti of crude words, names of heavy metal bands, and special local features, but it is unique along the railbed. There's a sign in white paint "art project don't distroy" with a white arrow towards a large mural. It shows a cartoon-style young man with blond unkempt hair, and bulbous veiny eyes. His mouth is open in a wide scream. The forested twin peaks painted in the background depict the same peaks visible south of the overpass. Superimposed on the background are the words "satan worship, aids, drugs, pollution."

Coming down the steep grade of afternoon into Shoal Harbour, dragonflies rise in squadrons from the roadbed. Marsh orchids, aspen, and larch on the left lean towards the river. Farther off is a pole line. Roof tops. Through the trees I can hear people whooping and splashing. Then the trees open and there is a man casting with a fly rod at the foot of a fish ladder. And on the opposite bank teenagers astride their ATVs, drinking beer.

The stouts practice tactical air manoeuvres on me until I feel like an air carrier. *Nyooom, nyooom* around my head one way, then release the throttle and allow the full momentum to carry them to the top of an arc, and drop like an arrow straight for me, then full velocity again, *nyoom* the opposite way, waiting for the deck to stop heaving so they can pitch and refuel at my expense.

*All that remains of Clarenville Station.*

## CHAPTER 38
# AT THE STATIONHOUSE

**3 AUGUST, MILE 130**

The back deck of the Station House Inn faces north, past the wrinkled trunks of the seventy-five-year-old trembling ash, to the evening-ruffled waters of Random Sound. A white smudge on the water is a distant boat. A half mile beyond that, several clearings on Random Island are highlighted among the trees. A glint of light marks a car emerging from the island, traces the pencil-line of causeway back to the mainland. The car disappears among the houses of Shoal Harbour, which hover between the descending forest and the wind-darkened water. Farther out, along the mainland shore, each house is a tiny sunlit rectangle.

This is where we meet in the warm evening air. There are two development workers: Brent Meade, who is young and enthusiastic, and Tom O'Keefe (the local rural development coordinator), older and openly skeptical. There's a cub reporter from the local newspaper and three former railway workers: Clyde Penney, a tall slightly balding man, Lindo Palmer small, thin, athletic-looking, and Ralph Balsom—everybody's bespectacled grandfather. While I pose for the reporter to take a few photographs, the men twitter about my clothes, especially the big crow's feather in my cap and the skintight spandex pants. A few jokes and then the scraping of deck chairs and polite conversation, while Station House proprietor Jean Durant brings coffee and food. Slowly we cut into the meat of our gathering. Brian Durant, Jean's son and owner of the Station House, joins us a little later. He's tall with thick curly hair and an intense stare. "He's very knowledgeable about the railway history, can tell you anything you need to know," Jean assures me.

The faces have changed but the stories are surprisingly consistent. They tell me how, in the last year of the railway, CN put in new ties and crushed stone east of Clarenville "to drive up costs." And all three are certain there was an overt effort on the part of management to undermine the service. They nod to each other when Lindo suggests the railway's days as the primary mover were doomed when the highway went across the Island, but all contend that the railway could have paid its own expenses. The leaves conspire overhead.

Clyde leans forward, hands on knees, "Sometimes thirty cars in Sydney—containers—for say, Port Blandford, well they'd put them on the train at Port aux Basques, haul them all the way across the Island to St. John's and then truck them back to Port Blandford." And there's no shortage of corruption stories about the railway workers. Carloads of timber would leave Clarenville and wouldn't make it the hundred miles to Avondale. One man hired out CN's own tractor to the railway. And there was the usual surplus of damaged goods. "Pilferage had to amount to millions," says Lindo, shaking his head. Gander Station used to be called the "Rogues' Nest," and there was a ring operating on the Bonavista Branch. As is often the case, the dishonesty of a few people brought the suspicion of senior management down on everyone. "When they served steaks they had to carry back the bones to St. John's to prove how many steaks was eaten," recalls Ralph.

In 1957 the Union of Locomoters, Firemen, and Engineers presented a brief to Cabinet. Ralph was part of that delegation. That was the meeting where then Premier Joey Smallwood predicted the railway's demise and the abandonment of the route in favour of the Trans-Canada Highway. But Smallwood underestimated the potential of the railbed, once the rails were gone, as a means to exploit the hinterland for recreation and raw resources. There are few places where the grass has had a chance to grow. All three men suspect that Joey made a deal with then-Prime Minister Diefenbaker to sell out the railway for a 90/10 federal/provincial cost split on the highway across Newfoundland. I'm suspicious of that reasoning though since Diefenbaker had so outraged Smallwood over his handling of Term 29 of the province's Terms of Union with Canada that Smallwood launched a nationwide campaign against the prime minister. Co-operation between the two seems unlikely. Besides, Pearson was prime minister when the TCH was completed. But their point is, more should be done to preserve the heritage.

Lindo was the stationmaster who received the last train orders for the unhappy duty of closing down Clarenville station. "Why is there no museum here? Bishop's Falls got seven million dollars when the railway pulled out. We got nothing." This is a bitter pill for the railway men. "They said there were no adverse effects. There were 130 people working here in the 1960s. Our mayor during the shutdown just didn't apply for the money in Clarenville. Places like Bonavista, Avondale, and Whitbourne have at least kept the station for a museum," says Lindo. "There is a lot of history here."

"The museum's a good idea. It would help show our past. People here could fill a book. The yard here could be a municipal park," says Clyde, but he's not so sure about preserving the cross-Island trail. "Those bridges are expensive to maintain. I don't see any way people can keep them up."

Lindo liked the idea of the T'Railway for skiing until he tried it a couple of winters ago. "I skied over the Gaff to Howley. I was the only railway man, so I led the party and they almost worried me to death asking when we were going to get to Howley. It's too boring to ski on that trail."

A forest for the taking.

## CHAPTER 39
# PIRATES

By 8:00 a.m. on the overcast morning of August 5$^{th}$ I am back on the road above Clarenville, past the Lower Shoal Harbour Trestle (Mile 126) up the steep climb east of Clarenville and past the top of the old communications road. Good-bye to Brent. It is just Joey, Clara and me again. But not for long. My burrowing companion, the Newfoundland Telephone sandworm, is back tracing a straight line of destruction past the stockpiled logs and on again beside the track and I follow like a dog heeling for its master.

Can humans grow accustomed to anything? The logs piled beside the track no longer offend me—provided the forest along the route is still intact. But the company they attract is what galls me: skidders and cranes and eighteen-wheelers. Perhaps if they just used short sections of the railbed? And then build access roads to harvest timber that is out of sight from the rail bed?

I telephoned Otto last night and he remains totally opposed to even considering the railbed as a road—a trailway it is, a trailway it remains. He sounded a little depressed. It seems to him as if we are losing ground in the struggle to preserve the rail line. But by the time we hung up each had managed to bolster the other's enthusiasm for our mission. He's a good man and I have a lot of respect for him and the tenacious way he has of focusing on a vision. I know what the title of this book is going to be now, but I'm afraid to tell him because I know he's not going to like it. I'll work "trail" into it somehow.

Yesterday, on my day off, I biked into the hills above Clarenville and then down the steep washboard they call Tower Road. On the way I met Ralph Short, from Deep Bight, stacking logs into the back of a pickup. He had several cords of wood there which he cut last winter for lumber. Ralph agrees with leaving the margins along the line, "but sometimes it only takes a few pirates to ruin it for everybody." He said that up until a few years ago there was a good forest behind Deep Bight. People were cutting wood there, "but not a lot." Then a few people collecting unemployment, or on the fisheries package, began cutting the wood for sale. "And now they've got the forest gutted."

Back on the trail, with Clarenville behind, power saws in the distance buzz like mosquitoes. A clap of thunder portends rain. Soon I am in some of the most extensive logging I have seen since the West Coast; a mile to the right, a mile to the left, and very little respect being shown for the margin of the railbed. A second thunderclap warns me to haul on the rain gear and prepare for the worst.

### Postcard from the hills above Clarenville

*The morning hangs heavily as I clatter up through the fog. Bird song and thunder hover, rolling on the breeze. Clouds sit on the tree stumps, cloak the forest in mist. Under the morning's threat of storm I hurry on, knowing the mosquitoes will sniff me out before I expel a second breath, knowing I have still 100 miles to go and more. The wind sweeps blackflies from my hair.*

*Think only of where I will stay tonight. Let the distance take care of itself, one step at a time. In the quiet before the storm, I hurry on. Thoughts of family, my sweet daughters darting barefoot through one of the few precious summers of their youth, sleeping under canvas and the starlit sky. And now the thunder crackles all around. Carry on, feel the energy of all those people who have shared their homes, their food, their lives with me for a moment. My home is five nights away, but tonight there is refuge beneath another stranger's roof.*

Boyd Soper waiting for a part to come in.

## CHAPTER 40
# HOW TO DROWN A HORSE

### 5 AUGUST, MILE 120

There in the wheel track, a pair of needle-nose pliers. Shoving them into my pocket, I round the turn and see two men in coveralls, oblivious to the drizzle, bent to their work in the back of a truck. It is parked smack dab in the middle of the track. To my left a rough sawmill shack, a pile of sawdust, and slabs of wood tell the story of these men. A few pieces of new white lumber are strewn on the black turf, a skidder parked to one side. The elder of the two men, perhaps fifty-five, climbs down from the truck, wipes his hands in a rag and walks a few steps towards me.

"How're you doing?" he extends his hand.

"Oh, I'm just out for a stroll. What about you?"

"Not doing very much. Damn skidder broke down. Gotta wait for a part," he says, half turning towards the truck where the other man has stopped filing the blade of a chainsaw and stands up to look at me.

"You're the guy walking across the Island are you? You're half way there then," the younger man says.

"I'm more than halfway, 427 miles done. About 120 left to go. So more like four-fifths of it is done. A hard old slog though, the odd day," I say trying unsuccessfully to draw a smile out of either one of them. He is Boyd Soper and the young fellow in the truck is his son. The usual questions follow about how far can I walk and why am I walking. Perhaps those questions are so frustrating because I still don't have a definitive answer for either of them.

"So, boys, I suppose taking the train off was a windfall for you?" The son goes back to filing the chain of the saw. Rasp, rasp, rasp.

"What'd ya mean?" says Boyd in a tone that makes me realize that I am out here in the woods, far from any help, at the mercy of anyone I meet, especially people with chainsaws.

"It gave you a road to get out here," I add hastily.

"Oh yeah, we'd have problems getting the timber out, that's why it's still here. We had a sawmill down by Beaver Pond there in 1961, right by the water," he says. With my eyes I follow his gesture down over the stumps and debris of the logged hillside behind their mill to the woods at the bottom of the slope.

In those days, after they had sawed the lumber they used horses or their own muscle to haul it up the hill on a tram car, stopping halfway up each time to re-lay the wooden rails because they did not have enough rails to reach all the way up to the track from the mill. Once they reached the railroad they would load a boxcar by hand. "One time I loaded a boxcar myself, right to the roof with lumber, and they wouldn't take her off the siding. I walked out to home, Northwest Brook, and contacted CN to see why they didn't take the car. They said 'you're overweight.'" Boyd pauses with a look of disgust. The rasping of his son file is the only sound. "Had to come back in, take it off. This ain't my way to get rich. But it'll get you a sack of flour when you can't get none," Boyd says, without a trace of a smile.

*Mile 118 runs through a wind-blasted area of marsh where the only thing taller than knee height is the sparse, wind-bent larch.*

Boyd has vivid memories from the early sixties of one horse that weighed in at 1,100 pounds. Many mornings Boyd would rise early to find the horse gone. "He wouldn't stay in the barn, he used to beat up everything. And he'd walk about four and a half miles out the track and I'd have to get up and walk out there and bring him back again," says Boyd, rubbing his fist in the palm of his other hand. Rasp, rasp rasp.

"That's a hard way to start your day."

"I had to do that, until one day I tied him on near the shore. Later my brother and me was coming down the pond in the boat and my brother said to me 'The horse is gone again.' And I said 'No sir, she's down in the hole now.' And when we come down she had the line on her and down between her legs and head all down in the water, drowned. After that, when we made up our logs, we had to push up the tram-load of lumber to the siding and it took us hours to do it. Work!" says Boyd and he looks at me sadly, as if I could never understand.

"I was glad she was gone though. She was a fucking nuisance." Time to be moving on. Rasp, rasp, rasp following me. Try not to run.

A few turns beyond Boyd's sawmill is Frost Mill Trestle, Mile 119.7. The trestle is just twelve ties wide, in excellent condition but the gravel shoulders are washing away. Here I take the first break of the day, let my legs hang over the side. The bed of the stream, where it runs beneath the track, is a concrete slab with two parallel rails embedded in it like the railbed and the sandworm. Then it hits me, the irony of a fibre-optics cable running along the rail line: our future and our past converging, running side by side along the same corridor.

Mile 118 runs through a wind-blasted area of marsh where the only thing taller than knee height is the sparse, wind-bent larch. Heavy wafts of fog haunt the barrens. There is a series of gullies where lichen-fringed trees grow thick. In one of these treed areas is a community of cabins. A sign "were da Veys stay" is planted in front of a two-storey cabin. Through the picture window I can see the entire bottom floor. A dozen or more cans of food are stacked on the table near the window. Plaid shirts and rain clothes hang from hooks near the door. A steep set of steps leads up to the loft.

About a mile east of the cabins the track crosses an old logging or communications-tower road. The map shows that the road leads out to the TCH, at the turnoff to North West Brook. Perhaps the road to Northern Bight Station? The crushed stone is very thin here and easier to walk on.

The fog finds its voice at Black Brook. Again and again it calls with the sharp laugh of a loon. The trestle (Mile 117) is forty ties wide and crosses high over the river. There is something about crossing over this trestle that is significant to me. My stomach tingles, but I can't imagine why. A sandwich and an apple later I am back on the trail, singing my fool head off. Today it has been mostly "Onward Christian Soldiers" except I only know the first couple of lines and the rest is nonsense or humming.

Another trestle, Little Come by Chance—Mile 113.7. I do not recall crossing so many brooks since the West Coast, but the scale here is entirely different. Out there the rivers are huge, with deep-cut valleys and large trees that dwarf me. Here, where the water tumbles in small brooks through a landscape of rock, ground-hugging berries and stunted scrub, I am a giant.

Melvin and Phyllis Eddy on the remnants of the Burin branch line.

# CHAPTER 41
# A PRIVATE PLACE

*Quiet minds cannot be perplexed or frightened,*
*But go on in fortune or misfortune*
*At their own private pace, like a*
*Clock during a thunder storm.*

– Robert Louis Stevenson

**5 AUGUST, 1:00 P.M., MILE 110, IRVING STATION,**
**GOOBIES, OVERCAST AND WARM**

The highway restaurant fills with customers gulping down food, asking each other the time, encouraging haste to get back on the road. I am in a time zone by myself, waiting for my local contacts to fetch me to North Harbour.

Dad will meet me there tonight, and tomorrow we start our four-day trek together to Whitbourne. In some ways I am jealous over sharing the walk with anyone. Like when Kathy told me my mother wants to walk from Manuels River to St. John's—my first reaction was "No. I want to do that by myself." And for a flash this morning, during the dry thunder above

Clarenville, I felt regret when I realized this was my last day walking alone for four days. But as the day trudged on I became more comfortable with the idea. And I did invite him—originally to walk the Gaff with me. I hope the tent is big enough for us both.

The crushed granite on this part of the walk is really beautiful. There is an overall reddish cast to the bed but stones of green, blue, purple, yellowish white, black, like rural lights seen from a jet, broadcast their presence from the red night.

Goobies has perhaps 100 houses near the old railbed. Coming into the village, domestic cutting, trees toppled onto the crushed stone, decaying debris from a long-fled sawmill, satellite dishes, ATV paths into the woods, garbage.

Where the track passes beneath the road it is a scramble up to the Burin Highway Overpass and then a half mile north to the TCH and the gas station. On the way I passed a man in shorts and a fluorescent green shirt, leaning against a guard rail. He had the longest teeth I had ever seen on man or beaver, stained brown with the gums pulled well back. We chatted briefly, me trying all the while not to focus on his teeth. Minutes later I could not remember a thing he said. Just the teeth like elongated chicklets.

After an hour-and-a-half wait, my contacts arrive at the restaurant. Heather, the coordinator for the local development association, is tall and in her late twenties, long curly hair, the car keys in her hand. Glenda Eddy is shorter, perhaps twenty years old, with shoulder-length blond hair. Heather is pressed for time.

We pile into the car, down the Burin Highway, over the railbed and six miles farther to the turnoff for fogbound North Harbour and Phyllis and Melvin Eddy's large split-level. They are Glenda's parents. The smell of baking bread greets us as I wrestle Joey in through the open door. Like her daughter, Phyllis Eddy is shorter than medium height and smooth skinned. She wears glasses that she frequently pushes into place on her nose, more out of habit than necessity, and her small mouth has a quick and savvy smile.

After supper Phyllis and Melvin take me on a driving tour of the old Burin Peninsula branch line. It ran more than twenty-five miles from the junction at Goobies as far south as Sandy Harbour River, but the only traffic it ever carried was the work train, before construction stopped during World War I. The first Burin Highway followed the railbed's winding course and the older houses in the settled areas are built on these crescents, shadows of the railroad, that curve away from the newer, straighter Burin highway. At Pipers Hole Park the old rail line has become a popular footpath. At the park, in an oiled-gravel parking lot, are dozens of cars with license plates from several states and provinces, even a few from Newfoundland.

Melvin pulls in and steps out, ready for a hike. No one mentioned hiking to me! But they both seem pleased so I say nothing. On we go for thirty minutes. There are still a few old ties visible in the ground. Melvin and Phyllis pose over a section of six or seven decayed ties long enough for me to snap a photograph. The forest has closed in overhead. In the rail bed protruding roots and large rocks demand nimble feet.

On the drive back to North Harbour they show me a big "drug money" house and talk about the smuggling going on along the boot of the Peninsula. Teenagers can earn $200 to $300 a night serving as spotters, watching for police while liquor is smuggled ashore. The locals talk about the smugglers as being a kind of Mafia, and the Eddys tell me it is ugly, but give no details.

After dark my brother Geoff, the man who so skillfully fashioned Clara for my hand, pulls his van into the driveway and Dad hauls his knapsack out of the back and into the house. Introductions all round, then Geoff is gone again into the fog and suddenly my father and I are a team, sitting at the Eddys' kitchen table, eating fresh bread and drinking tea.

## HISTORY SIDING NINE
## RECOMMENDATION 29

The last days of Newfoundland's railway history are, for many, the most controversial. Many former workers accuse CN of using tactics designed to drive up costs and drive away traffic.

In 1978, Dr. Art Sullivan headed a federal/provincial commission to investigate provincial transportation. Among the findings in his report was "Recommendation 29." It proposed phasing out the railway. Amidst immediate public outrage, Premier Frank Moores criticized CN for its hidden agenda to close the railway. The federal government appeared to honour their obligation as Transport Minister Otto Lang created the Newfoundland Transportation Division with a declared mandate to draft a plan for upgrading the services for Terra Transport, CN's Newfoundland assets.

In 1978 Terra Transport's daily service declined to one freight train each way between St. John's and Port aux Basques, and one weekly mixed freight and passenger train on the Bonavista, Harbour Grace and Argentia branches. But, for a brief period in the early 1980s, following aggressive sales of its new freight container shipping, the railway shipments increased. In the face of this success, Terra Transport applied to and got approval from the Canadian Transportation Commission to close the branch lines. In the fall of 1984, one hundred years after it opened, the Harbour Grace line became the last branch to close. Thirty-two railway stations were dismantled. All that remained operational was the main line across the Island.

By mid-1985, CN had lost ten percent of its annual 400,000 tons of freight. In September of that year federal Transportation Minister Don Mazankowski floated a trial balloon on the possibility of Newfoundland trading its constitutional right to a railway for unspecified federal money. Perhaps federal support for the railway was not all it appeared to be. Then, in November, CN Marine announced the end of priority rail car service on the gulf ferry between Nova Scotia and Port aux Basques, ranking rail cars behind transport trucks on the ferry.

In the meantime, encouraged by their own leadership, aging members of the railway unions accepted negotiated severance packages, a move that many were later to regret.

# ISTHMUS TRAIL
## GOOBIES TO WHITBOURNE

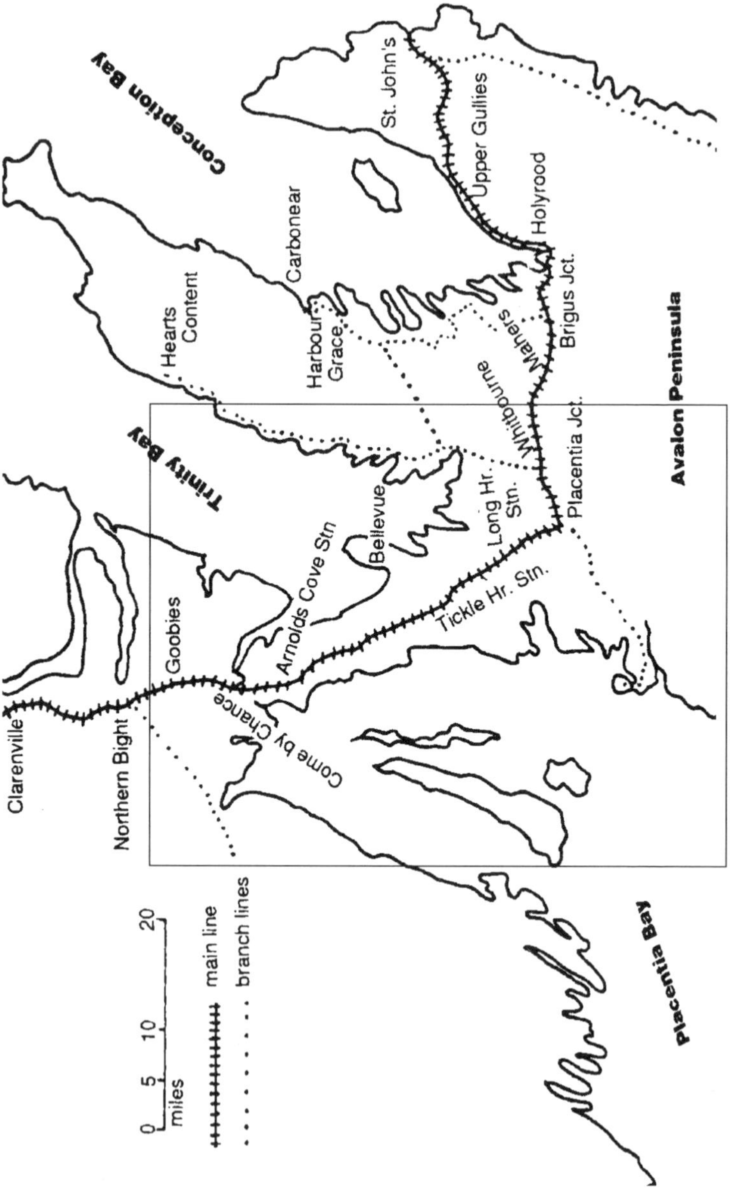
Conception Bay
St. John's
Upper Gullies
Holyrood
Carbonear
Brigus Jct.
Hearts Content
Harbour Grace
Mahers
Whitbourne
Avalon Peninsula
Trinity Bay
Placentia Jct.
Long Hr. Stn.
Bellevue
Arnolds Cove Stn
Tickle Hr. Stn.
Goobies
Clarenville
Northern Bight
Come by Chance
Placentia Bay
0 5 10 20
miles
main line
branch lines

# ISTHMUS TRAIL INTRODUCTION

By the end of June the mussels in the shoals off Bellevue are not as plump as they were in May, but that doesn't stop Ivan and Maxine Anderson from sailing their barge out to rake a bucketful for a boil up. That was how we spent the evening when I stayed with them during my trek in 1993 and it is still one of their favourite pastimes. But, despite the similarities with my previous visit, a lot has changed for the Andersons.

On this evening Maxine Anderson is speaking to me over the telephone. I can hear the television in the background. She tells me that, shortly after my first visit, the family moved to Italy for three years while Ivan worked on a project related to the manufacture of components for the Hibernia offshore platform. Their sons Mark and Jim spent some time in Italy before returning to the island. Both have since moved away and married: Mark to Denver where he runs his own business; and Chris to Toronto where he is a stay-at-home dad with two kids.

During the time in Italy, Anderson flew back and forth to keep their tourism operation, Fiddler's Green Cottages, open. She still manages them. And their business has grown. They bought the former Bellevue Beach Park which Ivan oversees—he's retired from the offshore industry. Among their many summer guests in the park is the occasional party of ATVers from the T'Railway, "but not many," says Anderson. "It's too far off the trail and they have to cross the TCH to get to us."

The scenery on the Isthmus Trail is unique with breath taking panoramas—that is, when they're not socked in with fog or masked in sheets of rain or blowing snow. The T'Railway Council isn't as active in this area as they are in other parts of the province—Executive Director Terry Morrison refers to it as "uncharted territory." But not for trail users. The route between Whitbourne and Goobies is one of the busiest sections on the trail for ATVs and snowmobiles. This is evident by the washboard condition of the trail.

Without regular upkeep, nature is taking a toll. In several places running water is eroding the right of way. The most severe of these, near Arnold's Cove Station, was repaired by the Eastern Trail Riders Snowmobile Club with funding from the provincial snowmobile federation.

Another type of erosion is evident along this route (as well as along the Trail to Avalon). That is erosion of the human kind. Despite the fact that the entire T'Railway is a provincial park, there's basically no patrolling or enforcement. And in heavily used areas that means trouble. Certain people have no problem backing up to the trail bed, loading the pick-up with ballast and driving away. Two places where this is particularly bad, according to local reports, are Placentia Junction and Brigus Junction (the latter is on the Trail to the Avalon). Also along this route you'll encounter people who park their trailer within the T'Railway's fifty-foot corridor and then shift the ballast from the railbed to make a driveway to their spot. Then they just shove a waste pipe into the ground without proper water treatment and presto—instant illegal cabin. You get a public road to your door. You never have to worry about permits or health regulations or legal enforcement of any kind. Probably cuts into the business of people like Maxine and Ivan. But, hey, it's the People's Road.

## CHAPTER 42
# OUR VALLEY

**6 AUGUST, MILE 102, COME BY CHANCE**

Dan Benson is nearing the end of his battle with cancer. There is a greenish tinge to his clean-shaven skin, his voice weak and sounding as if he needs to clear his throat. He tries to occasionally, but doesn't have the strength. Dan sits straight-backed, propped against the high wing-back of the couch. I sit on the other end of the couch, a leather-covered Bible between us. Crowded into the overstuffed living room with us are his thin and boisterous wife, Irene, his quiet sister and his brother-in-law John Dicks. Glenda Eddy is there too. She is a journalism student and asked to come along for the interview. She sits, notebook open, while I ponder an appropriate opening.

The whole morning was more of a struggle than usual. By 8:00 a.m. Dad and I had started from Goobies. The trail was in pretty good condition, just a thin layer of crushed stone over the gravel. The weather was foggy and warm and we soon left the traffic sounds behind. The rain came as if someone had turned on the garden hose and left it on for an hour. By the time we made the shelter on a stranger's veranda in Come by Chance we were both drenched. The development association office, where

Heather works, is in this community of several dozen houses. So I call on Dad's cell phone and Heather and Glenda arrive within minutes to take us back to the office. By the time Glenda and I leave to meet Dan Benson, Dad has on his second set of clothes and his socks and pants and other laundry are hung over the heaters.

The Benson bungalow is tucked into a hollow at the foot of a low hill. A Newfoundland Telephone van is parked in front and standing on his ladder is a man in blue coveralls, working on the wires leading into the house. Behind the house, about halfway up the gentle slope, a model steam engine large enough to seat a child is hitched to several cars and a caboose. Asleep in the dirt is a black dog, and behind it another bungalow. A heavyset man in his late sixties heaves himself up the concrete steps to the house.

"Dan Benson?" I say. He turns and studies me through his spectacles for a moment.

"No. He's inside. He's not very well," he says, in a tone that sounds to me like I should go away. But when I insist that Dan has agreed to see me, the man shrugs and leads us into the house, calling Irene. She is a thin and energetic woman in her late sixties with a tinge of a British accent. Irene ushers us into the living room and introduces us to Dan. The rail line is visible through the picture window, a few houses beyond that and then the forest rollicking back and up over the distant hills.

Dan starts talking before I can open my notepad. From 1937 to 1982 he worked on the eight-mile section from Mile 101, just east of Come by Chance, west down the Come by Chance Valley, past Powderhorn Hill to Goobies. Started as a teenager on a four-man crew, with his father as foreman. Dan began work during the most profitable decade in the history of the railway. The railway actually recorded an operating surplus and the number of cars loaded in St. John's increased from 150 to 228 cars a week. And much of the milling stock and the communications lines were modernized by the United States as part of their war effort on the Island.

As a section man, one of Dan's major jobs was cutting back the brush on each side. "Cleaned right down just the same as a lawn mower on the right-of-way down through that valley. Everybody who rode in the trains used to speak of it. Didn't they John?" and he turns his neck stiffly to look over at his brother-in-law. John nods.

"One crew trying to outdo the other," says John.

"Now they've got it ruined. Our valley is ruined down here," says Irene from her perch in the chair nearest the window.

Dan's nostalgia for the railway only covers the first twelve years of his career, until 1949 when Confederation brought Canadian National into the picture. "There was guys on the railroad, before CN, would go out and work all day for nothing. I'm talking about the Newfoundland Railway." Dan remembers when he first started work with the railway, there were up to seventeen trains a day passing through their section. "We were hauling paper from Grand Falls to Hearts Content and St. John's. When they built Gander we had a sand train going from St. John's to Gander." And of course during wartime there were the guns, munitions, military supplies, and personnel.

The section crews replaced ties, straightened rails, secured loose spikes, repaired culverts and washouts, and performed any number of tasks required to keep the trains on track and as close to schedule as possible. With trains running frequently and no way to communicate with the station, Dan says "it created some difficulties for the section crews working along the line. They'd flag their way most of the time but that was time consuming. More times we'd take a chance."

"So if you're on the track on the speeder and you hear the train coming...?"

"If we heard the train coming we'd jump," says Dan with a grin.

"And the speeder?"

"Smashed to pieces and drove out into the woods ... and the next day we'd get another one. There was no safety for your life or anything like that."

Dan's sister lets her knitting needles lie in her lap. "I know what I used to do. When Dad used to be on the speeder he used to go out in the mornings, and lots of times there'd be an engine coming from Whitbourne, and I used to go out and tell them my father wasn't home and to look out for him. Tell the driver and he'd start blowing then, he used to blow all the way up the valley. I did that a good many times."

"No safety in them days," says Dan again. He remembers stories of Joey Smallwood going through collecting twenty-five cents from each section man and they "never see nor hear tell of him after." (Smallwood's autobiography claims that he negotiated with Herbert Russell, general manager of the railway at the time, to halt a proposed wage cut. Smallwood also claims he sent copies of a new paper he was able to finance, The Labour Outlook to all 600 section men.)

"They say he got married after that and that's where he got the money from," says Irene, with a quick tilt of her head.

"He'd walk so many sections a day and then he'd go again. Sometimes he'd get a ride with the section men. One section man would take him to the next crew," Dan says. "Never heard tell of him after he got the money.

He said he got us a raise. But we never ever got a union in the Newfoundland Railway. Did we John?" says Dan, pushing his left elbow against the couch to look over at John.

"No. We went from twenty-five to twenty-seven cents an hour. That was the only raise ever we got," he says. Dan recalls an express conductor Harry Shortall who, after he retired, went through and tried to form a union.

"Only union we got was after Confederation," he says.

"What about the branch line they were putting down the Burin Peninsula? That never carried an actual train other than the work train. Is that right?" I ask.

"Father worked on that. He told me the work train got as far as the big cut this side of Swift Current. And she went off the track there one day when the boxcar struck the cliff. That was as far as the trains ever got. But they put the railroad over to Sandy Harbour River, just laid the ties and the rails. Never ever hauled any freight that way," says Dan.

"What do you think about the railbed now? Should we just let it grow over?"

"No, no. That's where the beauty is," says Irene. The man in blue coveralls appears in the doorway and Irene follows him into the kitchen.

"I think we should look after the right-of-way," says Dan. "They got all the right-of-way cut, slaughtered. We used to …"

"He's going to test the phone line there now," Irene interrupts.

I tell Dan I have not yet heard anyone who worked with CN say anything good about them. Dan agrees. "No you can't say anything good about them. The first thing they did when they took over after Confederation, they wanted to lengthen out the sections." CN ordered the section crews off the brush cutting and track maintenance and directed them to put up signs, put rocks around the base of the signs, and then paint the rocks. "We spent months and months at that foolishness, instead of working at the roadbed to try and keep it in shape."

"Where are all those signs now?"

"When the railroad closed down sure they cleaned everything. I got a few mile poles there. I was smart enough to get them before they got them," says Dan as the phone rings and he leans towards the side table to answer it.

"They're testing it. He's just testing. He's testing it. That's all right Dan," says Irene. Dan relaxes his grip on the receiver. The phone keeps ringing.

Dan says that just before the railway shut down, CN began to pay more attention to the condition of the roadbed. He feels, even then, CN's intentions were not for the good of the railway. "They knew it was going out and they started to spend a bit of money on it. They said 'We'll spend all the money we can on it to say it is going in the hole.' Cutting back on services. Terrible what they done with that. We sold it out. The money is gone now and we'll never get it back. Terrible what they did," says Dan and he wipes the corners of his mouth. The phone keeps ringing.

Irene recalls happier days. "On Sunday evenings you'd see people by the swarms coming in just to see the train go through. Wouldn't you?" she says looking at Dan for confirmation. "Sunday evenings?"

"Of course, at that time, there wasn't much more to see besides the railroad," says Dan and he chuckles weakly. "The railroad meant a great deal to Come by Chance, especially in the days before the Trans-Canada. We had the hospital here, no roads. People'd come in on the express line, see the doctor, and they'd wait for the train nine at night and go back again." The phone stops ringing.

Irene gestures towards the window to an abandoned building. "When my first husband and I came here from overseas in '46—my husband was in the army—we bought that place over there. At the time there was no place where a person could buy a drink when they got off the train. We started it up with that." Once the children came along the store was an extra burden, so Irene and her former husband sold it.

"This is the Garden of Eden. You couldn't get any better place than Newfoundland. You just stop and think now … out here the other evening there was a moose, right there," says Irene as she stands and walks to the window and points down at the lawn. The rain clouds of the morning are scattering and the sun is breaking through. Irene raises her hand to shade her eyes as she gazes out into the bright afternoon. "You can go and you can get rabbit; you can get a partridge; you can go get trout and salmon. You've got gardens of vegetables. What else do you want?" She returns to her chair and sits down completely at ease. "Over in England you can't catch a fish. You can't kill an animal. You can't cut a tree. Or else they'll have you in jail because you're not rich. Here you've got the Garden of Eden. It's free for you. It's built for man. But they are abusing it."

"Well, not everybody, there's a few pirates," I say thinking of the people I've met along the way who've spoken out for protection and preservation of the railway. But Irene disagrees.

"Not a few at all, there's a lot of them now. They got no respect for nothing." Her youngest son from her first marriage is a river-warden with the Department of Fisheries. "He gets lots of threats, but he catches lots of poachers," says Irene gathering herself up. Her son works night patrols, walking the treacherous shores of the North Harbour River. "I've seen him leave the Trans-Canada, with the night cold, black as pitch. He'd catch two or three fellas some nights. He caught a good one the other day, I'll guarantee you. That fella lost his car, he lost his engine; he lost it all."

"We got the subject changed now altogether," says Dan. He wants to talk railway. "It's the backbone of Newfoundland."

"What better thing can you do now, than stroll along part of that railroad? I knows places on that track now, my son look, it's just like a little park," says Irene.

"I think the right place for the government to spend a bit of money is keeping what we got. Just cut the brush so it wouldn't grow in and be lost."

Dan, Irene, John, and his sister, whose name I never did get, all agree that if it is not claimed for preservation, someone will take the railbed to abuse. They praise a local doctor, Pete Cleary, who has claimed much of the valley for cross-country ski trails. Earlier this morning Dad and I saw "ski trail" signs nailed to trees on the last two miles of our slosh into Come by Chance.

"You'll notice a difference between where that ski trail is and just up here by Come by Chance. He won't let them cut it, see. He said you've got to get permission from the government. But beyond that, they give them permission to cut," Dan shakes his head.

There are other ways to preserve the railway says Irene and she asks if I noticed the model train behind the house. "One winter when Dan didn't have anything to do he was down in the basement puttering around one day and he called up to me 'I know what I'm going to do. I'm going to build a train out of wood.'"

"What put that in your mind?" I ask Dan. He seems more withdrawn than when Glenda and I first arrived.

"I always loved the trains. I loved the steam engines, I loved the Newfoundland Railway. I wouldn't have anything to do with the CN. When I built mine I marked it all Newfoundland Railway." He finished it in a week and let his then four-year-old grandson play on it. The boy has long since outgrown the model but Irene says they get tourists with license plates from "all over" the U.S. stopping to photograph and videotape the model. Dan and the others believe that is evidence of just how valuable a tourist resource the railway could be. Local residents are so proud of Dan's handiwork they've displayed the train on a flatbed in several Santa Claus parades.

I can see our presence is draining for Dan, but as I rise to leave he gets another burst of steam. "I worked with the railway forty-five years and retired in 1982. Now I don't want to preach it again, but I got cancer of the gall bladder. Me and Irene married eight years ago and we had a wonderful life. We traveled Newfoundland from end to end. Every inch of her. Labrador. Eight good years," says Dan.

"It's so beautiful you know. It's a gorgeous little Province," says Irene.

"I suppose I got seventy-seven years in," says Dan.

"I've been up on the mainland too. I was there for twelve years. But I always come back here," she says.

"I got no regrets," smiles Dan.

Al Kearley taking a breather.

## CHAPTER 43
# FATHER AND SUN

**6 AUGUST, 8 P.M., TANKER INN, ARNOLD'S COVE**

Dad called it quits at Come by Chance. I think his feet were bothering him and his boots were soaked through: not the best way to start a four-day hike. He felt bad about quitting and I think he was wary of potential ribbing when he gets home. This is the first time I have really admitted Dad is getting older. It is hard to relate to someone I am proud of and embarrassed by at the same time. The embarrassment is really my doing, my failure to accept him on his own terms. But I have been warmed by his support and the effort he made to join me on this trek. It just was not meant to be.

Around the time Dad left the sun broke through and shone hard for the rest of the afternoon. About 3:00 p.m. I passed the 100-mile marker. Far downwind in the smelly blue haze, the flare-off stacks of the Come by Chance refinery were blazing. All the rivers swollen from the early rain. I considered taking a photograph of the stacks protruding from the barrens, but through the camera lens the flame was as small as the flare of a match.

About twenty minutes later I reached an underpass where the line ducks beneath the TCH on its approach to Mile 98.4. On either side of the underpass opening, scrawled in red paint "Wade don't go past the line or you'll be sorry." I know it was not intended for me, but it stopped me in my tracks for a moment. Under the highway, past the dozen houses of Arnold's Cove Station, over another trestle, alongside another gravel pit and a covey of grouse—four miles on to the end of the day's trail near Jack's Pond Provincial Park. All the campsites are flooded, but Heather, god bless her, spoke with the manager of the Tanker Inn and he donated a room for the night.

*The sun is bright through the clouds and the air thick with the moist, lingering breath of yesterday's rainstorm.*

Arnold's Cove is on the Placentia Bay side of the Isthmus of Avalon, which runs roughly north to south connecting the heavily populated (or should I say "less sparsely populated"?) Avalon Peninsula with the rest of the Island. To the east, not eight miles away, is Trinity Bay. Placentia Bay is to the west. Surrounded by the sea as it is, it's not surprising that Arnold's Cove is home of the largest fish plant in the area. There is also a new suburb built to accommodate the workers on the nearby Hibernia project.

I'm writing these notes in the restaurant of the Inn. The waitress refills my coffee cup and clears the table. I had ordered a fish platter; figuring the fish should be pretty fresh with the plant just down the road. But indeed they have not any. Adjacent to the dining room is a lounge and I can hear the click of the break from a pool table, loud country music, and snatches of slurred conversation.

When I think back on all the people's lives I have been touched by, I feel blessed, so lucky, so at a loss to thank them all. And I'm so lonely for Kathy, for her companionship, her wisdom, her breath, her flesh. And I am so damn excitable! I have flash-fantasies about almost every woman I meet, and hope it doesn't show in my eyes. A sure sign I have been gone too long.

The only other diners here, a couple, are two tables over. Just close enough for their conversation to drift to me. "Tickets bought, a room booked at the Airport Inn, I can't believe you're really going," she says, touching his arm.

"This week has zoomed by," he says and they hold hands, lean towards each other.

I have three cups of coffee before I can face my room. The telephone is ringing as I enter. It's Otto, his voice now a forgotten friend. The publicity from my trip is helping his efforts to push for the T'Railway and he has learned about a group promoting a Trans-Canada trailway. There is a conference in Peterborough, Ontario on the weekend immediately after I reach St. John's and can I go? "Are you kidding? Once I reach the city, I don't even want to think about the T'Railway for at least a month."

Around 11:30 p.m. the phone rings again. It's Dad. He wants to come out and spend tomorrow night with me in Bellevue and walk into Whitbourne the next day. I welcome the idea, but really do not feel like calling Maxine Anderson, who has invited me into her home for the night, and asking her if she will take in one more person. Maybe I am starting to get a better perspective on what I can ask for and what I should not. Instead, we'll meet the day after tomorrow at the Long Harbour Road intersection. I switch off the television, turn out the light and lay my head full of racing thoughts down to sleep.

I am tired the next morning. Must have been those cups of coffee; tea for supper tonight. In brush outside the window a chickadee mocks me: "drinkin' tea tea tea tea." I dreamed of being in a wheelchair on a long, long dirt road. I was trying to get back to the motel to catch a taxi, and I remember bumping through the potholes and over the stones, struggling to make the wheels go faster, but I just didn't seem to be getting anywhere.

Eric Rose, the taxi driver from Arnold's Cove, is honking outside my door 7:30 a.m. sharp. I am still shoving things into the knapsack as I clump out onto the veranda. The sun is bright through the clouds and the air thick with the moist, lingering breath of yesterday's rainstorm. On the ten-minute drive back to the park, where I will pick up the trail, Eric and I chat. When he discovers that I am "that fella" walking across the line he won't take any money for the fare. "You needn't mention me in the book neither. Just glad to help out."

Running alongside the rail line for miles ninety-five and ninety-four is the original pole line with a single wire strung between the poles. In a few places new poles have been erected. Around Mile ninety-five, Pole number six the fibre-optics sandworm swerves into sight and dives beneath the railbed. This is the first time I've seen it since it left the line yesterday around Mile 111. Four miles later I feel a growing rage inside, where I have felt serene for many days. Here the cable is actually buried beneath the rail line. The past and the future colliding under my feet. I don't know whether to curse the heavens or sit down and cry. It seems more like walking through a construction site than over a rail line. Littering the sides of the track are bits of tire, spent blasting caps, blasting wire, blasting mats. Blast it all! Every now and then I can see old ties and other railway detritus, formerly preserved in the crushed granite, now dug up and dumped beside the railbed. At Mile eighty-nine the fibre-optics slash veers off to follow the Trans-Canada. The rail line flows southeast under the TCH towards Little Harbour Road.

Just beyond the underpass, a section of track cuts a shallow S through the middle of a small pond. Though I have never walked through this section before I have seen it many times, a stone's throw from the TCH I remember once, as a child watching from the back seat of the family car, as a train burst from the summer forest, charged across the small pond and plunged beneath the highway. This past spring, during business trips, I have glanced through the car window, tried to imagine myself walking lonely stretches like this one, over bogs, across ponds, through forested valleys. A car drives past on the highway and I wave. There might be a child watching through the back window.

Must be getting close to the Little Harbour Road, there is a small dump less than a quarter mile to the south. Sudden commotion in the trees nearby and my heart pounds until several grouse tumble out of the branches twenty feet in front of me and fumble into the air.

What is it about certain places that make them special, sacred? I have stopped by a pond. The surface is smooth. Fish, too numerous to count, mostly small ones, leaping clear into the air, like drips of black water that hang an instant wet then drop to merge again with the mirror surface. The splash from a big fish ripples across the pond, swallowing the splashes of lesser fish. Spruce and birch tangled on the far side are reflected dimly. Tweep tweep of small birds. Patches of the fog lift. For a moment I stand entranced, and then Joey digs his heel in my back. I sigh with gratitude and resume the pounding pace.

Ahead in the fog a car horn blows and I shout back. It keeps blowing and for a time it sounds like a train whistle. After a moment the sound subsides and the shape of a pickup emerges, headlights like two angry dim eyes. There are three men in the cab, each wearing the obligatory baseball cap. The smell of alcohol greets me as the driver rolls down his window. He wears a red plaid shirt and two days' beard. There's an open two-four of beer on the floor.

"There's a big traffic jam up ahead is it? I could hear the horn going."

"No, we just seen a moose. Right there. Just right there. I was blowing the horn to see would he come out of the woods again.

"So what da ya got, a special moose-calling horn?"

"He came across the road and went on around the edge of the marsh." Their excuse for being here is to pick berries, but they had to give it up because the flies were too bad.

"Yeah that's why I keep moving. It's great for the mileage, boy, when the flies are thick. You don't stop too long," I say. As the truck fades out in the opposite direction, the flies, whose spirit we have invoked, come hunting.

## Postcard from the Isthmus of Avalon

*The large flat rock is warm against my back, the sun hot on my legs and body. Crickets scratch the silence. Just out of arms' reach a red squirrel sniffs for clues and darts into the bushes after my raisins. Big flies buzzing, gulls in the distance. Mosquitoes bump my skin's acrid repellant. All around, barren hills with small stunted trees crowding into the hollows. The hill directly behind me slopes a short distance to the north where the grunts and groans of small flocks of seagulls emerge, flying so low I can hear the wind in their feathers, like the sounds of clothes on a line. Below my feet the hill falls southward to where a kingfisher dives to nick the pond surface and veer off towards the shore. On the hill beyond the pond a large colony of roosting gulls flecks the air with their squabbling. Black power lines suspended above a more distant pond slice into a fog bank over Placentia Bay. Eighty miles to go.*

A retired fire engine.

## CHAPTER 44
# FIDDLER'S GREEN

### 7 AUGUST, 2:00 P.M., MILE 79

Just before the Fair Haven intersection there is a steep car park. Actually it is not so much a car park as an embankment directly off the railbed. But there are three cars parked there, all with doors open, windows smashed out, engines gone and bodies rusted. At the intersection I drop Joey, plop on top of it. If ever there was a "middle of nowhere" this is it. I'm standing at the crossroads in a broad rocky plain, a few low juniper and spruce, small gullies, broad sky. And two hours before anyone is scheduled to be here to pick me up. There's no service in the area so the cell phone Dad loaned me is useless here. And I am in no mood to sit around in the heat and the flies. About a mile down the road I can see a small clutch of cabins, a car in front of one. Joey climbs back onto my shoulders and we head north along the road. No traffic. Even if there was, I'd probably have to lie down in the road to get someone to stop for such a dirt bag as me.

At the cabin a grey-haired man in shorts lounges in the shade, sipping a dark drink. His cell phone can pick up a signal so I call Terry Fahey. He's with the local development association. Waiting in the shade the cabin owner tells me that even here the pirates have had their way. Last spring there was a guy caught netting fish one night on the pond back towards the track. He had over a hundred dozen in the boat when he was nabbed. "Haven't been able to catch a thing there all summer."

It is a three-mile drive north to the TCH and then another two miles down a steep incline to Bellevue, a small community spread out along a natural harbour in Trinity Bay. Maxine and Ivan Anderson run a tourist cabin operation there called Fiddler's Green. The family home is a large A-frame. Six cabins are arranged around the eastern perimeter of the property and a path leads down the short distance to the wharf where a small barge is tied. About a quarter mile across the water the ocean has pushed up a long reef of beach rocks, which divides the waters of Bellevue Pond from Trinity Bay beyond. When Terry pulls the car into the dirt parking lot, Maxine comes out through the door of the cabin nearest the water. Dressed in jogging pants and a tee shirt, she is stuffing a pillow into a pillow case and looks tired and dusty. She waves to Terry and me, tells us to go on into the house, she'll be with us when the cabins are cleaned.

The steps to the house lead to the back deck where a sliding door opens into the kitchen. Ivan is sitting inside at the table with a half-full bottle of wine in front of him. He invites us in. Ivan and Terry know each other by name but they shake hands. Ivan invites us to join him in his celebration and he rushes to get glasses. His dark-blond hair is cropped short and enhances the slightly flushed face. Having just resigned his position at the Come-by-Chance refinery to take a job with the Hibernia Project, Ivan is looking forward to this October when he and Maxine leave for two years in Italy. There he will oversee the construction of a component for the gravity-based platform.

When the drinks are poured, wine for Terry and Ivan, Pepsi for Terry's young daughter and me, the talk turns to the fishery and The Moratorium. No good news. Over the next hour or more Terry has a couple of drinks but Ivan is drinking furiously, consuming at least half of a second bottle.

After Terry has gone, Ivan suggests a trip on the bay in the barge and calls his brother Berkeley to invite him and his wife Chris and their two young daughters Holly and Rebecca to join us. Berk is tall and slim where Ivan is short and plump. Chris, too, is slim with long dark hair. The girls aged seven or eight, like most children, are an interesting mix of both parents. Over the next couple of hours before the boat trip, Ivan drinks steadily, yet he appears as sober as when I first arrived. The only change is that he moves more slowly and pushes his glasses back on his nose more often. On the wharf, Ivan holds the barge until we are all aboard then pulls on the skipper's cap. I am a little concerned and look around for life jackets. But Ivan executes a perfect launch, wine glass in hand, and heads up the saltwater pond to the "rattles," where the pond opens out into the bay.

The bottom is black with mussels and everyone takes turns with the rakes hauling clumps of the shellfish off the bottom to fill two five-gallon buckets. Maxine and I break the clumps apart, keeping the larger mussels and throwing the smaller ones over the side.

Just offshore from the mouth of the rattles, Ivan steams towards a low, grass-covered island. As we get closer, a cloud of gulls rise into a living halo. The stench of the island sticks inside my nose. Known locally as Dog Mackerel Island this is where, years ago, the local fisherman used to discard the by-catch of large tuna. Ivan laments the number of fish discarded here, fish which today bring up to $10,000 each from Japanese buyers.

Against Chris' protests Ivan runs the barge ashore and Berk, Maxine and the two girls splash to shore. Within minutes the children have each captured a mottled chick and return to show their mother. Once everyone is back aboard, minus the chicks, Ivan, still with glass in hand, steams back through the rattles. In the pond the children take turns steering the barge into the wind. They squeal with delight as they struggle to keep the boat heading up the pond. I am filled with a sense of guilt. What am I doing here with these strangers, without my own family? Tomorrow I walk twenty-four miles to Whitbourne and three nights at home, before I start the final fifty-six miles from Whitbourne to the feet of the Goddess of Industry statue, in front of the terminal in downtown St. John's.

After the mussel boil-up I say goodnight to my hosts and turn in early. Just before I sleep the hint of a smile seeps into my tired muscles. I realized something today, as I napped beside the track, the sun breaking through the fog, the many gulls commuting overhead between the bays on the isthmus, bawling commands that no one obeys. As I took all that in, I realized deep in my bones, more intensely than I ever felt before, that the Avalon Peninsula is my home. And with that came an even deeper sense of peace.

# CHAPTER 45
# "SURE, WHAT'S ON A BOG?"

**8 AUGUST, 8:00 A.M., MILE 77, OVERCAST**

This is my last day on the trail before Whitbourne, a two-day break, and the chance to sleep in my own bed for the first time in over a month. Yet it is only now, near the end of this journey, that I am coming to know anything about the trail, about myself. Little pieces fitting together: how to walk, how much I need to carry, how hard I can push myself, how to carry things, how to take care of my feet, what to eat and when.

It is almost ten miles from here to the Long Harbour Road intersection where Dad and I will meet at 10:00 a.m. The crushed stone is a single layer over the gravel. Occasionally a deserted camper-trailer or small cabin. Blueberry bushes and Labrador tea on both sides A few spruce and fir trees and countless rocks—grey, lichened, rocks stacked by retreating glaciers, scattered on the land, diverting streams and brooks, half hidden in the shallow ponds.

After an hour the fog is thicker and a fine drizzle begins. It is like traveling inside a translucent bubble with a fifty-yard radius that drifts along with me. Everything beyond is invisible. By the end of the second hour that familiar weariness is creeping in and the whole thing seems just a bit too much. My carbohydrate intake was low yesterday, but at least I slept well. Time for a sugar rush.

There are black campfire circles and chicken take-out boxes, here a bumper, there a muffler, here two hub caps, ee-ei ee-ei oh! The occasional pile of ties, some partially burned, the coiled wires visible. And small cabins that can fit into the back of a pickup truck are plopped like igloos on the landscape. The crushed stone is pushed aside now and the roadbed is a washboard of potholes.

A dented grey pickup pulls up on my left and the driver leans across to roll down the passenger window, says he is going about a mile down the track and do I want a lift. Ten minutes later Clarence Smith pulls in to where he and his wife Mary have a converted bus parked permanently beside the track. There is an all-terrain vehicle with six muddy wheels at the back of the lot. The bus is painted a deep blue. Mary has short wavy hair and she's dressed in loose clothing when she opens the bus door to see who Clarence has dragged home. She invites me in for a cup of tea.

There were very few cabins in here before the railway closed, says Clarence. When I ask him what the bogs are like with all the ATVers in the area, they both become defensive.

"Sure, what's on a bog? There's nothing up there anyway," says Clarence.

"Well it's mostly one track. People get in and follow the track. Sure what harm is that gonna do? Those people who say the bogs are chewed up, they're only jealous because they don't have a bog machine," Mary tells me with a knowing smile.

Back on the trail I have to step aside for traffic every few minutes, the most traffic I have seen since I started, with the exception of Skull Hill, west of Badger. But that was loggers, this is domestic traffic. You would never know this was once the railway track. It is now just another dirt road.

Half an hour late I round one more turn and there, 300 yards away, is Dad's car on the Long Harbour highway. The door opens, a familiar figure, still too far away to see his features, steps out and starts walking towards me. Nearby a man with short black hair and black glasses is leaning on a fencepost to which is nailed a white railway milepost with sixty-nine painted on it in black letters.

"Where are you walking from?" Chris Cooper asks. He's from Old Shop and has a cabin nearby.

"Port aux Basques."

"You poor thing," he says and genuine concern shows in his face. "That's some walk. When did you leave? You poor fella."

"Don't pity me. It has been an adventure," I tell him. Dad is almost within earshot now and I wave. There have been cabins here since long before the train shut down. Now it looks like a community. On the far side of the highway is a small village of trailers.

"I went past here this morning looking for the railway and I drove right past here, thought it was a road," Dad says. Back at the car he straps on his new hiking boots while I offer him advice on how best to bind his feet. He endures me patiently. My stepmother, Dianne, has come out with Dad and we chat until Dad's strapped in for the walk. I strip off my rain gear. Dianne agrees to pick up Joey at Fiddler's Green, so I give her directions. And then Dad and I are off.

My reputation has preceded me to the trailer village. Several people call to me to stop and talk. One woman snaps our picture and a small crowd of children and dogs follow us for a short distance. Then we are back in the woods and I hurry to keep pace with Dad, who seems bent on covering the sixty-nine miles to St. John's today, rather than the fourteen miles to Whitbourne. After I plead several times for mercy, he slows his pace and we relax into the walk, snapping pictures, chatting, and taking the occasional break.

Around mile sixty-three, just two miles west of Placentia Junction, there is a twenty-five-foot-wide washout about six feet deep, with grass growing down the sides. It has been like this for a few years. That explains why the traffic thinned out and finally stopped altogether the farther we got from Long Harbour Road. The ditch looks like it was excavated, perhaps to cut down on the traffic using this route as a road between Placentia Junction and Long Harbour, and to give some privacy to the cabin owners in the area. Of course it has not stopped the ATVs, just rerouted them down through the riverbed.

By 3:00 p.m. we reach Placentia Junction and lunch in the cabin of a man named Brewer, from St. John's. He has had a place here for thirty-nine years. There are a lot of cabins around and very little garbage. Brewer says that the cabin owners take care of the area. They are concerned about the T'Railway, because they are not sure what the implications are for their ability to access their cabins.

Where the track turns northeast for the final six miles into Whitbourne, the crushed stone becomes thicker again as the traffic forsakes the railbed for a trunk road from the Junction out to the Argentia Highway. The clouds and warm wind are holding. The way narrows as the alders close in. It is so narrow I am surprised when we see a small grey pickup rushing towards us. Dad and I push to the side to allow him to pass, but there is not enough room and he isn't slowing down. A woman on the passenger side appears to be knitting and, peering over the top of the steering wheel, is a small balding man. It is as if he doesn't even see us. No time to think: Dad leaps into the alders and I fall to the side, swinging Clara as hard as I can at the driver's side mirror. The mirror smashes, but the brake lights don't even flick as the truck continues on towards Placentia Junction. What was he trying to prove? What was I trying to prove?

The last four miles into Whitbourne pass without incident. We stop at the local police station to call for a taxi to the TCH, where Kathy will meet us at the gas station restaurant. The officer on duty offers to drive us, so we arrive at the restaurant in grand style aboard the RCMP cruiser. Amid curious stares from the other diners, Dad and I order pie and coffee. Kathy arrives before it is served.

## HISTORY SIDING TEN
## END OF THE LINE

In January of 1986 heavy runoff washed away a pier in the middle of Robinsons River Trestle on the province's west coast, dragging two spans of railway track into the churning torrent. Whether this could have been prevented or not by proper maintenance is open for debate, but records show three other large railway trestles in the area were in need of repairs. It took forty-eight days and half a million dollars to re-open the line.

This disaster was only one of many factors that must have weighed on Premier Brian Peckford as he struggled with how best to manage the province's dying railway industry. The right to a railway was enshrined in Newfoundland's Terms of Union with Canada. But the service had been whittled down to the main line. Railway cars had lost priority Gulf ferry service. And rate hikes for less than superior service were driving business to other modes of transportation. The only light at the end of Terra Transport's tunnel appeared to be the headlights of a transport truck.

The federal government had expressed willingness to buy its way out of the Terms of Union with money for road improvements. Peckford took that as his cue and negotiated not whether the railway would close or not, but how much the province would get for signing away its rights to the service. Negotiations over the railway's fate were dragging on even as the Robinson's Trestle collapsed.

That spring rumours about an imminent closure were gathering steam. Some maintained that the federal and provincial negotiators had agreed to one billion dollars but disagreed over the terms.

Then, in what appears to be a calculated gamble, the federal government announced the railway would remain in operation. Premier Peckford publicly welcomed the news even as the rumours of a termination agreement picked up speed. On 20 June 1988, the death knell of the railway in Newfoundland was delivered in the guise of the Newfoundland Transportation Initiative; an $800 million "roads for rails" deal. Ron Lawless, CN's president said it was the end of an industry that "served no significant function."

On 30 September 1988 the last train crossed the Island. And, less than a month after the diesel engines went cold in Port aux Basques, crews were pulling up the first rail in a remote area of the Topsails, far from the maddened crowd. Despite wide-spread protests and lobbying to leave the lines in place until a feasibility and opportunities study could be completed, the demolition continued at fever pace. Within two years the last of the ties and rails were hauled away on flatbed trucks and the People's Road was born.

# TRAIL OF AVALON
## WHITBOURNE TO ST.JOHN'S

228

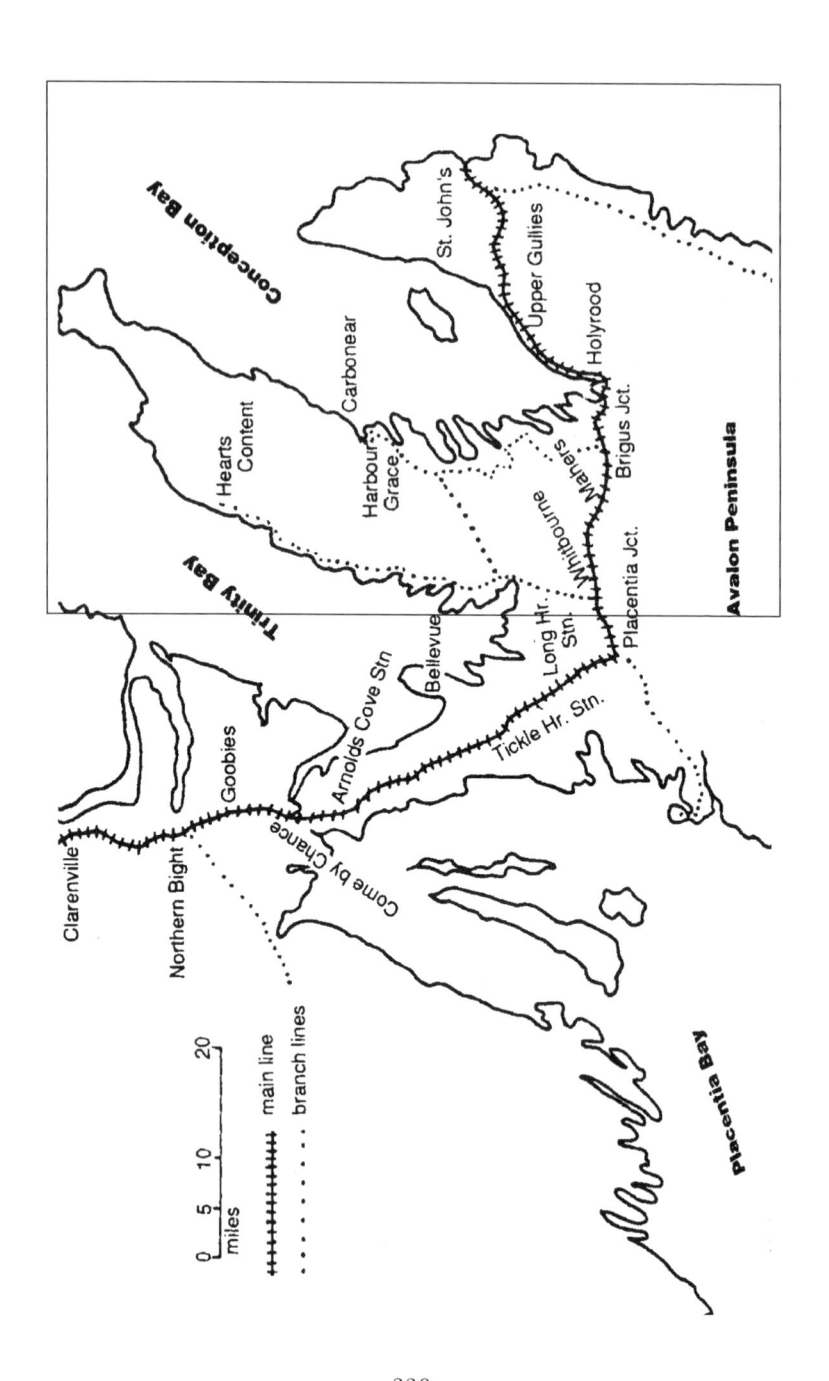

# TRAIL OF AVALON INTRODUCTION

The noon-day train whistle at the Avondale station blows every day at 1:00 p.m., reminding the residents of quiet Station Road that something is amiss. Over the past six years the railway museum and railway stock, including a section of original railway track, has fallen into disrepair as the Heritage Society disintegrated. Among the former members were Martin Hennessey and Alex Hicks who greeted me here in 1993. Both have since died. Others have either moved away or resigned because of other commitments. But, according to Mary Hicks, that is all about to change. She is president of the revitalized Heritage Society. Along with several of her sisters including vice-president Ann Hicks (who was married to Alex), and co-treasurer Katherine Kennedy, plus other local volunteers, they plan to "get the station back to where it was six years ago."

Although they have kept the station museum open Wednesday to Sunday for the summer season, Mary Hicks is the first to admit they have their work cut out for them. Her late brother-in-law, Alex, "is badly missed." An electrical engineer and railway buff he, "did everything around here," from managing and supervising the operations to setting the noon-day whistle.

Other items on the Society's agenda include retrieving the CN trolley from Trinity where it has been for the past year. But even when they get it back to Avondale, they won't be offering rides on the rails any time soon. "We just can't afford the liability insurance, and we have tried everywhere," she says. On a bright note, Hicks adds that the Dining Car, operated by Mary Buckle, has remained open serving, among other things, "the best cod tongues I've ever tasted."

Eighteen miles up the track is the western gateway of Trail to the Avalon. The Whitbourne town hall and museum, located in the former railway station, is one of the more active sites in the community.

According to Randy Noseworthy, the railway cars near the town hall— officially called rolling stock— have all recently been painted including the orange snowplow, the grey, black, and red locomotive, the rusty, red baggage cars, the white maintenance-crew car, and the orange caboose.

A retired teacher, Noseworthy's fascination with the railway continues unabated since we last met in 1993. He maintains his model railway in the basement of his Whitbourne home. He wrote and published *The School Car: Bringing the Three Rs to Newfoundland's Remote Railway Settlements (1936-42)*. And, among his filing cabinets full of papers, he keeps "a photographic and written log of the remaining historic railway stations and rolling stock." But, as Noseworthy admits, the log is about four or five years out of date—delayed by his moving back and forth to Wolfville in Nova Scotia where his daughter Janice lives with her family. And, while he's aware of the two new black and white aluminum signs on the TCH directing traffic to the Whitbourne Railway Museum, Noseworthy is not up to scratch on the latest issues related to the T'Railway.

One person who is aware of the condition of the trail, and of the issues related to its development, is Rick Noseworthy (no relation). A resident of Conception Bay South, an avid ATVer, and vice-president of the T'Railway Council, he minces no words when it comes to advocating for the rights of the Council and ATVs on the trail. One of his biggest concerns is how the trail is being carved up.

"Our fear is that we lose a piece here and a piece there and pretty soon there's nothing left. The T'Railway Council needs to have more teeth," he says with a mixture of concern and anger in his voice. "If we are going to manage the trail, then manage it. We have the agreements in place," he says referring to the Council's contract and trail lease agreements with the provincial government. "But we need to see follow-through from the government. Just like they let school boards run the schools." But, says Noseworthy, when a business goes to government to use the trail for logging or running fibre-optic cables or widening roads, bureaucrats ignore the Council. "Government should be saying to those people, 'Go back to the T'Railway Council.' But they don't because the Council is not considered a key player. We even had to fight to get on that committee for CBS," he laments. He's referring to the long running battle that may be coming to a head in Conception Bay South over ATV use in populated areas.

In 2007, a consultant's report, commissioned by the town of CBS, recommended closing the T'Railway to motorized traffic and diverting it to a bypass that would be cut through the forest to the south of the town. The T'Railway Council's input into development along the Avalon section of heavily-used trail, "will probably stop at the Holyrood-CBS boundary," says the Council's executive director Terry Morrison.

In the meantime there's a great deal of maintenance work needed. Many sections of this heavily-used trail are marred by motorized traffic. There are, according to Morrison, major washouts in the CBS area which will need immediate attention. Indian Pond trestle near the Holyrood generating station is continually battered off its foundations by the wave action from Conception Bay. Until recently, Newfoundland and Labrador Hydro kept putting it back in place, but the Navigable Waters branch of Transport Canada has ordered its repair or removal. With no further need for the structure, Hydro committed to remove it by early August of 2007. Another break in the CBS trail is the 500-metre gap just west of Manuels River. "Obviously, something will have to be done to remedy these problems," says Morrison, "but we'll have to wait and see who will take over responsibility." Motorized traffic is banned from the trail between Octagon Pond in Paradise and the Railway Museum in the former St. John's railway terminal. This trail has been refurbished as part of the Grand Concourse Authority's walking network in the greater metropolitan area.

Morrison sees the Trail to the Avalon as an interesting section because "you have a number of small towns in close proximity to the trail and they all have associated tourism opportunities, particularly Avondale," he says. "And the town of Whitbourne is a big supporter. We've helped them over the years with some materials and signage. I think they see the potential of the T'Railway with Whitbourne as a hub for all the ATV traffic in the area."

Patrols and enforcement is another issue for trail management in this more heavily populated region. For example, there are speed and age limits for ATV drivers on the trail but, according to Rick Noseworthy, "there is no one to enforce it. I can't remember the last time I seen a forestry officer on the T'Railway. They are in the parks but not on the trail. There are no wardens. But it's supposed to be a provincial park." The Royal Newfoundland Constabulary patrols the trail on the Northeast Avalon from Paradise to Holyrood once every three weeks. "There's nothing sustained, but kids don't know when they are on patrol and they don't know what adult is an officer. So that is helping," says Noseworthy. "The number of complaints we are getting is way down."

Photo by Randy P. Noseworthy

## CHAPTER 46
# AUTOGRAPHS FROM MAHERS

**11 AUGUST, 9:25 A.M., MILE 54,
WHITBOURNE TOWN HALL**

The former railway station has been refurbished as Whitbourne's town hall. Parked on an adjacent rail siding are several railway cars, all rusting around the edges. There is a brisk westerly wind stirring up tiny white caps on Whitbourne Pond. When the gravel parking lot crunches under our wheels, Julie and Sasha stretch and sigh in the back seat. I am out and opening the trunk before Kathy turns the car off. Eight people cluster on the building's steps in the cool bright light. I recognize Randy Noseworthy's tall slim figure and his moustached smile. A forty-year-old railway aficionado, he has organized this morning's sendoff for me. Randy introduces me to his parents and sister, to Mayor John Gosse, to the museum guide Mary Lou, to a local reporter, and to the town's historian.

The mayor leads a tour of the station house, which includes the town hall and a museum where we pause among pictures and memorabilia of the town's 100-year history. Although Whitbourne's population has hovered at 1,300 people for many years, it began as a major hub of activity in 1884. Originally called Harbour Grace Junction, Whitbourne was the turning point in the track from St. John's to Harbour Grace. Whitbourne was also the headquarters for the Reid Newfoundland Company until 1903 when the new Riverhead station was completed in St. John's.

In the museum Mary Lou presents me with a wall plaque bearing a line drawing of Sir Robert Bond's manor, the Grange. Bond was Newfoundland's Prime Minister from 1900 to 1909. Before assuming leadership of the Liberal party, Bond had served as Prime Minister William Whiteway's chief lieutenant. Among his accomplishments under Whiteway, Bond helped stave off bankruptcy for Newfoundland after the bank crash of 1894. Robert G. Reid was another key player at the time, using his Montreal connections to bring in the Canadian banks. (A canny move, considering he was paid in Newfoundland Government bonds.) This was the last time Bond and Reid were to work together for a common goal. In fact Bond was a vigorous opponent of the 1898 railway contract. When Bond retired he built his "gentleman's ranch," the Grange, on a small portion of a twenty-square-mile grant of Crown Land across the pond from Whitbourne Station.

*The grey of the old trees shimmers like smoke through the soft green branches of young trees.*

"That house was destroyed by the provincial government in the spring of 1953. They didn't have much vision of the historical potential of that," says John. "As late as 1960 there were forty-three items from that house stored in Confederation Building. Nobody in there can find anything. They can think where it might be, but they won't put it in writing," he adds.

John wonders if we should learn a lesson from Bond's redrafting of the contract with Reid. "I often think, you know," John hesitates, "you hear about the Churchill Falls contract, that it can't be changed, that gives away so much of this Province's wealth. Well the railway contract was changed, and as a result of that, control over millions of square acres of land reverted back to Newfoundland."

I am eager to get on the trail. So we pause for a few grip-and-grin photos, then I thank the send-off party, bid good-bye to my family and head up the track. The reporter stops me. Another interview, a few more photographs. Then for about a quarter mile Randy and I walk together. His interest, the history of the railway, is not so much a hobby as a passion. He had planned to write his thesis on the railway but by the time he was ready to begin "the train was gone. So for the past couple of years I've visited places to document what's left of the railway infrastructure and photograph it."

We part at Rocky River Trestle, where a dirt road intersects the track. As we say good-bye, Randy mentions his model train track and working models that I might like to bring the girls to see. For the next hour I push ahead, refusing to make notes or take photographs. I am in a strange mood, sulky and sultry. Crossing the marker for my 500th mile from Port aux Basques I feel anger erupting inside me. Maybe I'm angry because all the attention will soon be over. Dad told me the other day on the trail "You're a celebrity now, my son!" I have lost all perspective on where I am and what I am doing. I just want to get to St. John's, get this over with. But will it be over then? Or will I always be introduced as "the guy who walked across Newfoundland on the railway." All I am doing is walking, that's the weird thing. All I am doing is getting up in the morning and walking. So why the attention? I shake my head to clear the thoughts and look around.

The wind is cool, but it is clear, with high clouds. Fire swept through this area years ago. The grey of the old trees shimmers like smoke through the soft green branches of young trees. This is my last day in the wilderness because when I reach Avondale tonight only the populated shores of Conception Bay will separate me from my final destination. Still the odd plate, spike, bolt along the railbed. Still the odd Wade.

It just occurred to me why crossing the Isthmus of Avalon felt so significant. Because in a way that's what the rail line is: an isthmus. It stretches between the peninsula of our history and the island of what we can become.

It felt so strange being home. It felt changed: there was an air of decay about the city. It is going to take me a while to adjust. On the first day of my break after I reached Whitbourne, I didn't want to make notes. But finally, around midnight, I was able to scribble a few words:

> *Here, not here. This is the strongest sensation, being here but having to go back on the trail for three days to earn the right to stay. Exhaustion on my shoulders like a backpack. Napped all afternoon. Avoided my journal and hated to look at a map of the Island because my eyes keep tracking the route I've come. Remembering the pain. The stretch bandages I've used on my ankles since Badger are washed and dripping dry from the shower rod. As I write in the journal, scraps of paper with names and*

*address fall into my lap. People to thank.*

But this morning, after three days at home, I felt a shot of excitement when I looked at my walking stick and knew I'd be back in the woods today. Of course part of that is knowing it's only fifty-four miles from Whitbourne to the statue of the Goddess of Industry in front of the St. John's railway station.

In Mahers I stop under the early afternoon sun on a hill amid a meadow of fireweed. The track to the north of me is hidden by the flowers. Two women on ATVs flee the clouds of dust swirling inward behind them. This used to be a logging camp. Kids grew up here, like Peg Alcock. She and her three teenaged grandsons are on the covered veranda of a stained-wood house not more than five paces from the track. Peg's next-door neighbour Helen Smith is there too. They call to see if I am "that fella," and then invite me over for a cool drink. Peg shakes her head in the direction of another pair of ATVs ripping up the rail line. "So, I suppose they've been going ever since the railway ties have been torn up?" I ask.

"Before even they came up. I mean there's nothing but … the berries are gone, everything is gone," says Peg. She has a deeper voice than I expected from such a slight woman.

"There was always a road in but it ended right here, and years ago everyone would park here," she says gesturing to the dirt road behind her house. "And this little house, when that train would come, and you're in the bed, it felt like it came in through that side and out the other," she shakes her head remembering. "But we'd sleep through it. Babies and everything, we'd sleep through it. But now these days you can't get used to the ATV's, like you could the train. When I hear one, the body just stiffens right up, you know?" She draws deeply on her cigarette.

"I still have a bag of money out home that the train flattened out," grins Helen. "Pennies mostly. I got a nickel home that the train ran over and when it did, it put a hole in it. And I put it on my charm bracelet." Peg returns and hands me a glass of iced tea and a banana.

"I was out to B.C. this year and I had a five-hour train ride right through the country. It was absolutely gorgeous. When Leon was only small… that's the father of this fine young man," she says patting twelve-year-old Matthew on the shoulder, "we took the train, me and Mom and Leon and went to Argentia. And another day we went to Carbonear on the last train on that branch line. That was 1984. The conductor took the boys up and let them blow the whistle and everything, right?"

"I remember Matthew, for the last run to Carbonear, I had to get permission for Matthew to get off school. And he had to go back the next day and tell about his train trip. It was the only reason they let him go."

Helen asks me to stop next door at her cottage before I leave. Finally I cannot think of another reason to linger in the shade of the veranda, so I strap on my pack, pick up Clara and thank Peg for her kindness. "Wait a minute," she says and scoots into the house. She comes out with a small hard-covered book and a pen, then asks for my autograph. Taking their cue from that, the boys shove various pieces of paper at me to sign. I have never done this before, and I feel awkward, don't know what to say. So I pull out my journal from the pack and get each of them to sign their names.

Next door Helen gives me two copper-coloured featureless disks the size of an adult thumbprint—train-flattened pennies—and a bag of warm muffins. Then she introduces me to her husband and parents, all seated at a red picnic table. We shake hands, exchange a few words, then I snap a photo of them and get back to crunching stone.

By mid-afternoon I reach Brigus Junction. There at Mile 41.6 is a double trestle where I stop for a short break. It was from here that the steam engine left, just before noon on 11 October 1884 for a point near "Harbour Grace Junction." There—less than a month before the last spike in the Canadian Pacific Railway was driven—at 3:00 p.m. the last spike in the fifty-seven-mile line from St. John's to Harbour Grace was hammered into place after a speech by Prime Minister Sir William Whiteway. Passengers and freight could then rocket along at an average speed of twenty-two miles per hour between St. John's and the north shore of Conception Bay.

All is quiet today. The low hills slope gently back towards the circle of horizon. The few houses, homes to several generations, look well kept. There is no traffic, not a child is visible. From behind a bramble fence the disembodied bark of a lone dog, my only witness, until the very edge of the village. There a man is working beneath the hood of his car. He glances up, sees me and stops, calls out to see if I'm "that guy" and invites me to tea. But, even though I don't have Joey with me, his hunger top get to the end of the trail spurs me on, so I wave thanks and continue on towards Avondale.

Just outside Brigus Junction the sandworm whiffles through the wood and swerves into the middle of the railbed. The plants, ploughed flat, are limp but still green. After a half mile of this, through the heat waves ahead, a rhinoceros-like mirage rolls across the railbed and then it is gone. Just beyond is a TCH overpass. There is the rhinoceros again, rolling in the opposite direction. It is a steam roller flattening gravel over the railbed. A tandem dump truck drives through the underpass. The TCH is being widened here and it looks like another section of the railbed has been claimed. I snap too many pictures of a crane loading the trucks with dirt which they dump on the railway.

The descent towards Avondale is steady and agreeable. Small streams are as sweet to the ear as the quick water is cool to the throat. The bushes are low near the track and allow a panoramic view of forested Dock Ridge to the left and the coloured smudges of civilization in the far distance. At Brigus Pond Outlet, 38.9 miles from St. John's, trout fins cut V's in the water as my shadow falls on the pool beneath the small trestle. Fatigued from the last sixteen miles, I climb down slowly and stretch out on a large flat rock, the sun presses warmly and I ignore the flies.

A feeling of serenity washes over me. Perhaps is it because, for the first time, my body senses the journey's end, senses its ability to carry on to that end, perhaps it is just a moment of peace in stark contrast to the seething rage that boiled in my boots earlier today. The tension drains from my muscles and I lie there with a foolish grin on my face for what seems like an hour. But, when two kids stop their ATV on the trestle to fish in the river, my watch tells me it has only been fifteen minutes. The boys are startled to discover a man stretched out beside the water. And I am not inclined to move or to speak, so after a few moments, without a word, they straddle their vehicle and head back the way they came.

A few moments more and I hear again the stutter of ATV engines. Only these are a long time approaching. Puttering down the track, one behind the other, from Brigus Junction, two ATVs, each with a driver and a passenger and each towing a trailer. Two people are sitting in lawn chairs in the trailer of the lead vehicle. The rear trailer is stacked high with camping gear.

They are two families from Grand Bank on the Burin Peninsula. They left Goobies three days ago. The lead driver introduces the group. "I'm Jerry Trimm, and the wife Elaine. That's Dave Osmond and his wife Judy. And that's the kids Rhonda and Adam," he says pointing to the two teenagers in the lawn chairs.

Yesterday they went through Brigus Junction and on down the Carbonear branch line as far as Bay Roberts. "It's hard going because there's a lot of traffic. They call it the Old Track Road. But it's a nice trail to keep open for hikers or bikers and skidooers," says Jerry and the others agree. He wonders how long it will be open. "We seen a difference since yesterday. We passed through under the Trans-Canada just fine on the branch down to Bay Roberts. But on the way back today they had the rail line blocked off. It was nothing but the muck there by Gushue's Pond

Park where they're putting in the four lanes for the Trans-Canada."

"So what put it in your mind to do the rail line?"

"We just likes nature. We've tried all the parks and all that every year," says Dave. He is the same age as Jerry, a little shorter, with close-cut dark hair and a round face.

"We've been trying to get this done now the last two years," says Jerry. "We're always in the great outdoors. We're always at it, summer and winter," grins Dave gesturing around us at the hills. "Instead of driving on the Trans-Canada we decided to take the bikes and go."

"A couple of people from Grand Bank done it last year. And if they keep tearing up the railbed there's not too many more people going to get the chance to do it," says Judy shaking her blond shoulder-length hair. "We were lucky now to get this far." She says the garbage is bad in places, and the car wrecks. "Especially where you get into the more populated areas. Too bad."

"But we're going all the way to St. John's. Next year now we'll probably go the other way towards Grand Falls," says Dave.

"So what'll you do now, drive to Chester Dawe's and turn around?" I ask knowing that there is a long chain link fence around that lumber yard, blocking the track.

"No, we'll get around there somehow. When we gets there we'll size her up. Nothing will stop we. There's always a way of getting around," says Jerry.

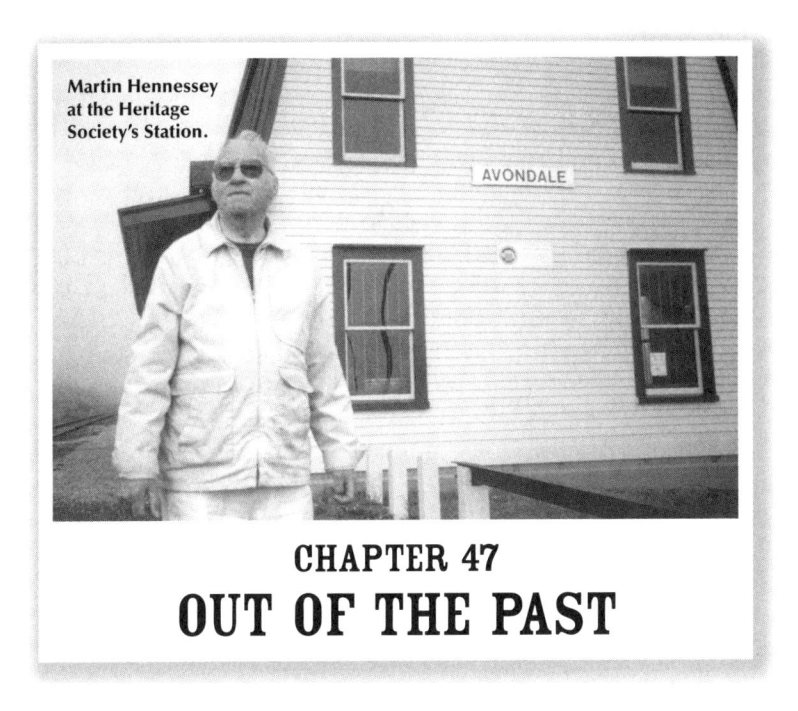

Martin Hennessey at the Heritage Society's Station.

# CHAPTER 47
# OUT OF THE PAST

**11 AUGUST, 4:45 P.M., MILE 39**

Avondale is like most of the older communities in Conception Bay. The main highway twists its way among a disconcerting mixture of mansard-style homes, bungalows, modern gas stations and convenience stores. Side roads, usually named after the families that owned the land, climb the gentle hills back from a community of 700 people. There is a higher proportion of new homes along these roads. Avondale is even typical in its Station Road. Where Avondale is unique is in the 1.8 miles of original rails and ties that stretch from the restored Avondale Station southwest of the site of the former watermill. It is the only intact section of the main rail line left in the Province.

What a strange experience, walking with the uneven gait demanded by the B-grade ties or balancing on the rusty rails. An ATV path runs parallel to the track. There are no words for my mixture of joy and sadness, to be walking once more on the track as I remember it from boyhood. No buddy here now to help balance on the rail. Shortly after five I galumph around a turn and there, half a mile away, is the bright yellow and green Avondale Station. Several railcars and a caboose gleam with fresh paint.

Between here and the station grey skeletons of railway cars lie flat, the wheel trucks gone, stripped to the frames—an elephants' graveyard. I poke my head through the open door of a vandalized siding shed, holes punched in the walls, railway hardware scattered over the floor.

Two young women walk towards me from the station. They are university students working as summer tour guides in the train station museum. It is "boring" here during the week but gets busy on the weekends. A white-haired man in a white windbreaker—despite the afternoon heat—steps out of the station when we arrive. One of the students introduces him as Martin Hennessey, chairman of the heritage society.

"Did you find the heat today?" says Martin. There is a twinge in his accent that I cannot quite place. After a soft drink and a few hot dogs from the station-house kitchen, I'm in a more chatty mood.

"So many other communities wanted to keep the rail line but only Avondale managed to. What was it that you did?"

"We sat on the track and wouldn't let them pick it up. We have pictures to show you ... this is August 11$^{th}$, 1989 ... all we've been doing is maintaining it. We put in new spikes every spring, level it, measure it, and make sure it stays there. But for what? Don't ask me. When we got these speeders," he says pointing to the trolley cars parked on the siding nearby "we thought we'd be running a little rinky-dink railway like they do elsewhere. But we haven't been able to afford it. The insurance alone is over $3,500. That's to put passengers on wheels. And we had six fine days last year and so far we've had four or five this year. So we wouldn't be able to pay for our way. We couldn't reason it through."

Alex Hicks, tall and skinny with a full head of black hair, joins us. He is a heritage society volunteer, and though he doesn't look to be more than fifty, he is retired and spends a great deal of time working at the station. "A little tiny place like this, population 680 counting cats and dogs, there's no corporate sponsors you can tap on the shoulder, but we kept this place."

"We have a great concentration of railway people on the Avalon Peninsula," says Martin.

"A majority of them, by jingo," says Alex. "The government railway colour when the railway went into bankruptcy was maroon. The old clapboard that's left here on the front of the station, if you scrape it the maroon paint is there. It's like old fashioned barn red—#242 American red is the match colour now, the rust red—the yellow and the green were the Reid Railway colours. But they never operated east of Whitbourne," says Alex. I know this is wrong. Reid took over the entire line after Bond renegotiated the railway contract in 1901. But I am more interested in hearing what Alex has to say. "Up in Whitbourne they had the roundhouses and the shops. There they used to assemble the steam engines that came in from Baldwin in the States."

"Reid operated west but they didn't get too far before they got into trouble," continues Alex. "But they still got land rights and mineral rights and all the rest of it. Ian Reid still got his business going and Reid Newfoundland is still in the phone book. He's still a member of our heritage society," he says raising his bushy eyebrows in Martin's direction.

Alex takes his toolbox and heads for the engine, where he is restoring his train whistle. Then I ask Martin for a tour.

There were only twelve telephones in the Avondale area in the 1920s. So the train station, with its telegraph operator, was a hub for communication and transportation. The operator's terminal is preserved as it was at that time. Martin seems more in his element inside the station where he leads me from room to spotless room. "This is the waiting room and it is all the same, the stove, the benches around the wall there." Then a series of framed newspaper clippings on the wall attracts my eye. The pictures show ceremonies over the years at the station. Martin points out some of the visiting dignitaries.

"There's Norm Doyle, a former cabinet minister. He's no longer in politics. That's Eric Gullage, another former cabinet minister. He's no longer in politics. Maybe that is one way to get out of politics. Get mixed up with the heritage," he laughs.

The freight shed, which measures about thirty feet by twenty, has been converted to a meeting room. Artifacts hang on the walls. "People keep donating things," says Martin, by way of explanation, "we issue receipts." With enough seating for forty people, the freight shed is a popular meeting place. "We charge a minimal rate to cover the cost of electricity. No profit. There's a great danger of running in the hole," says Martin.

Up the narrow stairs to the second floor. "Nobody bugs you here. This is where the stationmaster used to live. We've changed it all over to washrooms and an office and another place for meetings. These are the original birch floors, not a bad job eh? But the walls are different. It's perfect for us," he says and runs his hand over the back of an overstuffed couch. The patter of ATVs outside. Looking down through the window I see the Trimms and Osmonds. I last saw them parked in the meadow near the old mill and assumed they were going to camp there for the night.

Back outside Alex has pulled one of the speeders onto the track. He hitches a covered trailer to it as Martin and I come out. "Thought you might like to go for a ride," he smiles. He invites the Trimms and the

Osmonds on board as well. They pile into the trailer and I get in the front with Alex. Martin elects to wait at the station. The six-year-old speeder has less than 1,000 miles on the odometer. It belonged to Newfoundland Telephone when they had lines that followed the track. The trolley jerks into motion and we rattle on up the track. The speeder drives with a standard gearshift just like a car, its top speed seventy miles an hour. Alex hold the speed to between ten and fifteen miles an hour.

Alex points to the train car skeletons near the first turn in the track. "Now you see those old cars? We're going to build one like that, the old wooden passenger cars, and put it on the line."

Clack-clack, clack-clack, clack-clack.

Then he points to the river running alongside. "We're going to put in a trail so we can take people up to the head of the falls. Right there at the end of the rail there is a spring that is ideal for drinking.

"After the rails came up they pulled a lot of house trailers in along and set them up as cabins. See the space right there at the end of the track? Somebody needed four ties so they came in here one weekend last month and took the ties right out from under the rails.

"That building there to the right used to be the old watermill," says Alex pointing to the graying shingled building with all the doors and windows gone. "Nothing left of it. Vandalized, cannibalized. It's unreal. That building is only about ten years old. It's an exact copy," says Alex. The old one collapsed but they still had the drawings. So when the government was "throwing out money hand over fist there, under the job strategy programs," about twelve years earlier, they applied for the funding and rebuilt it. They had to bring in twenty-four foot timber from British Columbia. "There's not a thing left in there now. Most of the equipment is stored. Except the turbine was there and darned if they didn't back in a crane one night and take it. And that thing weighed tons, by jingoes."

Clack-clack, clack-clack, clack-clack.

*8:55 p.m.   Martin Hennessey's kitchen, Avondale*
  From my notebook:
  If this trip has been a lesson for me, how might I sum it up?

1. There's nothing like controversy to get a microphone shoved in your face.
2. Television carries a lot of short-term impact (but is also more long lasting than I expected).
3. Radio coverage is very limited.
4. Walking hurts.
5. The current bureaucratic system of government is incapable of responding in a rational manner to any issue except perhaps saving its own skin.
6. I myself do nothing. Through me a higher power takes action.
7. Big words may cover your ass but they can also be turned against you.
8. Prepare for all interviews.
9. During the interview let the interviewer ask questions then say what you want to say, your rehearsed message.
10. Life is sweet, live well.
11. Giving and generosity are sacred.
12. Newfoundlanders despise their culture.
13. Newfoundlanders cherish their culture.
14. "If it moves shoot it, if it grows chop it down."
15. I abhor party politics.
16. "It's not what you do but the final tally that counts"—I don't believe it.
17. All people like stories and facts.
18. Never make decisions when you are tired or hungry.
19. Anything is possible, one day at a time.

All seems so obvious. And it only took me thirty-seven years to learn it.

Trawling the wind.

## CHAPTER 48
# A RIDE ON THE GHOST TRAIN

### 12 AUGUST, 8:02 A.M., AVONDALE STATION, MILE 35

Almost came off without Clara. Martin and I were just saying goodbye when I discovered she was missing. Twenty-one miles to Manuels River today. The bright disc of the sun through the fog gives the land an eerie glow, like intense moonlight, the trees an iridescent green. The fog is cold through spandex. Maybe I should have a little more self-respect and wear real pants. I get my legs pumping for a while until I warm up. I imagine how this terrain might look if I was sitting on the train, what I would see and hear.

"All aboard."

I can almost hear steam hissing from the engine up ahead, as the carriage jerks forward a couple of times and then settles into a steady motion, continuing on slowly. I whistle as I come to the first turn, gathering speed. Smoke and embers billow from the stack several cars ahead.

There through the window on the left is the low rock outcrop called Lees Pond Mountain draped in a shawl of fog. The low spruce and birch flow by in slow motion. To the right, spiders string beads of light along the bank of a small gully. Robin song like needles of sound. On the left the land dips and there lies the blue-green expanse of Conception Bay widening towards the eastern horizon.

The engineer would have to grind the brakes before rattling across Harbour Main Brook, Mile 34.4. The fog has burned off now. There is a guy and his Afghan hound walking down the path. And the landscape is all very familiar. As a boy I picked blueberries in those low hills woven with thickets of alders. But I do not remember the train.

Suddenly we burst across Holyrood River North Arm, brakes grind again, across the Conception Bay Highway and along the north side of Terrys Mountain. Some larger rocks have rolled down onto the track. Once these were a hazard, but our train of thought does not hesitate, pushes effortlessly past the rocks. Conception Bay is just below us now, the salt air tingles my arms. On the opposite side of the inlet are large homes, with yachts tied to the wharf. The property belonged to the late Chester Dawe. Immediately below on this side of the inlet, a fishing quay. There is a man down there hammering. He would hear the train from there, might stop and wave to the engineer or to the people waving from the passenger cars. Today he remains focused on his work. Snatches of country music drift up from his radio.

Out around Joys Point, and south again briefly to Main Beach, at the southernmost tip of Conception Bay. Here at Holyrood South River, Mile 29.5, a brief stop to gulp water from a well, stuff a few sandwiches and off again on a gently curving six-mile stretch along the southern shore. The north shore drifts slowly away, the forest becoming less distinct until it is a mat of green, the houses dabs of coloured rag woven into the mat. In the middle distance Salmon Cove Point, the lighthouse barely discernible among the rocks. A sailboat gives a wide berth around Harbour Main Point and heads east out the bay. A gust of wind wrinkles the surface of the water, rushes towards the shore 100 feet below. The heavily wooded land climbs steeply up from the waterline to the track. To the right the land slopes less steeply. In one section, for half a mile or more, a 100-yard-wide swath has been cut from the forest. Levered by erosion, huge boulders tumble slowly towards the track and silt fills the ditches.

On a rocky ledge at sea level lie several boilers from the old steam engines dumped on top of one another. The large rusty cylinders were probably discarded by the railway in the 1950s, when the diesel engines began to lumber over the narrow gauge line. On down the straight stretch, past the oil-fired electrical generating station. It roars jets of steam that fan out like clouds and drift quickly away with the sea breeze. None of the men working in the yard look up, none see the ghost train charge from the forest and out onto the beach. Conception Bay is immediately to the left, a dark blur in the heat of the day. Here the sea has strewn large rocks onto the track, rammed them beneath Indian Pond Trestle. Fog hangs over the far side of this greater bay and caresses the abrupt cliffs of Bell Island. The wind off the water is cool, so I roll down my sleeves and button up my coat.

At Seal Cove Trestle, Mile 23.1, huge boulders block the way for all traffic, except the ever-creative ATVers who squeeze around the boulders and across the trestle. On we chug, along the coast between waves and small ponds. Lance Cove, where I learned to swim, where my brothers and I pulled bottles from their saltwater corrals of beach rocks, gulped down Keep Kool Orange and RC Cola. The once-secluded pond is now a waterfront for large homes with two-car brick driveways.

Another half mile to the sandpits. Washers, car parts, old train parts. On the beach scattered rusty equipment, broken glass, remains of cars. Past a concrete-manufacturing plant. Stockpiles of smaller crushed stone spilling over onto the railbed; high cones of sand overlap the track. Front-end loaders, people walking around, cement trucks. On top of one of the silos is a Christmas star. And there is a building spewing silt into a pool, right next to Lance Cove Pond.

By 1:30 p.m. I am over the Upper Gullies Trestle and there is something new: manhole covers in the rail line, as the track widens to a dirt road. On through Upper Gullies where Ted McCarthy, the brother of my sister-in-law Colleen, waves from the back of an ATV. Then to Kelligrews and a brief stop at Station Road. There a road crew is laying waterlines beneath the track. Just up the road lives Noreen Tilley, sister to a boyhood girl-friend of mine. It is a decade since I have seen her. The bungalow looks a little run down, but Noreen has the same quick smile and light feathery laugh I remember. Noreen's ten-year-old daughter looks so much like her aunt Janet, the one I dated, that my eyes wander back to her face several times.

An hour later the ghost train whistles, so I say my good-byes and start on the last four miles to Manuels and the final night of the trip. In Foxtrap, as the track turns inland for the final charge over Topsail Hill and into St. John's, huge boulders are piled beside the track to discourage the starving bay from eating the land. Perched like a siren against the granite I see a woman. She stands and walks towards me. From her black hair, and the way she walks, I can tell it is my mother. The ghost train dissolves and I am back in my life. I had assumed the man beside her was her husband, Mike. But he is a stray she found along the track. The smell on his breath is of alcohol and his eyes are unfocused. Mom introduces us and then as quickly as she politely can, leads me down the track. I look back once. The stray is still sitting there, slack as a sack, but now there is a black dog with its head in his lap.

The next hour is surreal for me as my estranged mother and I walk through the landscape of my childhood, chatting lightly, stopping to drink, or for her to light a smoke, and then pressing on across the highway in Foxtrap, through Long Pond, dodging ATVs, along the section of highway in Manuels and past Berg's Ice Cream Parlour where the four-lane highway has wiped out half a kilometre of rail line. Then, inland again to the trestle that passes so high above Manuels River. This is a sacred place for me. I grew up on the banks of this river, watching in awe as the waters raged in spring, swimming at the Drops and the Canyon every summer and fall, in winter risking the ice, taking refuge here all year round.

The author with daughters Julie and Sasha and friends.

Photo by Katharine Kearley

## CHAPTER 49
# THE LAST SPIKE

**13 AUGUST, 9:00 A.M., TOPSAIL POND**

For the first time in years I spent the night at Dad's house, sleeping until almost 8:00 a.m., gulped some breakfast, and then Dad gave me a lift out to Topsail Pond, Mile 11.6. It is slightly overcast, though warm and not likely to rain. That is good for the turnout at Bowring Park, where Kathy has organized a welcoming party to accompany me the final two and a half miles into St. John's. With Clara clicking smartly at my side, I soon leave Topsail Pond behind. Then out of the forest and into the industrialized area around Octagon Pond. I begin to fashion my message to the media, replaying it on the tape recorder and repeating it until I cannot get it wrong.

On through Paradise, where front-end loaders have eaten their fill of crushed stone. Then over the chain link fence at Chester Dawe's lumberyard where the rail line is fenced off. Under the TCH one final time, through an industrial park, past a sign forbidding motorized traffic, skirting Mount Pearl, and down along the farmland of Brookfield Road towards Bowring Park.

I arrive at 11:40 a.m. There is no one there. I lie back in the grass. I had expected that everything would look new, that I would be flooded with new insights, but all I feel is relief, mingled with regret. I have enjoyed all the attention. Then a man calls my name. It is my uncle, Sheldon Legrow, a part-time photographer, there with his bag of tricks to capture the event on film. Then a boy of about twelve or thirteen years arrives. He has read about the walk and wants to join me. Kathy comes over the bridge.

"What are you doing here?" she calls to me. "The media's not coming for another ten minutes. You're not supposed to get here until then." We hug and then she sends me back up the track with instructions to get out of sight and then make my re-entry.

Taking Julie and Sasha by the hand, I walk back the way I came until the underpass is out of sight. Several of my co-workers walk up the track to join us. I am trying not to think now, trying to just walk, be here. Trust my memory for the statement I have rehearsed. I hug the girls, chat with my co-workers and watch the second hand drag itself around the dial.

Twelve o'clock. Time to go.

Rounding the turn into Bowring Park I see it has changed. Directly beneath the underpass are people carrying cameras, microphones, pens and paper. Behind them a crowd of people, some on horses, some on bicycles, many on foot. Some of them wave banners welcoming me home. I feel overwhelmed. Kathy and I hug again. The media group tightens around me and I hear myself deliver the rehearsed message, then make a small speech to friends, relatives, co-workers and supporters. I hand over the Port aux Basques spike and the town pin from the mayor of Port aux Basques to Mayor Shannie Duff of St. John's, and then head off amidst the crowd for my last push on the trail of the Newfoundland Railway. I forget to make notes, forget to take pictures, forget the tape recorder, the blisters, the bad knees and the politics of the T'Railway and just walk right off the map.

The scene at the terminal is a bit of an anticlimax. I have walked rather slowly so the crowd has dispersed. Julie and Sasha take rides on the two horses. Kathy and I sit on a curb and chat with the few people still milling about. The Goddess of Industry statue is no longer in front of the station. She rests under wraps around the corner from us on the old platform, awaiting restoration.

## HISTORY SIDING ELEVEN
# SURVIVING FORMER RAILWAY STATIONS IN NEWFOUNDLAND

*Compiled by Randy P. Noseworthy, August 6, 2007.*

**Surviving main line stations**
- Avondale
- Badger (moved from original site)
- Bishop's Falls
- Caribou
- Clarenville
- Glenwood
- Grand Falls
- Port aux Basques
- Spruce Brook (moved from original site)
- St. John's
- Whitbourne

**Surviving branch line stations:**
- Argentia
- Bay Roberts (moved from original site)
- Bonavista
- Carbonear
- Clarke's Beach
- Harbour Grace
- Lewisporte
- Port Union (moved from original site)
- Spaniard's Bay
- Victoria (moved from original site)
- Western Bay

**Replica of former station:**
- Port aux Basques (Railway Heritage Centre, a replica of the original c. 1898 station)

Neil Dawe at Indian Pond Trestle.

# EPILOGUE
## TO THE ORIGINAL VERSION

### 30 APRIL 1995, 2:20 P.M. MILE 23.8,
### INDIAN POND-DUFF INTAKE TRESTLE

Slob ice jams Conception Bay, lifting and settling with the tide. In the distance, halfway between this shore and the north side of the bay, two icebergs bask in the early afternoon sun, one angled and steep sided, the other lower and flat on top. From the railbed Neil Dawe, a friend of mine since boyhood, scans the white glare of the bay for seals. "Oh my God, look out at that iceberg Kearley, there's people on it." He hands me the binoculars and points towards the low berg. What seemed no more than a dark smudge to the naked eye expands now to seven people. I watch them pick their way in single file down the side of the berg to the ice field where they "copy" from pan to pan.

We are here to inspect the trestle where Indian Pond drains into the bay. Neil is keen to discuss the competing demands on the T'Railway and how they affect him as a landscape architect with the Johnson Family Foundation. That philanthropic organization is spearheading the ambitious Grand Concourse T'Railway development in St. John's. By the year 2000 they plan to have 200 kilometres of interconnected trails throughout the metropolitan area. The former railbed will be an important part of that development. Neil walks over to the trestle and leans against a chain-link fence. There is a similar fence across the other end of the trestle. All the ties are missing, the metal beams of the structure are clearly visible, the clear blue-green river is ten feet below. A white sign wired to the fence declares in red letters: "Closed. Unsafe for public use." "The old assumption is that industry and recreation are mutually exclusive," says Neil. "But I don't believe that. With the right planning, industrial and recreational uses can complement each other."

Despite the fence and sign, this trestle is evidence that what Neil says may be true. On the opposite side of the pond the tall smokestacks of the Holyrood oil-fired generating station cough soot and smoke. Newfoundland Hydro, which owns and operates the plant, became very concerned about this trestle last winter. At the height of the worst storm of the season, waves smashed the fifty-foot iron structure off its abutments blocking the stream. Since the generating plant channels water into the pond, it is in their interest to ensure that the pond is well drained. So Newfoundland Hydro brought in heavy cranes and re-installed the trestle, minus the ties.

Neil scans the bay again through the binoculars watching the small party picking its way across the ice. I use the time to reflect on some of the many events that have affected the railway since I finished my trek, twenty months ago.

On a personal level one of the most significant events was Otto Goulding's resignation from the T'Railway Committee in the fall of 1994, after years of volunteer work lobbying for the T'Railway. The most significant event for the development of the trail is the provincial government's formal announcement (on 28 March 1995) of their intention to declare the main line of the railway a linear park. That is the vital—and long anticipated—hinge on which all future development of the T'Railway swings.

As part of the deal for taking over the main line of the railroad, the provincial government received seven million dollars from CN for culvert and trestle maintenance, but that is only a small portion of what may be needed. Mike Buist, the assistant deputy minister with responsibility for the T'Railway, believes corporate support must be a major component.

Roger Grimes, the Minister of Tourism and Culture, agrees with the need for corporate involvement but he also believes community support is essential. "This will be largely community driven," he told Eric Legge, the new chair of the NLRDC's T'Railway Committee at an April 1995 meeting. "If communities aren't on board this won't work." As far as the minister is concerned, the priority is to have an uninterrupted passageway across the Island. "Imagine a groomed snowmobile trail from Port aux Basques to St. John's," he said.

But even when the line is declared a provincial park there are many unresolved issues. Who is to oversee the development for consistency? Who is responsible for maintenance? Should there be an overarching organization? If so, is the T'Railway Committee the best organization to do that? How is it to be policed? Why are the branch lines excluded? Will the linear park come under the Province's new "master plan" for park development? Can communities on the railway opt out? How are conflicts resolved where municipal and provincial uses of the T'Railway clash? The list of questions is long. But at least now people know which department they can go to with their questions, even if the answers will have to wait.

A related development on a much broader scale was the June 1994 launch of the Trans-Canada Trail (TCT)—a proposed 15,000 kilometres of shared-use recreational trails from St. John's in the east to Victoria, British Columbia in the west, and north from Calgary, Alberta to Tuktoyaktuk, North West Territories. Newfoundland could be one of the first provinces with its province-wide trail in place.

While these events are taking place at the national and provincial levels, changes with more immediate impact continue along the railway. Industrial and recreational demands are daily shaping the T'Railway, for better or worse. For example, a small section of the railbed in Port aux Basques has been set aside for Irving Oil to develop.

The major trestles on the West Coast, over Robinsons River, Crabbes River, Fischels Brook, and Flat Bay Brook remain passable but it is difficult to say whether the rivers are undercutting the main piers. These must be inspected by divers. How long can we afford to wait? It cost CN half a million dollars in 1986 to repair Robinsons River Trestle when one of the midstream piers listed due to undercutting. What would it cost to repair the same damage today?

The Stephenville Crossing town council and the provincial government have co-signed a wetlands conservation stewardship agreement restricting development in the nesting areas along the track. Hayward Young, mayor of the Zing when I passed through in '93, must be pleased. This clears the way for full protection of this important nesting site for large numbers of migratory birds that are rarely seen on other parts of the Island. Bud Hulan, MHA for the area, is now a member of the provincial cabinet, and no doubt is still dispensing stories from his days as a chemist.

The Trans-Canada Highway expansion north of Corner Brook continues to stampede over the railway, despite resistance from residents in towns such as Pasadena. As a consolation, the T'Railway Committee of the Newfoundland and Labrador Development Association has a letter from the current provincial Minister of Transportation, John Efford, stating that, wherever the railway is taken for road purposes, the government will construct another section of T'Railway to maintain the integrity of the cross-Island route.

The Deer Lake town council remains determined to exclude the T'Railway from their community. Cabin owners are still driving back and forth along the railroad to their cabins at Pond Crossing and the Gaff. But for how much longer? The government's announcement of the linear park has cabin owners like Maxine and her sister concerned about continued access to what is for them literally a birthright. Another danger is the large stands of timber out there. The logging companies know the rail line is the cheapest access route.

The announcement, 28 March 1994, stated specifically that snowmobiles and ATVs will be permitted on the trail. This complements new ATV legislation which restricts their use on wetlands, forcing ATV users off the bogs and onto forest paths and backwoods trails. ATV traffic on the T'Railway has increased as a result.

Certain commercial uses are still permitted on the T'Railway. More fibre-optic cables are buried under the roadbed. And Fred Thorne and Classic Stone have special permission to continue their quarrying operation in the Topsails. In 1994 his company became partners with another company and set up a secondary processing plant in Buchans to cut the huge stone blocks into headstones, counter tops and tiles.

Despite attempts by certain sectors of the federal government to claw back half of the seven million dollars granted to them in 1989 as part of the euphemistically named "CN Diversification Agreement," the Bishop's Falls Development Corporation (BFDC) continues, with some success, to encourage the development of new industries in the town. Bill Sterling, who remains as executive director, believes the town's future is in the industrial sector and not in tourism. And the provincial declaration of the intention to create the linear park really does little for the BFDC. They own several buildings in the train yard which they would like to develop, but, because they sit on former CN land, the whole waterfront area on the Exploits River is frozen until the government declares its intentions.

Bill says they do have one unique tourism opportunity: to construct a loop park between Bishop's Falls and Grand Falls using the former

Newfoundland Railroad and the roadbed of the old Anglo-Newfoundland Development Company line, which runs along the Exploits River.

People in the community on the south side of the Exploits River still use the trestle as their main bridge to Bishop's Falls.

Glenwood's cloverleaf, which took out the train underpass, is still unused, except by logging trucks. The small Glenwood train station remains standing, though vandals have burned down the nearby storage shed. The trestle across the Gander River to Appleton is a popular route for people on foot, ATV or snowmobile. Gander has developed the rail line through town as a hiking and skiing trail and has constructed an alternative route around town for the ATVers and snowmobilers.

Last summer I revisited Gander to interview Clar Lannon, the former track supervisor, but he was no longer a reliable source because of debilitating memory lapses. I cursed myself then for not making more time on my trek to talk to him. It is startling how easily our history slips away, one person at a time.

Loggers in the central area are more aggressive than ever and have even graded several sections of the rail line. The most recent incident occurred in April 1995, on the ten-mile section between Terra Nova Village and Port Blandford; and this after the government had declared its intention to make the route a linear park. Yet, until the rail line is actually designated a provincial park, Minister Grimes admits government is powerless to prevent such action or to punish the culprits.

A few months after the interview with Dan Benson in Come by Chance he died from cancer. It was a privilege to have met him and witnessed the real love he felt for the pre-Confederation Newfoundland Railway. He helped me to understand at a deeper level what we lost when the railway closed.

At the intersection with the TCH just outside Brigus Junction, the overpass is gone completely now, but it is not impassable. They installed a culvert, like the one between Bishop's Falls and Norris Arm, that is large enough for ATVs.

The Avondale Station museum and track continues its tenuous existence. Alex Hicks, who took me for the speeder ride there on the only remaining section of the main line, is now mayor of Avondale and still very much involved with the railway station. When I called him in April of 1995 he told me that last year alone they had 3,500 out-of-province visitors sign the guestbook. The track is still in excellent shape and they have built two passenger cars—a twelve-seater and a six-seater—to pull behind the speeder. This year they will offer regular rides up and down the track.

The Avondale train whistle works too, thanks to Alex. He has placed a timer on it, so the whistle blows at noon every day. The ghost of the train lives on. But Alex is not certain what will come of the government's declared intention to make the T'Railway a provincial park. He feels too much will be left up to the municipalities. "The department of tourism sends us out boxes and boxes of tourist information that we give out for free. Yet when we want to get a few small highway signs to help people find us, government wants forty dollars a month for every sign," Alex said. "A few years ago the government used to give us more than 2,000 dollars for every mile of road in the community. Now we only get 400 dollars. That's not enough to pay for asphalt patches," he lamented. So he is not sure how Avondale can help realize the government's intention of a linear park. One thing for sure, the rail line is a popular route between Avondale and Ocean Pond. Every $24^{th}$ of May holiday it is more like a back road than a trail.

Around the shore of Conception Bay the railbed is more vulnerable to wave action than anywhere else along the entire main line. This includes a quarter mile section in Holyrood and a longer section through Conception Bay South, from the generating station to Foxtrap. The damage to Indian Pond Trestle shows just how destructive wave action can be. Since the council finished laying the water lines and manholes, the hard-packed railroad through Conception Bay South supports a steady train of pedestrians, bicycles, and off-road vehicles.

The area with the most competing demands for usage is the first half mile of the T'Railway, from the dockyard at the head of the St. John's harbour west for a half mile to the Leslie Street bridge, along the Waterford River. This land remains in federal hands. On the south side of the river the property is just a narrow strip of scrub brush. The property on the north side of the river—known as Riverhead—includes the former Newfoundland Railway freight yard and the St. John's terminal. The Riverhead station was designated a heritage site in the summer of 1994.

The current minister of Transport Canada has yet to announce how these lands will be used. According to Doug Oldford, Transport Canada's regional director, the content of that announcement may depend on the fate of the dockyard, up for sale at the time of writing. I called Oldford late in April for an update on plans for the former rail yard. He confirmed that the province's jurisdiction over the T'Railway begins a half mile west of the terminal at the Leslie Street bridge—although the Coast Guard has fenced off the first 100 yards or so. According to Oldford, there is not much chance of opening up the north side to a T'Railway. The property includes a compound for new cars trucked in for the city's dealers and a container freight yard leased by Oceanex, a major container shipping carrier. Oldford believes these kinds of uses could be dangerous when combined with a trailway, but admits it is not his role to figure out how the area ought to be used. "I had to wend my way through mazes of multiple applications and then make my recommendation to the minister," he told me. "Industry and recreational uses are not mutually exclusive but it really depends on the nature of the industry. The groups who want a claim on this space should lobby at the ministerial level since the final decision rests with the minister." He believes the south side of the river, removed from the historic property would be a "better route" for the trail.

Neil sits on an overturned dory, Indian Pond Trestle behind him. He has heard Doug Oldford's arguments before. And he doesn't buy them. St. John's will be the starting point of the trans-Island and eventually a Trans-Canada Trail. He contends that to allow the trail to begin anywhere other than at Riverhead would be to miss an opportunity.

Neil's calm determination reminds me of my mentor on the other side of the Island—Otto Goulding. Two years ago, at a lunchtime meeting in Corner Brook, I wondered aloud if the T'Railway could happen. Otto looked as if I had stung him. "Never give a foot when you know you are right... And if we keep our determination we can make this T'Railway into a multinational tourist attraction."

Now, with the linear park so close to official recognition, Neil says we need to think big in terms of what the trail can offer. "It will pass through caribou herds, through pristine valleys, along the coast, and through the heart of the interior. Think of the potential, hallmark events such as international bicycle or dog-team races from Port aux Basques to St. John's. It's time to stop underestimating our potential," he says. Neil believes government is finally waking up to the possibilities. "There *is* a way to negotiate safe access and that is just what we intend to do."

Out on the bay the party of people are much closer. The man in the lead pokes the ice pans with a gaff as they slowly make their way shoreward.

# ENVOY
## TO THE ORIGINAL VERSION

### LAST NOTES: BEAVER POND

A shimmering twig pitches on the end of my pen. I can see its proboscis darting in and out like a small tongue—oops, he's flown. What a day... road weary from the moment I woke up, I am here now with my feet soaking in the cool, lapping waters of Beaver Pond, just seventeen miles of wilderness between me and Corner Brook to the north. A small spruce nearby wears all my freshly washed clothes. Not a sound but the water, the buzz of stouts and one hand slapping. The setting sun shines straight across the pond. The rail line is just behind me. The crushed stone is heavy here, few signs of traffic. On the far side of the pond, reeds fade to bushes to tall spruce and birch.

Swimming alone always unnerves me. But tonight I stripped and dived shallow through the few lily pads, surfaced and turned immediately and swam to shore. I lay naked for twenty minutes or more before scrambling into my clothes because I imagined I heard a car on the road bed. Unseen trout plunk in the pond.

As I sat quietly in the tent to escape the last onslaught of flies before dark, I kept thinking I could hear the distant beat of rock and roll.

Listening carefully to see if I could tell the direction of the source, I realized the beat was coming from inside my chest. Outside, my voice echoes so sharply that the first report is like a tape of my own voice, then five or six more echoes before silence. A band of crows on the other side of the pond are bawling at each other.

At 6:00 the next morning the loudest sound is mosquito buzz and bird song. Beneath it all, silence. The fog is lifting, offers a brief glimpse of blue sky. Breakfast is a banana Dan Conway gave me, bread from Ruby Gillam, Rick Larishe's apple and my tea. I am down to my last bit of audio tape, my last half-roll of film, and the only pen I have is running dry. The last of everything and I still have a long day before I reach Corner Brook. Air ruffles through feathers, whistles in my ears as a loon swoops low overhead and disappears blackly into the mist.

## SUGGESTED READING

Chafe, W.J. *I've Been Working on the Railroad: Memoirs of a railwayman*, 1911-1962. St. John's: Harry Cuff Publications, 1987.
*Encyclopedia of Newfoundland and Labrador* s.v. "railway stations," "railways," "Reid Newfoundland Company," "Reid, Robert Gillespie."
Hiller, James K. *The Newfoundland Railway 1881-1949.* Newfoundland Historical Society, Pamphlet Number 6: 1981.
Hiller, James K. "Going for Broke." *Horizon Canada* 3 (Sept. 1985): 740-744
Hoddinott, Claude. "The last days of the Newfoundland Railway," *Canadian Rail* 419 (1990): 202-204.
Locke, Peter D. "Czar of Newfoundland: A profile of Sir Robert Gillespie Reid." *Canadian Rail* 419 (1990): 183-195.
Locke, Peter D. "Coastal Steamer and Branch Railway Line Revenue Competition in the Reid Newfoundland Company," *Canadian Rail* 419 (1990): 196-201.
Newfoundland and Labrador Rural Development Council. Special Transportation Issue, *The Rounder* (January 1977): 90-102.
Noel, S.J.R. *Politics in Newfoundland.* Toronto: University of Toronto Press, 1971.
Northland Associates Limited et. al. *The Newfoundland T'Railway: Opportunities and Feasibility*, volume 1. Gander: Newfoundland and Labrador Rural Development Council, 1992.
Northland Associates Limited et. al. *The Newfoundland T'Railway: Resource Assessment and Opportunity Analysis*, volume 2. Gander: Newfoundland and Labrador Rural Development Council, 1993.
Penney, A.R. *A History of the Newfoundland Railway: Volume 1 (1881-1923).* St. John's: Harry Cuff Publications, 1988.
Penney, A.R. with Kennedy, Fabian. *A History of the Newfoundland Railway: Volume 2 (1923-1988).* St. John's: Harry Cuff Publications, 1990.
Noseworthy, Randy P. *The School Car: Bringing the Three R's to Newfoundland's Remote Railway Settlements (1936-1942).* Whitbourne, Newfoundland, R.P.N. Publishing, 1997.
Smallwood, Joseph R. *I Chose Canada: the memoirs of the Honourable Joseph R. "Joey" Smallwood.* (pp. 152-160). Toronto: Macmillan Company, 1973.
"Spent Bullet." *Time Magazine* (December 29, 1967): pp. 9-10.
"The History of the Newfoundland Railway," *The Newfoundland Quarterly* (October, 1901): pp. 5-6.